ADVENTURES WITH
POSTPARTUM DEPRESSION

A MEMOIR

COURTNEY HENNING NOVAK

For Pippa

PROLOGUE

If I raised my arms in the air and threw Pippa as hard as I could against the hardwood floor, her skull would crack open and her brains would splatter all over the floor.

I gasped and held Pippa closer to me, as if the very thought of throwing her could rip her from my arms. Why did this keep happening? I loved my daughter.

Didn't I?

What a silly question. Of course I loved Pippa. I had loved her since the moment I learned I was pregnant.

Then why did I keep thinking about throwing her against the floor with all my strength? Why did I keep seeing images of her brains splattered across the room? And why was it getting harder and harder to push the dark thoughts away?

I collapsed on the pink glider in the nursery and patted Pippa's back. "It's okay. It's okay, baby girl, it's okay."

Pippa continued wailing. Though it did no good, I kept patting. Maybe she just had an epic burp stuck in her little tummy. I could never tell when she was cranky and when she was just gassy. All her cries sounded the same: loud.

Maybe it wasn't a burp. What if one of my hairs was wrapped

around one of Pippa's tiny toes and cutting off circulation? I had seen an article about that on Facebook. A baby cried and cried and her mother had no idea that one of her hairs had gotten tangled around a toe and by the time she noticed, it was too late. The toe had to be amputated.

I put Pippa on the changing table and bent over her hands. She was shrieking now, but I had to act quickly before it was too late. I checked her fingers and toes. No errant hairs. I checked them again. Still none. Pippa was wailing, but I could not stop. I checked her thighs, her forearms, her neck. Part of me felt like I was losing my mind, but the other part of me did not care.

I had to know.

I thought I was being extra-vigilant. My baby was only four months old. Anything could hurt her. Anything could kill her. Surely all new mothers took these sorts of precautions.

I was wrong, though. I was not being extra-vigilant to keep my baby safe. Of course, I wanted her to be safe and healthy, but that was not the reason I was checking for anything that might pose a threat to her safety.

I was checking to make myself feel better.

Most of the time, I vibrated and buzzed with anxiety. A ticker tape of worries constantly ran through my mind. My shoulders ached as if I were carrying around extra weight. My stomach twisted and groaned. The blood in my body seemed to be rushing faster than usual through my arteries and veins.

Except when I was checking. When I was examining Pippa's body for stray hairs, or crouching down to check that the stovetop burners were lit, or unlocking and relocking the front door a dozen times in a row, I calmed down. For those brief moments that I was checking something, my body felt still and calm. I felt like myself.

Finally satisfied that a hair was not cutting off circulation to one of Pippa's fingers or toes, I picked her up and tried to soothe her again. Her screams got louder. She was going to scream and scream forever and ever and nothing would make it stop unless I threw her as hard as I could—

No no no! I pushed the image out of my mind but too late. I had already glimpsed the horror of Pippa's skull cracked open and felt the relief of imaginary silence.

I was a monster.

I blinked away tears and patted Pippa's back, counting to one hundred and then back down to zero.

It must be the insomnia. The insomnia had started a month ago. I could sleep only three hours at night. The rest of the night, I lay awake in bed, my skin crawling from the constant buzzing of nerves, my mind refusing to slow down. I wanted so desperately to sleep, but my body seemed to have lost the ability to perform that most basic of functions.

If I could stay strong for just a few more days, surely the insomnia would end and I would become the mom Pippa deserved.

Who was I kidding? The insomnia was never going to end. I had given birth to a beautiful, healthy baby girl but now my body was broken, shattered into a thousand pieces. No one could ever put me back together.

Thank God, I was wrong about that too.

A FEW DAYS LATER, I finally made an appointment with my doctor. She told me that the dark thoughts, the compulsive checking and the sleepless nights was *not* something that all new mothers experienced. She gave me a diagnosis – postpartum depression – and asked me to admit myself to the hospital for psychiatric care. I agreed and in less than seventy-two hours, I felt like a new person, a phoenix risen from the ashes.

After four days in the hospital, I was ready to reclaim my life. I worked with a cognitive behavioral psychologist to dismantle

3

my anxiety and confront the traumatic parts of my illness. Within a few months of my hospitalization, my psychologist and I decided I had made a full recovery from postpartum depression.

But I was not done.

For almost my entire life, I had forced myself to live within narrow parameters that I thought would make me successful, like studying hard, going to law school, and working at big law firms, but the things that were supposed to make me feel happy made me miserable. Looking back, I know now that my sensitivity to hormonal fluctuations all but guaranteed that I would experience postpartum depression. The way I had been living my life, however, turned an illness into a crisis.

During my recovery, I did some intensive soul-searching and discovered new ways to feel like my most authentic self. I stopped worrying about what everyone else thought and started listening to my intuition. I filled my life with joy, meaning and fulfillment.

This is the story of how postpartum depression was the best thing that ever happened to me.

THE GIRL WITH HYPOCHONDRIA

"You have a cold," the doctor said.

"That's it?"

"That's it. But."

The doctor flipped through my file. I waited for the death sentence. Cancer? A tumor? Something too exotic to diagnose?

"You seem to come here for a lot of minor complaints. Colds. Headaches. Food poisoning. A spider bite."

It had been an impressive spider bite. A circle of skin on my left calf had turned pink and warm to the touch and swelled up to a diameter of at least two inches. My skin had never reacted so violently to a bug bite. I'd had to show the bite to a doctor *just in case.*

The doctor snapped my file shut. "I think you should see a therapist. Your student insurance covers ten visits."

Therapy? Me? What if my friends found out?

Therapy was for bored housewives and people who could not get their shit together. I did not fall into either category. I was an Ivy League student, writing a senior thesis about the publication of Benjamin Franklin's *Autobiography* and headed to law school next year. I barely ever cried.

Clearly, though, I was doing something wrong if this doctor thought I needed to talk to a therapist. "Okay," I said as he handed me a sheet of paper with information about the college's mental health services. I felt like I should say something more to convince him that I was a normal, successful student who rose above her emotions, but the words got stuck in my throat.

Maybe I could use therapy to learn the right way to act so no one would ever again think my feelings were getting the better of me.

My NEW THERAPIST ushered me into his office. He seemed old—in his early thirties, at the very least—and was wearing glasses, a white lab coat, and grey slacks. The blinds were drawn.

I sat down on a chair on the other side of the room and took note of the large box of tissues on a nearby table. Hopefully I would never need them.

"So why are you here?"

"One of the doctors suggested it. He said I've been coming to the student medical center too often."

"Do you think you've been coming too often?"

"All my friends think I'm a hypochondriac, so maybe."

"What do you hope to accomplish in therapy?"

"I want to stop acting like a hypochondriac."

"Why?"

"Because hypochondriacs are weak and pathetic. People laugh at them."

What I meant was that *I* thought hypochondriacs were weak and pathetic. *I* thought feelings were silly and degrading.

I have tried to understand where and how this aversion to feelings started.

Maybe I learned it from the movies. I watched a lot of *Star Wars* and *Indiana Jones* growing up. The heroes almost never took a moment to linger on unpleasant feelings. If someone important died, they got sad for 2.3 seconds before throwing back their shoulders and facing the next attack from Darth Vader or Nazis.

Maybe I gleaned it from books. I favored big fantasy adventures like *The Lord of the Rings* and just like the movies, those stories did not dwell on messy feelings like sorrow and loneliness. Even if a character cried, I only had to flip through a couple of pages to get back to the adventure. The message I internalized about life was that emotions deserved very little attention from a heroic character.

Then again, maybe my overdeveloped sense of independence contributed to the way I avoided crying. From an early age, I wanted to be able to do things all by myself. In preschool, I learned how to read. In kindergarten, my mom gave me *Ramona and Her Father*, a book with chapters and almost no pictures. We sat down on the couch and started to read the book together, but after a few paragraphs, I pulled the book away, insisting I was going to read it by myself. The girl who wanted to read by herself would have loathed asking her parents to help her navigate messy feelings. I had to handle my emotions alone.

Except I did not like the way I felt when I was sad, lonely, embarrassed, or rejected. I learned to shove those feelings away. It was better to listen to some cheerful music and do my homework than to let myself cry when I was dumped two days after my first kiss or when I found out my friends had dressed up in their fanciest clothes and had "prom" at a diner without me.

Whatever the reason, by the time I was in the office of my first therapist, I was determined to be strong and rise above any ugly feelings that might try to ruin my day. Even if that meant acting like everything was fine when my eldest cousin died.

AFTER SEVERAL SESSIONS, the therapist observed that my medical complaints had started during the spring of my freshman year.

"I guess so."

"Did anything happen before the spring that might have triggered your fear of dying?"

"Um," I thought out loud. "I don't think so."

The therapist waited.

"My cousin Kim died."

"Tell me about that."

I took a deep breath. I had barely spoken of Kim's death since it had happened. "It was January. I was a freshman. I saw Kim for the last time ever on Christmas Eve . . ."

On my dad's side of the family, I was the fifth of sixteen grandchildren. Three of my cousins lived in Michigan, but the rest of us were born and raised in Los Angeles. Family gatherings, from barbeques to baptisms, were frequent and crowded with cousins. Christmas Eve was the most important. Since before I was born, everyone had always celebrated Christmas Eve at my Uncle Phil and Aunt Berta's house. Aunt Berta made lasagna, there was this amazing pink Cool Whip "casserole," and the house was crowded with about thirty cousins, aunts, uncles and family friends.

"Kim was sick. But not sick like she was going to die. More like sick because she had had the flu for a week."

I was hanging out with my cousins Emily and Julie on a couch near the Christmas tree. As kids, we had played tag in the backyard with our brothers. When we felt too old for tag, we played poker with pennies and nickels. Now that we were in college, we just liked to sit and gossip. Emily, Julie, and I had gone to the same all-girls Catholic high school and our classmates were always up to something amusing.

Kim came into the living room. She was thirty-one, and I was not quite nineteen. Despite all the family gatherings, I did not know her very well. I had been the sort of kid who wanted to hang out with other kids. I was not interested in grownup lives, and with our age difference, Kim always seemed like an adult to me. I assumed I would get to know her better when I was older myself and we had boring grownup stuff, like mortgages and grocery lists, in common.

Kim was helping her mom get dinner ready. We chatted while she snapped open a tablecloth and smoothed it over a folding table.

"How are the college girls doing? Anyone have a boyfriend?"

We bantered, and Kim coughed into her arm.

I winced sympathetically. "I heard you had the flu."

"Had?" Kim laughed. "Try the present tense. This has been the longest flu of my life."

"Christmas Eve with the flu must be fun."

"Oh, it's fantastic." Kim smiled. "But it's worth it. This is the first year that Timmy kind of understands what is going on."

At two and a half, Kim's son was the baby of the family.

"Then what happened?" My therapist dragged me back to the present day.

"That was the last time I ever talked to her. A couple of days later, she was hospitalized. I wanted to visit but my parents vetoed that idea. But the doctors discharged her and said she was doing better. I came back to Dartmouth for the winter quarter. I forgot about Kim being sick…"

I started to cry and reached for the tissues. I had rarely cried in front of anyone. Hell, I had barely ever cried in solitude.

My parents had called my dorm room on a Sunday morning, waking me up. Kim was gone, they said, she had died the day before, in her sleep. I remember crumpling forward into an origami position of shock—elbows on knees, head in hands, legs numb.

"But the doctors said she was fine. They discharged her from the hospital."

"I know." In the background, I thought I could hear my dad

9

crying. He had been only thirteen years old when Kim was born and made him an uncle.

I sobbed so hard, my chest hurt. My roommate got out of bed and hugged me from behind.

"Can I come home for the funeral?"

"Of course. Dad already called the airline. There's a flight that leaves Boston this afternoon. Can you get packed in time to catch the eleven o'clock mini coach?"

I disentangled myself from my roommate's hug and forced myself to stop crying as I talked travel logistics with my parents. Then I got in the shower and sobbed alone. I was in brand-new emotional territory. My great-grandmother had died when I was seven; my childhood dog had been put to sleep shortly before my senior year of high school; and that was it. I was not prepared to deal with death, not when I was in New Hampshire, far from my home in Los Angeles, in front of friends I had known for less than four months. Especially not with my lifelong aversion to crappy feelings.

I did not cry for Kim again—not even during the funeral. But now, in my therapist's office, I found I was crying and in need of the box of tissues. For a moment, my chest felt lighter, as if a darkness were leaving my body, but then my brain got involved and resisted the rush of emotions.

I sniffled and pulled myself back together.

"Sorry about that."

The therapist shrugged. "That's fine."

I was horrified with myself. If I had to be a person who did therapy, at least I could be the sort of person who smiled and acted fine during said therapy.

BY OUR NEXT APPOINTMENT, I had everything figured out and

explained it all to my therapist. "I've been acting like a hypochondriac because Kim died suddenly and unexpectedly."

"Oh?"

"She had been taking diet pills that damaged her heart. Fen-phen." Kim died in January 1997. Less than a year later, the Food and Drug Administration pulled fen-phen off the market. "But at the time she died, we had no idea why she had been sick, so I became anxious that I too might collapse and die without warning. That's why I've been running to the student center for every medical symptom."

The therapist nodded and tapped his pen against a clipboard. I remember how smug I felt, coming to that conclusion about my anxiety. My conclusion, however, was just a rushed and amateurish attempt at concocting a psychological explanation to put a bandage on the emotional equivalent of a severed limb.

"The next time I get stressed about a medical symptom, I just need to remind myself that I'm being a hypochondriac. Then I can talk myself off the ledge."

The therapist tapped his pen even faster against the clipboard.

"So I don't need any more therapy. I've resolved my issues. I'm cured."

With a completely neutral tone of voice, the therapist said, "You think you have resolved all your issues?"

"Yes. Now that I know what is happening, I can control it."

If I had known the problems my hypochondria would create after I had my first child, I might have been willing to invest a little more time in therapy. Then again, I would never have believed how badly my efforts to conceal my hypochondria would backfire.

LOVE AND MARRIAGE

"So you guys have season tickets?" I asked.

"Yes, we got them last year." Nathan jumped to his feet. "What's the flag for?! He wasn't offside!" He sat back down and leaned closer to me. "When a player is offside, it means—"

"You can't kick the ball to the guy playing offense if there's no one from the other team between him and the goalie."

"That's right," he said, turning to make eye contact. "I'm impressed."

"I played soccer as a kid. Until eleventh grade."

"Why did you stop?"

"I thought four AP classes and being editor of the lit mag would look better on college applications. When did you start playing soccer?"

"I never played. We didn't have soccer in my town."

Teddy had mentioned that Nathan grew up in rural Nebraska, but it had never occurred to me that a town could be too small for soccer.

We were not on a date. I was merely attending a soccer game with Nathan, his best friend Sean and my friend Teddy. Teddy and I had become friends during our first semester of law school when we bonded over a plate of french fries and a discussion of the cute boys in our section. This was her latest attempt to play matchmaker and end my dating drought, which was now on par with an Old Testament–style Egyptian famine.

Teddy had actually been trying to arrange this meeting for the past year and a half, ever since Nathan started working at her firm. She was a busy lawyer, Nathan was a busy lawyer, and I was a busy lawyer. Aligning our schedules was near impossible, especially since we all lived in different parts of Los Angeles County. During the time that Teddy had tried to arrange a date, Sean told Nathan, "If it turns out you guys actually are soul mates, you are going to be pissed that you missed out on having all this time together."

But when I look back at it now, I'm not pissed. I'm grateful. If we had met any sooner, I would have subconsciously sabotaged any chance at a serious relationship. Don't get me wrong. I *wanted* to find my soul mate, fall in love, and live happily ever after. Emotionally, though, I was not ready.

That's why I was giving therapy another go, this time with a licensed clinical social worker named Sheila. In college, my hypochondria had been glaring enough for me to realize that I might benefit from a little therapy, but I had only dipped my toes into the tide pools of my issues. A couple of years after law school, my failure to ever venture beyond a second date had made me so desperate, I was willing to wade into the surf and splash around with my feelings. Now, after more than a year of talking about all of the reasons I avoided dating—my anxiety, fears of rejection, and avoidance of messy feelings—I was watching a soccer match with a man my friend insisted I was going to marry.

He wasn't my type.

The four of us—Teddy, Nathan, Sean, and I—had met for dinner beforehand. As soon as I saw Nathan, I knew it would never work: I preferred my guys tall and lanky; Nathan was tall but built for football. At least I would get to cross "attend a professional soccer match" off my bucket list.

It seemed pointless to make conversation, but Teddy was paying attention and would ream me if I spent the entire game sulking. Also, I had told Sheila about this set-up, and she would want to hear what happened.

Under Sheila's tutelage, I had ventured into the world of online dating. According to her, going on dates signaled to the universe that I was ready and willing to meet the right guy. More than a dozen times, I had exchanged witty emails with a guy who seemed promising online, but then, we would meet for coffee or drinks and the potential would fizzle. I was starting to feel like maybe my fear of rejection was winning. Maybe I had met Prince Charming a dozen times but convinced myself the chemistry was missing so I could stay home and knit another scarf. Knitting never made me cry.

"So . . ." I took a big sip of my soda. "I hear the Galaxy signed Beckham."

"Yeah, he starts next week."

"Do you think he'll be a good thing for the team?"

"He better be, for all the money we are paying him."

"Isn't he one of the greatest players?"

"*Was.* He's old now. He and Victoria probably just want to hobnob with all the Hollywood stars."

"That's right, he married a Spice Girl. I nearly got expelled over an incident involving a Spice Girl act in our high school talent show."

Nathan turned away from the game. "This I have to hear."

I was on student council and in charge of the activities that created school spirit. My friends wanted to dance to the song 'Wannabe' and I didn't make them audition. They were, of course, the grand finale. Some girls from a junior high school were visiting and watching from the back of the auditorium. My friends danced the way people danced.

I could feel myself getting angry at the memory. "It's not like they were doing a strip tease but they were moving their hips, and the dean of students was scandalized."

"Why? Did the guys get rowdy?"

"I went to an all-girls Catholic school."

"Oh, so you were supposed to be prudish and virginal?"

"Exactly."

As I continued the tale of how the dean thought I had ruined the school's reputation, Nathan listened intently, ignoring the game on the field. This was refreshing. Every time I had gone on a date, the guy had just wanted to blather on about himself. Nathan and I were actually having a conversation.

While Nathan was distracted by Sean, Teddy whispered, "So? It's going well?"

I blushed. Was it going well? I had never had such an easy time talking to a guy, but that was probably because Nathan wasn't my type. I didn't feel any pressure to flirt. Still, I liked the way I felt sitting next to him. I could so easily lean against him . . . But no, Teddy was just an overeager matchmaker. Nathan and I did not have that essential "spark."

During the second half, a few players started elbowing each other as they scrambled for the ball.

"Woo hoo hoo." Nathan clapped. "Things are getting chippy now."

"'Chippy'? What does that mean?"

"It means the players are getting a bit belligerent."

"Huh." I dunked a chip into fluorescent nacho cheese. "'Chippy' is such a fun, cheerful word. It should mean something good."

"Yes, like, 'This ice cream is very chippy.'"

"Exactly!"

We had our first in-joke.

A blob of the luminescent cheese dripped onto the cuff of my grey sweater.

Nathan pointed. "That stuff is probably toxic. You'll have to burn the sweater."

"Then you shouldn't have spilled the cheese all over me."

"Me?" Nathan feigned shock. "That was all you!"

"I'm sure you caused some sort of disturbance in the atmosphere that caused me to drip it on my sleeve."

"So you admit it was you!"

What was happening? It was as if we were flint and steel, striking against each other, creating a shower of sparks. If this soccer match lasted much longer, a flame was going to ignite.

"This is Guitar Hero," Nathan said.

"The guitar is the controller?"

"Pretty awesome, right?"

"Suuuuuure." In college, one of my friends had had the original NES system with all my favorite childhood games. We spent as many Saturday nights playing Super Mario Bros. 3 as we did going to frat parties (probably more). The new video games, however, seemed too testosterone-driven for my taste. I avoided them at all costs, but Nathan and I had been dating for about two months now, and it was becoming more and more clear that Teddy was right. This man was my soulmate. For Nathan's sake, I was willing to feign a little excitement as he jammed colored buttons in time with the colors flashing on the screen.

He handed me the big plastic guitar and showed me how to position my fingers. I sighed. How long did I have to pretend I liked this game before I could propose an ice cream outing?

The song started. The screen lit up with colorful circles and I pushed a button. My fingers were nimble on a keyboard when I was composing angry missives to opposing counsel and tapping out emails on my Blackberry, but now they felt slow and awkward.

"Don't pay attention to the score," Nathan said. "I was even worse my first time."

"How can I pay attention to the score when I can't even pay attention to the song?"

"Stop talking, just play. You've got this."

I kept jamming the buttons, praying the song would end, but then I got into the groove. My head bobbed along with the music, and I got lost in the game.

I had forgotten how much I loved to play.

In my last year of college, when my anxiety was bursting to the surface through bouts of hypochondria, I still had fun. My friends and I went to bowling alleys and truck-stop diners; played whiffle ball, Frisbee, and board games; and went sledding on the golf course at midnight, wearing trash bags and flinging ourselves down the hill. During law school, though, I forgot to have fun. Instead of hypochondria, I channeled my anxiety into studying and getting the best grades possible. When I took a study break, it was to watch a movie or log a few miles on the treadmill—relaxing, perhaps, but not the sort of fun I'd had in New Hampshire.

The song finished. I sat for a moment, savoring the tingling feeling in my chest, arms, and neck.

"What did you think?"

I leaned toward Nathan and gave him a kiss. "Can I play one more song?"

"Of course!"

ONE TUESDAY MORNING IN JULY, Nathan casually suggested a trip to our favorite botanical gardens. We had been dating for two years and fifty-one weeks. (Nathan gets defensive if I round up to three years.)

"Ooh, yes. The gardens are open until eight. You know I've been wanting to go."

When I got home from work, it was a balmy ninety degrees in Pasadena. I assumed we would scrap the garden outing for something involving air-conditioning, but Nathan was still dressed nicely in his work clothes and eager to go.

An accident had turned the freeway into a parking lot. I touched my palm against the hot window. "Maybe we should go another night."

Nathan gunned the car toward the off-ramp. "We can take surface streets!"

I leaned back and hummed along to the music. Life was good. A couple of months earlier, I had quit my job with a big law firm (about seven hundred lawyers throughout the country) and joined a firm of less than a dozen attorneys. I was willing to accept the smaller salary for a better quality of life. I still had my apartment in Brentwood but almost never went there anymore. My mail was forwarded to Nathan's house in Pasadena, and I had told my landlord that he could use my apartment to practice his electric guitar. It was a win-win: his wife got some peace and quiet; and I did not have to worry that vagrants had turned my apartment into a meth lab.

My car's fuel light clicked on a few miles away from the garden.

"Oops, I forgot about that." My stomach rumbled. "Maybe we should get gas and dinner."

Nathan gritted his teeth. "We can get gas after the garden."

I thought Nathan's resolve to get to the garden was a bit out-of-character. He was the sort of guy who wanted to watch television and maybe float in the pool after work. I, however, did not pursue the thought for more than a second. Maybe my subconscious was trying to keep the rest of me in the dark so I could be surprised by what was about to happen.

The garden was unusually busy. Kids were screaming and running around as a band played music on the main lawn.

Nathan seemed concerned. "I had no idea it would be so crowded. I wonder if we can find anywhere private."

"It doesn't matter." I clasped his hand in mine. "I just love being here."

We walked over an orange bridge in the Japanese gardens. As we climbed up a steep hill in a wooded area, the din of the children's concert faded to silence. We had the back half of the garden all to ourselves.

"I love this place," I said, "it's so magical."

For the most part, our relationship was easy. I once knew a couple who took unicycle lessons together because they had nothing in common. Nathan and I did not need unicycle lessons. If anything, we enjoyed too many of the same activities, from wine tasting in Santa Barbara to gardening at home.

We loved to make each other happy. I cooked Nathan's favorite meals and listened to his complaints about the Huskers. (My next book should be called *So You Married A Nebraskan: How To Be A Supportive Wife During College Football Season*.) Nathan was willing to try any restaurant that struck my fancy (unless it was sushi) and fully supported my move to the small firm.

We had talked about the future (usually while floating around the backyard pool) and knew we wanted to spend our lives together. Marriage, though, was still an open issue. I had been ready to get married since our first anniversary of dating. Nathan was moving a little more slowly on that front. I thought I was fine waiting, but one month ago, I had started crying hysterically while getting ready for work and ended up in Nathan's lap, arms around his neck, sobbing that I could not take the uncertainty anymore. Nathan had already made up his mind to propose and had no idea I thought we might not get married.

Walking around the garden, I was no longer worried about our future. Crying on Nathan's lap had made me feel a lot better.

If Nathan needed a little more time to get his mind around the commitment of marriage, I could wait. He was certainly worth it.

Nathan steered me toward a spot that overlooked acres and acres of forest and, beyond that, the mountains. Looking back, I can see he was a little nervous, but at that moment, I was too content to think anything of it. He took my hand in his and started talking.

"Courtney, the past three years have been wonderful. You make me a better man. You are so sweet and beautiful but so strong. I never thought it was possible to find such an amazing woman."

I smiled and nodded, touched but utterly oblivious to what was about to happen.

Nathan got down on one knee.

"Courtney, I can't imagine living my life without you. Will you marry me?"

For a few seconds, I was speechless. Of course my answer was yes . I did not have to think about that, but I seemed to have lost the ability to speak. When I finally could, I stammered, "Oh my God, oh my God, oh my God."

"Is that a yes?"

"Yes! Yes, yes, of course, yes!"

Standing over the gardens, I felt as if I had reached my "happily ever after." The second round of therapy with Sheila had surely resolved all my issues. From here on out, with Nathan at my side, everything would be easy.

My adventures, though, had not even started.

LET'S MAKE A BABY!

Nathan folded his hands as the waitress walked away with our menus. "I guess we should talk about kids."

I burst out laughing. It was Monday morning, only a day and a half since my dad had walked me down the aisle while the DJ played the theme music from *Star Wars*. We were now having breakfast before running errands. There had been an ongoing issue with the front lawn's sprinklers, and Nathan did not want the grass dying while we were on our honeymoon in Maui. I was more concerned with stocking up on sunblock and procuring magazines for tomorrow's flight.

We had gotten married in Pasadena just a few miles from our house. My body was still glowing from the sheer joy of that evening: exchanging vows while my cousin Julia officiated; dancing the "Hava Nagila" with all our family and friends; playing with the boas and top hats in the photo booth; and twirling around the brick courtyard to a Bohemian dance number that involved lots of accordions.

"We don't need to talk about that yet." I patted Nathan's hand. "Let's enjoy the honeymoon first."

I was not trying to dodge a difficult conversation. We had

already decided we wanted to have children before we even got engaged.

"It's just that we are not getting any younger."

"I know. I'm not saying we need to wait until our forties." I was thirty-two. He was thirty-one. "I just think we only get to be newlyweds once, so we should enjoy this before we leap into the next big phase of our life."

"That makes sense. I don't want to rush you. Besides, if you change your mind and don't want to have kids, I will support you no matter what. It's your body. I don't want you to feel obligated to have kids for my sake."

"Thanks, babe." I peeled the top off a miniature half-and-half container. "Where should we go first? Home Depot or Walmart?"

"So what do you want to do today?"

"I don't know. Anything. Except the Coke museum."

My college friend Kendall laughed. I had dragged her and several friends to the World of Coca-Cola in Atlanta during college. Dartmouth required all students to attend school during the summer of their sophomore year. Most students went home for the long Fourth of July weekend, but Los Angeles was too far for a weekend trip. Kendall had convinced a bunch of us to go to her hometown instead. I was excited to visit Atlanta but had one condition: I had to go the Coke museum. Kendall had pleaded for us to do something else, *anything* else, explaining the museum was a big boring advertisement for the soda brand, but I could not be swayed. Sometimes we can learn only by making mistakes.

"Let's go wine tasting." That was Jason, Kendall's husband, speaking. Jason and I had met our very first day of college, when we were assigned to the same pre-orientation hike in the woods.

I frowned. "They have wine tasting in Atlanta?"

"Of course," Kendall said. "Georgia is the wine-making capital of the South."

Sometimes I am gullible. "Is that true?"

Kendall laughed. "I have no idea."

I had flown to Atlanta for a long weekend with my college friends. Nathan had stayed home because I did not expect him to fly across the country to listen to Kendall, Jason and me reminisce about our college days. The Aires, a Dartmouth all-male a cappella group, was performing at a local school. I swear, I did not schedule my trip around a college a cappella group, but Kendall and I had some serious feelings about the Aires. Nathan would be much happier in Pasadena having breakfast at our favorite Mexican dive restaurant and playing Dungeons and Dragons.

As we drove to wine country, I sat in the back of the car with my friends' seven-month-old baby, Annie. I made silly sounds and played peekaboo to amuse her.

Babies usually left me feeling hollow and bored. Inevitably the mother wanted me to hold her baby, and then I had to feign admiration while wondering when I could politely pass the baby back.

But not Annie. Or more accurately, she had evoked the "hot potato instinct" when I first met her, but after a few hours, I'd found myself enjoying her babbling company.

Nathan had asked about kids only once after the honeymoon. I had told him that I was not ready to get pregnant and would let him know when I was. He had assured me that I should take all the time I needed and would fully support any decision I made.

I had plenty of time to think. The job with the small firm had eventually made me even more miserable than the job with the big firm. I had resisted the idea of quitting, terrified that people would think I had waited for Nathan to propose so I could stay at home all day and eat bonbons. Nathan, though, told me repeatedly to stop worrying about what other people would think and pursue my dream of being a writer already. A few months before our wedding, I'd finally quit. Since the honeymoon, I had been working part-time from home, doing legal writing for a plaintiff's attorney and using the rest of my time to write a novel. Lately, my life seemed to be divided into three parts: part-time creative writing, part-time legal writing, and full-time worrying about whether I truly wanted to have a baby.

When I asked myself if I wanted to have a baby, my inner self jumped up and down and screamed, "Yes! Yes! Yes!" My lawyer brain thought that was too easy. Surely such a momentous decision required a little more thought.

And so, I thought. I read all the books I could find that addressed the weighty matter of choosing to be a mother or not. Then I wrote, pondered, and reflected in my journal. Between my history major and legal career, I knew how to weigh and analyze evidence, but those skills were not helping me answer the question at hand. How would I ever know that I absolutely wanted to be a mother?

The Atlanta visit was a nice vacation from that nagging question.

One afternoon, we stopped by the grocery store, where I pushed Annie around in a shopping cart. I stopped in the produce section and dramatically picked up a pineapple. Her eyes widened in wonder.

Jason drove me to the airport for my flight home. One last time, I sat in the back with Annie. Before I left, I kissed her forehead and whispered, "Good-bye, Annie. I love you." I had not planned on saying that but realized as I spoke the words that they were true.

I had my answer.

Except that answer gave rise to yet another question.

THE HUMMINGBIRD PERCHED on the stick. I raised it a few inches off the ground into the air. It started to flap its wings.

"That's it, little guy, you've got this."

It hovered in the air for a few seconds and then crashed back onto the grass.

"That's okay, maybe you need a little more rest and nectar."

An hour ago, I had discovered the hummingbird lying on the sidewalk in front of my house. I assumed it was dead but, upon closer examination, discovered its chest was moving. A quick internet search suggested the hummingbird had fallen from its nest and was now stunned. It would need nectar before it could possibly fly again.

I had raced to the hardware store and procured a hummingbird feeder and a gallon of red nectar.

My neighbor Alice pulled into her driveway.

"What are you doing?"

"I found this hummingbird."

She gasped. "Oh! It's so tiny and perfect."

"I think it must have been trying to fly a little too early."

"Poor baby."

Alice dropped her purse and settled on to the sidewalk next to me. We had been neighbors for over a year now, and Alice often updated me on her pregnancy status. It amazed me how easily Alice spoke of her struggles with infertility. She was a breath of fresh air, but at the same time, her honesty made me squirm. Since she wanted to talk about pregnancy tests and IVF, her very presence made me think about babies.

Nathan and I had been married for eight months now. Ever since I had returned from Atlanta a month ago, I knew I wanted to have a baby, but now I was struggling with another dilemma: *Should* I be a mother? It did not seem fair to bring a baby into this world unless I would be a good mama.

Nathan got home a little before twilight. He made a nest at the edge of our garage, and I transferred the bird to its evening quarters. We went inside for dinner and Mario Kart. Every twenty minutes or so, I paused the game and went back outside to whisper reassurances to the hummingbird and offer it another sip of nectar.

The hummingbird survived the night and even managed to flop itself eight or nine feet away from the garage. I found the contact information for a hummingbird expert in Hollywood, and she told me to take the bird to the Humane Society. There was legal research that needed my attention, but this was more urgent.

A couple of days later, I called the Humane Society to see how the bird was faring. It had peeped on the drive over in its little shoe box bed. I knew it was going to be fine. I provided the case reference number and waited as the volunteer tapped it out on a keyboard.

"It died yesterday."

"Oh. Thank you."

I hung up the phone.

Lowered my head into my hands.

And wept.

When I'd first quit the small firm, I'd started writing a fluffy comic novel about a disastrous wedding. After a few months of writing, it morphed into a more serious story about a woman whose twin brother died in college. My grief over Kim's death had finally found a way to bubble to the surface. By writing about a fictional character's loss and how it affected her, I was able to come to terms with my own feelings.

As I wept for the hummingbird, I also cried for my cousin. My tears were not enough to cure my anxious tendencies. The anxiety was far too deeply embedded in my body, mind, and soul to be so easily resolved. But I did cry enough to answer the question of whether or not I would be a good mother. At least, that was what I thought was happening: that I truly needed proof that I would be a good mother and the fact that I could feel so much love for a hummingbird was the proof I sought.

What was actually happening, I realized later, was a little more complicated. The questions of whether I would be a good mother and whether I actually wanted to have a baby were delay tactics. So long as we weren't trying to get pregnant, whether or not we had a child was in *my* control. As soon as we started trying, I opened myself up to the possible pain of infertility, miscarriage, premature delivery, and a baby with health issues. I lost absolute control. That was terrifying.

Something about the hummingbird's death took away that terror. Less than a week later, Nathan and I started trying to have a baby of our own.

———

MY GENERAL PHYSICIAN scribbled some notes on my chart. "I'd like to get an X-ray before I order physical therapy," she said.

I had hurt my back while testing beach chairs at the drugstore. The pain had subsided after a couple of weeks of painkillers and heating pads, but after a cross-country flight, it had flared up again.

"Sounds good," I said. "Oh, by the way, we've been trying to get pregnant."

My period had come and gone three times since we started trying and was due again in a few more days. I assumed that since I knew so many women who suffered from infertility, I would struggle with it as well. At a recent checkup, though, my obstetrician had said we should try for a year before worrying about that.

"I don't want to give you an X-ray if you are pregnant, so let's do a urine test."

I peed into a cup, certain that I would be getting an X-ray in ten minutes. Back in the examination room, I flipped through magazines and berated my heart for daring to beat a little faster.

A nurse opened the door. Avoiding eye contact, she said, "The doctor will be with you shortly."

My heart sank. At least Nathan had promised I could have a herd of dachshunds if we could not have children.

The door opened again. This time it was the doctor, smiling as if she had won the lottery. She was waving something around in her hand, but for a moment, I could not process what it was.

Yellow.

Square.

Paper.

A yellow sticky note. It was a yellow sticky note.

And what was that scrawled on the sticky note?

Was that . . . ?

Could it be . . . ?

A plus sign?

I jumped to my feet.

"I'm pregnant?!"

"Congratulations!"

The doctor's phlebotomist drew my blood to confirm the urine test.

"This is so perfect." I had never been so happy to let someone stab me with a needle. "I wanted to get pregnant after a year of marriage and our anniversary is next week."

"Ooh, you should wait until your anniversary to tell your husband, and then you can surprise him with a onesie for his favorite sports team."

"That's a great idea."

As soon as I stepped out of the building, I called Nathan. There was no way I could wait a week to share the news.

———

"WAKE UP, BABY!"

The image on the ultrasound screen stayed in the same place.

The doctor, a man in his sixties with a Caribbean accent, wiggled my stomach around with the ultrasound scanner. He was an obstetrician who specialized in ultrasounds. My regular obstetrician did not have any concerns about my baby, but she sent all her patients here during the second trimester.

Nathan had been excited when I called him with the news that I was pregnant. My excitement soon morphed into another feeling: awe. I had to drive home from the doctor's office and realized I was no longer driving for one. If something happened to me, it would also happen to my baby.

My parents were on vacation in New York when I learned I was pregnant. My sister, who is ten years younger than me, was also in New York, studying art business. I decided to surprise them with the big news when they were back in California and ordered mugs that said "World's Best Grandpa," "World's Best Grandma" and "Best Aunt Ever."

I gave them the mugs on a Sunday in early August. I was seven weeks pregnant, and my mom nearly fainted when she realized what her gift meant. Everyone was so excited, we decided we had to call my brother Matt and sister-in-law Sara right away. No one bothered to calculate the time difference between Los Angeles and South Africa. Let's just say that my brother was less than thrilled when I woke him in the middle of the night. (Even Peace Corps volunteers get cranky.)

"Your baby," the specialist said, "do you want to know the sex?"

"She's a girl." During the first trimester, I had gotten an expensive blood test called the Ashkenazi Jewish panel because my mom is Jewish. It was a genetic test to rule out recessive disorders like cystic fibrosis and Tay-Sachs that are common among the Ashkenazi Jewish people. Insurance did not cover the test, so to make the $800 bill more palatable, my obstetrician made sure the test results included the baby's sex.

"She is indeed. She does not want to wake up."

"I didn't realize babies sleep inside the uterus."

"Oh yes, they sleep, and your baby seems very determined to stay asleep in this position so I can't check her measurements."

"That's okay. I just like getting to see her." Though I had no idea what I was actually seeing on the ultrasound screen.

As if reading my mind, the doctor pointed at the grainy blob. "This is her head."

"Her head."

"These are her hands."

My heart skipped a beat.

"Come on, baby, wake up." More jiggling.

"Do all babies do this?"

"Babies often get into the wrong position, but your baby is taking longer than usual to wake up."

"Is that bad?"

"Bad?" The doctor chuckled. "She's stubborn. Like my daughter. Which is good when she is a woman, but not so easy on the parents. Ah, there she goes."

I felt awful—nauseated, constipated, and the pain in my back would not subside—but as the doctor measured my daughter's limbs, all those crappy feelings faded away. I was going to be a mom! That grainy blob on the screen was my baby!

Besides, the first trimester was nearly over. Surely my hormones had done their worst. From here on out, it would be easy street.

My hormones, though, were just getting started.

4

PREGNANCY, AKA A FANCY WORD FOR "HELL"

I settled my feet on a stack of pillows and clicked on the nightstand light. "Okay, baby girl. It's week twenty-eight. Let's see what the third trimester has in store for us."

I cracked open my favorite pregnancy book and started reading about Braxton Hicks contractions and delivery. I could not wait for this pregnancy to be over.

In the first trimester, I had discovered that morning sickness was not always limited to the morning and could in fact last all day. Once I got my arms around the fact that a man had probably coined the phrase "morning sickness" in order to get his wife back into the kitchen and making supper, I started counting the days to the second trimester, when the all-day sickness would end. The sickness, however, did not abate until several weeks into the second trimester. When it did, I was so relieved, Nathan and I planned a trip to Orlando to visit family and have some fun. The nausea returned with a vengeance as I was drinking a virgin strawberry daiquiri by the pool. (I'll never drink another daiquiri.) I prayed my stomach would return to normal after the birth.

The constipation was even worse than the nausea.

Around week seven, I felt my bowels grind to a stop. I did everything I could to reboot the system. I guzzled prune juice, various pink and green potions that my obstetrician recommended, and walked around our block. The pain was so bad that if my bowels had felt inspired during one of those walks, I would have gladly squatted on a neighbor's lawn.

Day three of the Great Constipation Ordeal, I could not pee. My bladder was ready to burst from all the prune juice I had been imbibing, but no matter how I squeezed or crouched above the toilet, only a few drops would trickle out. My obstetrician told me to go to the ER for a catheter.

A concerned doctor listened to my stomach with his stethoscope. "Well, I believe you when you say you've been drinking prune juice. I can hear a lot of activity in there."

That sounded promising.

"But unfortunately, your plumbing is all blocked up and nothing is coming out until we deal with that."

That sounded less than promising.

"Pregnancy can be so hard. I remember my wife had terrible constipation during her pregnancies. I could give you a catheter, but I think if we relieve the constipation, then your bladder will sort itself out."

A kindly nurse arrived quickly and asked me to roll onto my side. This was my first experience with an enema, and I actually thought the nurse was going to squirt a liquid solution up my derriere. I was more than a little surprised to discover what an enema actually entailed.

The nurse patted my shoulder. "Try to lie here for ten minutes before using the bathroom."

That would obviously not be a problem. After three days of constipation, I doubted the next ten minutes would bring any relief.

Three minutes later, I practically skidded into a wall as I made my way to the bathroom down the hall. The constipation crisis was over.

My humiliation, however, was just getting started.

By the time we left the ER, it was eleven o'clock on a Sunday night. The doctor had given me a prescription for a bladder infection (because if a pregnant lady shows up with constipation, I guess her urine needs to be tested as well). I wanted to fill the prescription immediately to keep our baby safe, but our local pharmacy was closed for the night. We had to drive to the next city to find a twenty-four-hour pharmacy and wait another hour to fill my prescription. Not only were we both exhausted, we were famished, having left for the ER before dinner.

As we waited and waited, I wandered the store. In the gastrointestinal aisle, I spotted a box of enemas. The warning on the box cautioned that pregnant women should not use the enema unless directed to do so by a physician, and my physician had told me to go to the ER, but I still blamed myself. I had been living off white bread, cheddar cheese, and more white bread to manage the nausea. I should have known that would make me constipated.

My cheeks burned. Was this all in my head? Was I being a hypochondriac? Since college, I had done my best to conceal the hypochondria, but I knew the truth. If I got a headache, I worried it was a tumor. When I got a cold, I fretted my immune system was collapsing. And though I knew in my rational brain that I was extra-sensitive to arachnids, I still suspected every spider bite was actually a flesh-eating virus.

Everyone – my husband, obstetrician, the nurses and doctor at the ER – must think I was so pathetic and weak for needing to go to the hospital for a little constipation. I should have been stronger and found a way to resolve the problem on my own. Hospitals were for severed limbs and deadly viruses. They were not for hypochondriacs who overreacted to something simple like constipation.

I resolved to do a better job of being the master of my body.

AFTER THE ER TRIP, I started eating double-fiber bread and apples to make sure my bowels stayed happy. This aggravated the nausea, but between puking and constipation, one must always, always choose vomit. A little before Thanksgiving, though, I got cocky. I was halfway through the pregnancy and sick of nausea. Surely I could mix some bland foods with the fiber.

Then again, maybe not.

This time, I ended up in my obstetrician's office.

"I could do a catheter—"

"Last time, I just needed an enema. That relieved all the pressure and then I could urinate."

My obstetrician winced. "I don't have any enemas—"

"That's okay, I brought one," I said, pulling the box out of my purse. (I was a Girl Scout.)

My doctor inserted the enema, I waited as long as possible, and then . . .

Did you know enemas do not always work?

Enemas do not always work.

"I was afraid this might happen," my doctor said. "I wonder if you have MS."

"Multiple sclerosis?" I yelped.

Was I dying? Would my baby be okay? Would Nathan have to be a single dad? And for the love of all things holy and sacred, could we please do something about the constipation before we sorted through the possible neurological underpinnings?

Not to worry: that was next.

"Since the enema did not work, I'm afraid I will have to manually extract the excrement."

I turned onto my right side, and the doctor lifted my paper

gown. When she put her gloved hand up my rectum, it hurt, but the humiliation was far worse than the pain.

As the room filled with the smell of my poop, the doctor said, "I'm a little concerned. You say you can't have a bowel movement, but your feces is actually quite soft. Based on your description, it should be hard."

To my ears, it sounded as if the doctor did not believe me. She was probably just puzzled, but in my already humiliated state, I assumed she thought the constipation was a figment of my imagination.

Tears filled my eyes. I had tried to poop. Believe me, I had tried. Pregnancy hormones do crazy things. They make women weep, drool, fart, and even eat dirt. In my case, the hormones had made the business of bowel movements a little more difficult. Still, I blamed myself.

"I'd like you to see a gastroenterologist to rule out something more serious."

Lovely. My obstetrician seemed to share my view that I was either a hypochondriac or dying of an obscure illness.

A month later, a gastroenterologist assured me the constipation was just a pregnancy symptom. "It's severe but still on the normal spectrum."

"So it's not MS?"

"No, you don't have MS."

Relief flooded my body.

"You will most likely experience more constipation and hemorrhoids after childbirth."

And there went the sense of relief.

"Is there anything I can do to prevent that?"

"I'm going to give you a list of things you can do while you are pregnant, but constipation after pregnancy is inevitable."

Oh good, I thought as I left the office. Another opportunity for me to be utterly humiliated and act like a pathetic hypochondriac.

I THUMBED through the third-trimester pages, noting topics of interest.

"Braxton Hicks contractions, that sounds sci-fi . . . oh, vaginal discharge, lovely . . . frequent urination. Even more frequent than it already is? Well isn't that exciting."

There was an entire chapter devoted to breastfeeding. I had already bought several books about the lactation arts and registered for a breastfeeding class but made a note to read the chapter with a highlighter and pen. There were also several chapters devoted to labor and delivery. Those would require meticulous study.

My hand flew to my stomach. Pippa had started kicking. Even though my uterus registered every thump, it was still cool to feel the force of her foot banging against my fingers.

We had picked her name weeks before her first kick, a few days after the expensive blood test revealed we were having a girl. It was a Saturday in early September, and Nathan was watching college football while I flipped through some baby name books. After a couple hours of entertaining various names, we agreed that "Pippa" sounded right.

I frowned from my spot on the couch. "So do we have to name her 'Philippa'?"

"Of course not. That was holding!" Nathan turned back to me. "We will just name her Pippa."

"I like that. But since 'Pippa' is quirky, let's give her a solid middle name, like Ann."

Nathan paused the game. "You know I love the name 'Ann.'"

"But it has to be 'Anne' with an E."

We had not told anyone else, but ever since that Saturday, our baby's name was Pippa Anne Novak. Of course, we said we were open to other names. We still had over two trimesters to discuss, but there never were any other contenders. Now, with just one trimester to go, she was most definitely Pippa Anne.

Pippa was still kicking. "Are you going to be a soccer player? Or a dancer? I'm so excited to see who you want to be."

I spent a lot of time these days lying in bed, surrounded by pillows, and reading pregnancy books. The law firm I had been working for from home had recently hired some new attorneys. My services were no longer needed. I was going to be a stay-at-home mom and was ready to be done with the law, so the timing could not have been better.

A little before Christmas, I had finished the first draft of my novel. My sister had read it and given me a ton of ideas to make it better, and I had created an extensive checklist of revisions I wanted to make. Those, however, would have to wait until after the baby arrived. Revisions and nausea do not mix. But hey, at least newborns nap a lot. There would be time enough for writing once Pippa was here.

"Meconium? Poop that's like tar? Gross. We'll just let Daddy change those first diapers, okay?"

Pippa kicked. We were already coconspirators.

I flipped through the chapters about the first weeks with a newborn.

"Oh, here's some ideas for the registry. I don't think we need a diaper bag, do you? No, they are too frumpy. What about a baby carrier? Would you like me to carry you in a sling?"

Pippa stopped kicking. She was saving her strength for the midnight hour.

"The baby blues . . ." I skimmed a few paragraphs. "Pippa, this says 80 percent of new moms get the baby blues. Well, that is not going to happen to Mommy. You'll see, Mommy hardly ever cries. I'll be so happy to finally have you here in my arms, I won't have time to be sad."

I turned the page. A heading in bold immediately grabbed my attention: "**Postpartum Depression.**"

For a moment, it seemed as if someone had hit the pause button on the universe. I stopped breathing, and everything became very, very quiet. I can't explain why or how, but it was almost as if some part of me knew what was going to happen after Pippa was born.

I started to read—"extreme sadness, low energy, crying episodes"—but quickly turned to the next page. Sitting on my bed, twenty-eight weeks pregnant and reading up on the post-partum period, I was not about to pay attention to irrational premonitions or put any silly ideas into my head. It was bad enough that I had to worry about postpartum constipation. My inner hypochondriac would have a field day if I knew the symptoms for postpartum depression.

"How are you doing?" The obstetrician had just arrived to check on my progress.

"The contractions just started hurting again. I need the anesthesiologist to give me another refresher."

I was in a private labor and delivery room at the hospital. The room was larger than any room at our house and had dark wood paneling on the walls. It felt more like a nice hotel room than a room for giving birth.

Nathan and I had been in this room, sleeping and watching movies, for the past eighteen hours. My water had broken the night before, a little after 11 p.m. I had been asleep and woke up to use the bathroom. After I finished peeing, a trickle of water kept coming out of me. My due date was eleven days away, so my first thought was that I had broken my bladder. It took me a minute to realize what had happened, and when I did, excited adrenalin flooded my body.

I would have run to wake Nathan if I had been capable of

anything more than a waddle. He was out of bed before I could finish the sentence, "I think my water broke."

My contractions had not yet started, but my obstetrician told me to head straight to the hospital. This did not surprise me. At the beginning of the pregnancy, I had tested positive for Group B Strep Infection, a bacteria that tons of healthy women have in their digestive tract. The bacteria can occasionally make a newborn sick, so my doctor had warned me multiple times that I would need to take antibiotics intravenously as soon as my water broke.

On our way to the hospital, Nathan played Europe's *The Final Countdown* on his phone. Our baby was coming!

Before I was admitted to the labor and delivery ward, the nurses had to confirm that I was actually in labor. I had a queasy feeling I was going to be sent home with an admonition to stop pissing myself. A nurse, though, tested the liquid coming out of me and confirmed it was amniotic fluid. She hooked me up to a machine and said I was in fact having regular contractions. Every time the machine registered a contraction, more liquid whooshed out of me. Still, I felt nothing.

I was a goddess. Contractions could not hurt me!

Ten hours later, the contractions were so bad, I wanted to die. My sister called. We had talked several times since my water broke. During the first several calls, I sounded cheerful and upbeat. About ten hours into labor, though, I sounded as if I had been possessed by a demon. At least, so my sister says. I myself have no memory of that conversation.

All I remember from that stage of labor was the delivery nurse's suggestion I wait a little longer for an epidural. I was only four centimeters dilated, and she thought I should wait until I was at least five centimeters. My obstetrician, however, had told me to get the epidural as soon as I wanted. I was not going to be a hero and wait for the five centimeter mark. The anesthesiologist had applauded my aversion to pain as he administered the epidural.

Now it was 9 p.m. Approximately twenty-two hours had passed since my water broke, the pain was back, and I wanted it to go away. My obstetrician, though, thought otherwise.

"You are ten centimeters dilated." She was standing at the head of my hospital bed. "It is time to push. It will be a lot easier if you can feel the contractions."

"But I want another epidural."

"Honey," the nurse said, "you will be able to push better if you can feel the contractions."

I looked at my doctor. "So it's better to feel the pain?"

"I think so."

"Okay."

And that is how I, a woman fully committed to having an epidural, entered the final stage of labor sans pain medication.

5

IN WHICH MY ADVENTURES WITH POSTPARTUM DEPRESSION BEGIN

Theoretically, I was supposed to "push" whenever a contraction started. The labor and delivery class had glossed over this part, the teacher insisting everything would make sense when the time to push arrived.

That time had arrived.

Nothing made sense.

With each contraction, I experimented with a different technique. It was like trying to do a squat without the benefit of ever seeing how someone actually performed that exercise. After several tries, I finally did something right.

"That's it, Courtney, that's it," my doctor said. "That's exactly how you need to push."

I panted and looked at Nathan. He smiled. Then I noticed the nurse was busy by my tush, cleaning up a mess.

Poop. She was cleaning up my poop.

Various authorities had warned me that I would probably poop on the delivery table. But I am a well-mannered woman, thank you very much, and my manners include holding doors open, saying please, and never, under any circumstances, pooping on a table. Besides, my poor obstetrician had already had to yank feces out of my intestines. Surely she had experienced enough of my poop to last a lifetime.

When the next contraction started, I got shy. I tried to push without pooping. It was a bit like trying to do a squat without using any thigh muscles. The contraction ended, but no one cheered.

This went on for at least an hour. Every now and then, I would let go of my inhibitions and push with all the muscles usually responsible for pooping. My doctor and nurse would hoot and holler and tell me to do it again. Then I would go back to worrying about pooping on the table and for the next several contractions, I would try to push out the baby while preserving my dignity.

About two hours into active labor, after a successful push, the doctor said, "I can see it, I can see the top of your daughter's head. Nathan, do you want to come see?"

No, I thought, he does not. We had discussed this and agreed he might be forever scarred if he looked at my lady parts during labor. But before I could register what he was doing, Nathan had scooted away from me and looked.

"She has hair! Lots of dark hair!"

When he returned to my side, he was trembling with excitement and looked radiant. As I watched, he transformed. One moment, he was a theoretical father. The next, he was an actual dad, head over heels in love with his daughter. My heart skipped several beats, but at the same time, I was jealous of Nathan. He looked radiant, but I felt empty and hollow inside. The pain of active labor had drained away all my good feelings.

Now that she had crowned, I assumed Pippa was seconds away from arriving. After all, that's how it happens in the movies.

Movies lie.

For another hour, I pushed and pushed and felt contractions ripping my body apart. Then, after nearly three hours of active labor, I accepted the truth: in order to push my baby into the world, I would have to poop all over the place. But I was exhausted and felt too defeated and pathetic to push.

As if she was reading my thoughts, my obstetrician said, "Courtney, you can push for ten more minutes, and then I have to do a C-section."

What? A C-section? After three hours of this hell?

I pushed and roared and pushed and forgot about everything but the contractions and the pushing. It did not matter how much poop got on the doctor.

Ten minutes later, the nurse placed Pippa on my chest.

I HAD BEEN ANTICIPATING this moment for nine months. It was the moment the heavens would part and fireworks would erupt and everything would be more joyful than I could possibly imagine.

The hospital ceiling stayed intact.

No fireworks exploded.

And though I searched for it, I could find no joy.

But here was my baby, my daughter Pippa, so I looked down at her and tried to memorize the moment. Her eyes were wide open and dark blue, almost navy, and from the way she looked at me, she seemed already to know that I was her mama.

My eyes glided down her body—head covered with black hair, plump lips, little scrunched-up shoulders, legs that seemed impossibly long for someone so small, and toes that were absolutely perfect. I wanted to hold this tiny creature forever.

But I could hold her for only a minute. Then a nurse whisked Pippa away to be poked and measured.

My doctor smiled apologetically. "I'm sorry, Courtney, but I need you to put your legs back in the stirrups so you can deliver the placenta."

Nathan shouted updates from the other side of the room. "She is so beautiful! Ten fingers. Ten toes. Oh her ears, they are so cute. She is amazing. So amazing! They are putting her on the scale. She weighs seven pounds and twelve point five ounces."

Some sort of enthusiasm from the mother seemed warranted, but I could think only about how much my legs hurt.

"Do you want to see the placenta?"

Not really, but before I could react, the doctor was holding my placenta high in the air, directly in my line of vision. It looked very *Game of Thrones*.

The doctor told me I had second-degree tears. The vaginal muscles had ripped during delivery. (Try not to dwell on that point if you can.)

"I need you to keep your feet in the stirrups a little longer," she said, "so I can stitch you up. But you can hold Pippa while I work."

A nurse returned Pippa to my arms, but my entire body was shaking from exhaustion. "Nathan, please hold her and give her some skin-to-skin contact." I did not want to drop my newborn.

Nathan removed his shirt and sat down on a chair about five feet from the hospital bed. He placed Pippa tenderly against his chest and held a blanket over her to keep her warm. After a moment, he laughed. "She's trying to latch on to me! You can try, baby girl, but I promise you won't get any milk from me."

I laughed as if this were the most magical moment of my life.

Inside, I felt empty.

What was wrong with me?

During that moment, when I was one of the newest mothers in the world, I thought I must be some sort of monster. But now, after lots of reflection, I know the truth: nothing was wrong with me.

I felt empty because I had given my all to bring my daughter into the world. The epidural had worn off when I needed it the most; my feet had been up in stirrups for over three hours; and my vaginal muscles had ripped. My feeling of emptiness was a vast improvement over the pain, misery, and fear of childbirth.

Still, I'd expected to feel some emotional fireworks upon meeting my daughter. Wasn't this supposed to be love at first sight?

Well, it was love at first sight, or rather, love at first *sound*, but that moment had happened three trimesters ago in my obstetrician's office when I'd heard Pippa's heartbeat for the first time. The obstetrician had moved the ultrasound machine's transducer probe around my bare stomach, a frown creasing her brow, and then her face had relaxed. She'd turned up a dial and the sound of a galloping heartbeat had filled the room.

My baby's heartbeat.

My heart had done somersaults and my lungs had felt so full, it was as if I might float all the way home. My baby. My baby! After that, I was fully in love with my baby. Every subsequent kick and ultrasound made my heart expand a little more. I did not need to see or touch my baby, and I certainly did not need to experience any fireworks, to be in love. But in the delivery room, looking at Pippa for the first time, I did not have the energy or capacity to think those things. All I could think about was how my reaction to Pippa's birth fell short of the Hollywood standard.

Meanwhile, my hormones were busy crashing. During pregnancy, my estrogen and progesterone levels had been much higher than usual. Within the next twenty-four hours, they would plummet back to their normal levels. For some women, this hormonal crash is a trigger for postpartum depression.

I had never done well with hormonal fluctuations. I could handle PMS, but the birth control pill had nearly destroyed me. When Nathan and I were first dating, I took one brand of the pill for a year, and even though my obstetrician at the time told me I would bleed a lot less during menses, my menstrual flow instead became even stronger. I tried switching to a different brand, but that only increased the intensity of the bleeding even more and, worse, gave me dramatic mood swings that made me cry hysterically—usually at dawn, to Nathan's delight, and for no reason at all. After six months on the second brand, I decided to quit, and the next time my period started, it was as if I had never taken the pill.

Looking back now, it seems so obvious. My body was sensitive to hormonal changes, and I already had plenty of preexisting issues with anxiety. Of course I was going to have postpartum depression.

ALL I WANTED to do was hold Pippa in my arms forever. After the doctor had sewed up my battle wounds, I had reclaimed my baby and held her for a second time. This time, I maneuvered her toward my chest and she eagerly latched on to a nipple and started to suck. Oh thank goodness, I thought, she is breastfeeding. I will be a good mother.

I ran a fever during the last hour of labor, so when Pippa was done breastfeeding, the nurses whisked her away for two hours of observation in the nursery. An orderly wheeled me to a room in the maternity ward where Nathan and I promptly crashed.

But even asleep, I could sense that something was missing. I woke up exactly two hours and seven minutes after the nurses took Pippa away for observation and shouted for Nathan, still asleep, to get our baby back. (I know, I know. It is so weird that I can remember that Pippa was gone for two hours and seven minutes and yet have no idea what I had for lunch yesterday.)

Pippa seemed to have gotten more beautiful while she was gone. I could not get over her almond-shaped eyes. When she was awake, I studied the color of her irises. When she closed her eyes, I marveled at her dark, dark lashes. Nathan had a hard time convincing me to put her back in the cradle so I could get more sleep.

My parents and Grandma Shirley arrived in the late morning for the beginning of hospital visiting hours. Pippa had turned them into first-time grandparents and a brand new great-grandma. As soon as Pippa seemed to be done breastfeeding, I proudly passed her to my mom. This seemed like a good time to feel some excitement.

All I could think about were my bowels.

I had started obsessing over my need to move my bowels a few hours ago, about seven hours into motherhood. Of course, at that point, I had nothing to poop. I had taken care of that situation on the delivery table.

That did not stop my anxiety from turning constipation into an obsession. While my parents and grandma gushed over Pippa, my brain fretted.

When would I poop?

Was I already constipated?

Would I need manual extraction again?

What if that didn't work?

I did my best to ignore the questions and enjoy our visitors. Pippa was lying stomach-down across my mom's legs, getting her first back massage to relieve gas. I thought I should be bouncing with excitement. After all, I had been so happy to tell my parents and siblings that I was pregnant. But now that my parents were here, snapping photos, and my siblings were sending excited emails and texts, the excitement felt so far away, it might as well have never happened.

Only the threat of constipation felt real.

BY AFTERNOON, I was certain that I had to poop. I had devoured a large breakfast, an even larger lunch, and multiple desserts. But every time I tried to have a bowel movement, I got nervous. Could I burst the stitches the doctor had sewn into me if I pushed too hard? Then I would imagine my bladder tumbling into the toilet and abandon the effort.

I got angry with myself. I was supposed to be bonding with my daughter, not worrying about my bowels. Surely all other mothers gracefully navigated these first postpartum hours. I berated myself as if I were spending every minute in the lavatory. That was hardly the case. The first day of Pippa's life, I spent all of fifteen minutes away from her. Most of the time, she was in my arms napping, breastfeeding, or both. I sang her lullabies, admired her toes, and cooed whenever she opened her eyes. My first day as a mother was mostly tender and sweet.

My anxiety about constipation, however, was an ever-present vibration in my personal atmosphere. It did not prevent me from bonding with Pippa, but it did keep my body humming with an edge of fear. And what had started as a single buzzing bee in the morning turned into an angry hive by day's end.

Around midnight, twenty-four hours after I had given birth, the night nurse tiptoed in to check my vital signs. Pippa was asleep in a cradle at the foot of my bed. Nathan was snoring on a cot near the door.

"Please," I whispered, not wanting to wake husband or infant, "I still haven't had a bowel movement and constipation was a big problem during pregnancy and I know from the way I feel that I'm going to need an enema."

I had mentioned the constipation issue at least a half dozen times to the day nurse, who was not impressed. The night nurse was much more sympathetic. She offered to fetch me a stool softener, and I gratefully accepted.

I thought I was solving an immediate medical concern, and that was indeed the case. But on a deeper, darker level, my anxiety, previously manageable, was increasing so much, it was interfering with my basic needs. Pippa and Nathan were both fast asleep. Exhausted from childbirth, I should have been sleeping as well. Yes, I felt a twinge of constipation, but the discomfort was on par with an itchy knee. The situation could have waited until morning. It was probably mostly a figment of my imagination.

The anxiety that had always been so manageable, that had given me the edge that made me a successful student and lawyer, had tipped into new territory. It was going to take a lot more than a stool softener to make me feel better.

"CAN I STILL HOLD HER?"

The nurse nodded curtly. "Yes, of course. You can take her out for feedings, but the rest of the time, she needs to be wrapped in the blanket. Make sure the eye mask stays in place."

Nathan transferred Pippa from her cradle to my arms. The biliblanket was made from thick, clear plastic. It was plugged into the wall and glowed blue.

The blanket crunched as I tried to find a comfortable position. I studied Pippa's face. Her skin still looked pink to me, but according to her blood test results, it was actually tinged yellow with jaundice. It had been less than nine hours since the nurse had given me a stool softener, and already my anxiety had found a new way to stay busy.

The paper mask covered half of Pippa's face, so I stroked the top of her head, the only part of her body I could safely touch without compromising the light therapy.

"Babe, that doesn't look comfortable," said Nathan. He was sitting on a fabric folding chair with armrests and cup holders that we had brought from home.

"It's not," I sighed. "How am I supposed to get skin-to-skin contact? I'm supposed to get as much as possible. It's important for breastfeeding."

"You got plenty of skin-to-skin with her yesterday, and you'll get tons more whenever she needs to nurse."

"I guess so," I said. I let Nathan put her back in the cradle and turn off the light so I could try to nap. In the dark, the biliblanket glowed an even deeper, more brilliant shade of blue.

"She looks like something out of a sci-fi movie," Nathan said.

"She's our little sci-fi burrito."

My heart was pounding as I tried to rest. At least Pippa had to be a sci-fi burrito for only one day.

THE INSURANCE COMPANY had decided it was time for my discharge, but the pediatrician wanted Pippa to stay in the nursery for another night. The biliblanket had not been intense enough. Pippa needed extra therapy from a light box, a big, clear container with a lamp at the top. It looked a lot like the sort of contraption that cook churros and pretzels at the zoo.

This was not part of the plan. We were all supposed to go home together, as a family of three. Nathan and I were not supposed to abandon our baby.

"You can stay until midnight if that makes you feel better," a maternity nurse suggested.

"Yes." I nodded. "And then we can come back at three to breastfeed Pippa."

I looked to Nathan for approval. "Whatever you want, babe," he said.

The nurse said, "That's fine, if you want, but you also need your sleep. We already have to give Pippa formula to help with the jaundice. You can come back in the morning after you have slept."

I hesitated. It was as if the room were crowded with the ghosts of breastfeeding experts, all of them wagging their fingers at me, urging me to be strong and not miss a single feeding.

But I was so tired. I had gone into labor a little before midnight on Saturday. I had labored all day Sunday, giving birth a little after midnight on Monday. Pippa had been the sci-fi burrito on Tuesday. Now it was Wednesday, and I could not remember the last time I had slept longer than three hours in a single stretch. My body needed some deep restorative sleep.

"We'll be back at six," I said. Pippa would miss only one nursing session. I could wake up at three and pump.

But once we got home, shortly after midnight, I could not bear the idea of setting up the pump and all of its bits and pieces. Surely the universe would forgive me if I let myself have a little uninterrupted sleep. I set my alarm for six in the morning and closed my eyes, assuming I would be asleep in seconds.

Except my body was too wired to sleep.

For two hours, I tossed and turned. The authorities had warned me to sleep whenever I could, but no one had told me what to do when a toxic mixture of guilt and anxiety—for leaving my baby, for not stopping the jaundice, for not being a breast-feeding superstar—pressed so hard against my chest that sleep was impossible.

BY MORNING, the guilt and anxiety had spread until they had contaminated all my thoughts—as if someone had repro-grammed my brain and changed the default settings. When my alarm pinged, instead of yawning and hitting snooze, I leapt out of bed (or did the best approximation of a leap that a woman with second-degree vaginal tears can do) and woke Nathan.

Now, on top of my guilt for abandoning Pippa, I felt guilty for waking Nathan.

According to what the discharge nurse had told me the night before, we were right on time for Pippa's first feeding of the day, but by the time we got to the nursery, Pippa had already been fed and put back in the Blu-ray player. My anxiety soared.

"Go have breakfast," the nurse said, "and come back in an

hour. Then you can cuddle her as much as you like while we wait for the blood test results."

The cafeteria was serving french toast covered with a tragic banana mush. As Nathan scraped away the mush, I felt responsible because I had ordered my breakfast first. By choosing the french toast, I had given it my vote of confidence. Now poor Nathan was eating a revolting breakfast because of me.

He hates me, I thought. He doesn't love me anymore. With every bite of breakfast, my adrenaline increased.

We ate in silence. We had been together for nearly five years and spent hundreds of waking hours together in companionable silence—sitting on airplanes, floating around our pool, driving to Santa Barbara, waiting in lines at Disneyland, and in a myriad of other places. But this silence was terrifying.

"Why did they have to put this banana mush on the french toast?" I said, feeling like the nerdiest girl at the bar making a pass at the movie star.

"I don't know, but it's disgusting."

His tone of voice said, I agree, this banana mush sucks, but inside, I winced and thought, He hates me, it's my fault this food is so gross. I felt an intense need to say something clever and interesting, as if our entire relationship depended on it.

"It's like cat vomit."

"Yep," Nathan said.

We were doomed.

Or at least, that was how the postpartum depression made me feel. I had no idea that I had postpartum depression, but looking back, I know that's what was happening. I cannot pinpoint the exact moment my symptoms turned into an illness. It's a bit like trying to determine when a snowball becomes an avalanche, but I strongly believe the snowball first started rolling as I tried to push Pippa into the world. By the time we were having breakfast in the hospital cafeteria, I had entered the postpartum depression zone.

Postpartum depression is a tricky illness. In the past, when I'd had a cold or the flu, I felt miserable but was still the same person. The common cold never made me question my relationship with Nathan. The flu did not make me hyper-analyze everything about his body language, down to the way he breathed.

But that was what postpartum depression did. Practically overnight, it shattered my sense of self. When we were dating, I often drove myself crazy with doubts about Nathan's love for me (thank you, *Sex and the City*), but those doubts had been gone for several years. My postpartum hormones resurrected long-dormant fears and increased their intensity by a power of ten. Instead of seeing my sweet, loving husband, I saw a man who emanated hatred and disdain for his lazy failure of a wife.

And the postpartum depression was only getting started.

6

THE FIRST SIX WEEKS

"How are you doing?"

"Wonderful! I'm doing great." I knew exactly what the obstetrician was doing. She was trying to sniff out a whiff of postpartum depression.

As if on cue, Pippa started to scream. She sounded like a siren portending the world's end, but the obstetrician seemed unperturbed by the noise. Instead, she looked concerned for me. I willed myself to appear calm and collected.

"But how do you feel?" she pressed.

"I feel great."

I was at my six-week postpartum appointment and given my history with hypochondria, did not want to say anything that would lead to a misdiagnosis of postpartum depression. Still, my doctor seemed to think I had it.

In hindsight, I realize my appearance might have tipped her off.

I usually got my long brown hair professionally cut and highlighted every two months. During pregnancy, my obstetrician had assured me that I could continue getting my hair highlighted, but I was not taking any chances. What if some chemicals seeped through my scalp, got into my bloodstream, and hurt my baby? If I was not getting my hair highlighted, I might as well skip the haircuts too. I had read about postpartum hair loss and reasoned it was better to have as much hair as possible in case half of it fell out.

By the time my water broke, my hair was straggly and a mix of greys and faded highlights. Three hours of active labor did nothing to improve my look: the ponytail holder fell out, and my hair got tangled into a sweaty, salty mess. During my first post-partum shower, I was too tired and defeated to drag a comb through the knots.

Six weeks later, I still felt too defeated to deal with the hair situation. Eventually, I would buy detangler and conquer the knots, but that was still several weeks away. My obstetrician must have been more than a little alarmed by my hairstyle.

"Are you happy? Getting enough rest?"

(My hair was truly frightening.)

"I am doing wonderfully. I didn't even have the baby blues. I haven't cried. I've been so happy since Pippa arrived."

When I said I was happy, I was trying to convince myself as much as the doctor. The part about crying, though, was true. I had not cried since Pippa's birth aside from the one time I started crying at one in the morning from pure exhaustion. That didn't count. That was not the baby blues. I assumed that whether or not a new mother had the baby blues was the ultimate barometer of her mental health; that postpartum depression was an exten-sion of the baby blues.

In a few months, I'd know better.

By the time of this six-week appointment, I had postpartum depression. I had not experienced any symptoms that would get me locked up in the mental ward (those would come soon enough), but looking back, I can see the red flags.

There was my new obsession with germs. Previously, my hypochondria had always been limited to symptoms I had, or thought I had, never extending into mysophobia, or fear of germs. Postpartum depression had helped me make the leap from hypochondria to mysophobia.

The first day of Pippa's life, while my parents and grandma were visiting us in the maternity ward, I scrolled through the online options for face masks. I needed a cache of masks for visitors who might arrive at my house with coughs and sneezes.

"I can't tell which one is good enough."

"I'm sure they are all fine." That was my mom, a woman who was always vigilant about her children's health. When everyone, including the pediatrician, insisted my sister simply had the flu, my mom was the one who piled everyone into the car to go to the hospital. Three hours later, the nurses were prepping Katherine for an emergency appendectomy. Now that her first grandchild was here, you could be sure my mom was not going to let anything endanger Pippa's health.

"But even the ones that are supposed to be good enough for surgery are not 100 percent effective."

"Courtney, if it's good enough for surgery, it will keep Pippa safe."

"You don't know that." I spent another hour agonizing over the options before settling on the best bad choice. Then I fixated on my next fear: unwanted visitors.

"What if someone wants to visit and they are sick?"

My mom had Pippa stretched across her legs, facedown, and was patting her back. This seemed to help her burp. "Courtney, no one is going to visit when they are sick."

"But what if someone wants to visit and they are already sick and contagious but they don't have any symptoms yet? Or they think it's allergies? A cold can kill a newborn."

I was imagining droves of Hennings, aunts, uncles and cousins from my dad's side of the family, descending upon our house unannounced.

"If the Hennings ask, do you want me to tell them you don't want visitors?"

"Yes. Be nice about it. But if anyone asks, discourage visitors."

The message must have been effectively delivered, because almost no one visited. Just my parents, Nathan's parents, my siblings, my grandma, and one cousin. I have a lot of aunts, uncles, and cousins in Los Angeles who would have loved to meet Pippa, but they steered clear.

So the mysophobia created another red-flag behavior: isolation.

———————

"SORRY, MY HANDS ARE COLD." The obstetrician had opened my gown and was gently touching my abdomen.

"It's okay," I said.

I had dozens of questions about my abdomen. Various nurses had shown me how to check my uterus and make sure it was shrinking, but their instructions made no sense. I could never tell what part of my body was stomach, what part was uterus, and what part was flab. I wanted to ask my doctor if my uterus had shrunk back to its regular size, but talking seemed like too much work.

I like people, I like talking, and lately, my life had been lacking in the conversation department. I chatted with Pippa throughout the day, but so far, she was a lousy conversationalist. I usually enjoyed talking with my obstetrician and should have been looking for ways to prolong the interaction. Instead I could not wait to be alone again.

When my parents and grandma visited, I usually retreated to my bedroom to sleep. I was exhausted from breastfeeding Pippa in the middle of the night, and sleep is essential to health, physical, mental, and spiritual; but even when I emerged to feed Pippa,

I hated talking. It seemed like an unnecessary burden. In reality, I was turning into a people-hating hermit.

Postpartum depression had changed my personality.

Just the previous week, my parents, sister, and grandma had wanted to visit during the weekend. I protested. Four visitors? At the same time? That was too much stimulation for Pippa. On the phone, I told my mom that anything more than two was unreasonable.

"Okay." I imagine my mom must have taken a deep breath at this point. "Just your father and sister will come."

"Thank you." I felt so relieved. "Thank you. I have to look out for Pippa."

A couple of days later, my mom called again. "Would it be all right if your grandma also comes to visit this weekend?"

"What? Grandma?"

"She's going back to New York in a week and she'd like to see as much of Pippa as she possibly can before she goes."

I gritted my teeth. "Fine."

When Nathan got home from work, I exploded. "This is ridiculous! They turn the house into a circus. It's too noisy and crowded with all of them here. My mom is being so manipulative."

Less than two years earlier, the morning after our wedding, we had about thirty people over to our house for bagels and donuts. The house had not seemed too crowded or noisy then. One newborn later, I could not tolerate the idea of being visited by three of my favorite people in the world at the same time. People who bathed the baby, trimmed her fingernails, and brought groceries. People who whisked away the dirty laundry and brought it back clean and folded.

It was not my mom who was being manipulative. It was the postpartum depression. It had manipulated me into a new person.

"ARE YOU STILL BREASTFEEDING?" The obstetrician gently examined my chest. Over in her stroller, Pippa was still wailing.

"Yes, exclusively."

I spent hours every day with Pippa suckling at my breast. The experts said a baby should be fed on demand, so every time she whined, I offered her a meal. Then once she had latched on, I could never tell if she was actually eating or just using me as a pacifier, so I let her linger as long as she liked. Each meal lasted at least an hour, and since she seemed hungry every other hour, I spent approximately half the day anchored to my chair.

I thought good mothers exclusively breastfed their babies. I was wrong (more on that later) but at the time of my six week checkup, that was what I believed. That explains why when my obstetrician asked if I was breastfeeding Pippa, and I said "exclusively," my stomach heaved from guilt and anxiety. I still felt bad that we had supplemented Pippa's meals with a little formula when she was diagnosed with jaundice. I remember the sucker punch of guilt that I felt in my gut when the pediatrician reported the jaundice on day two of Pippa's life. The pediatrician mentioned that we needed to supplement with formula because I was not producing milk yet, and I immediately (and incorrectly) blamed myself. It was my fault that Pippa had jaundice.

Pippa's jaundice was not my fault, but I had always had a propensity to feel guilty about things that were out of my control. In the second grade, when my vision started to fail, I assumed I had sinned and was being punished by God. My hippie parents were not at all religious, but after becoming less than enamored with the local public school, they had sent me to Catholic school. Impressed by an Old Testament God who sent floods and leveled cities, I hid my shoddy vision for two years. Every time I had to take an eyesight exam at school or the doctor's office, I cheated. I got close to the Snellen chart, memorized the lower rows of letters, and bluffed my way toward twenty-twenty vision. By the fourth grade, though, no amount of squinting could help me decipher the blurry smudges on the chalkboard. When I finally confessed my poor vision to my mom, and she laughed and said I had inherited my dad's vision, I felt as if I had escaped damnation.

Guilt, though, is its own sort of damnation, and six weeks postpartum, I was in guilt hell.

After Pippa's jaundice, guilt hijacked my body. I felt guilty when Nathan got up with Pippa during the night so I could sleep a little more. Surely he needed his sleep more than I did. I felt guilty when my smartphone died and I had to race out on a Saturday to buy a new one. Surely I should have anticipated that and procured a new phone when I was pregnant. I even felt guilty when, after holding Pippa for hours in the evening (she liked to cluster-feed), I passed her to Nathan so I could go to the bathroom. My bladder should have been stronger.

At six weeks postpartum, I had no idea that the guilt I felt was extreme or that feeling guilty is a symptom of postpartum depression.

"EVERYTHING LOOKS like it has healed nicely."

The obstetrician was talking about my vagina.

"So it's okay to have sex again?"

"Yes, all activities are fine, including sex."

My vagina had been cleared for takeoff, but I still felt sore and tender in my pelvic region. I assumed I was supposed to be excited to rejoin the ranks of the sexually active, but my vagina felt differently. After the trauma of childbirth and second-degree tears, it was going to take more than six weeks for my body to be ready for sex.

When Nathan and I did have sex, it was painful. It became

another source of anxiety. Most of the time, I worried we were not having enough sex. Then, when we were having sex, I worried the doctor had sewn me up a little too vigorously. Would I feel like a virgin forever?

My poor body just needed more than six weeks to heal.

To be more precise: my vagina needed eight months to heal.

I'm not trying to be lurid or sensational, but my thoughts on sex were another red flag. My doctor did not know how I felt. All she could see was the way my wounds had healed. Based on what she could see, my vagina was indeed ready for sex. Based on what I could feel, though, the only thing my vagina was ready for was hibernation.

A very extended hibernation.

I did not tell my doctor that everything was still sore in the pelvic region. That felt . . . inappropriate. Remember: this was not just any doctor. This was my obstetrician. A professional trained to take care of vaginas. Yet I felt too embarrassed to talk about my vagina with my vagina doctor.

This was new. I had never been ashamed of my female anatomy. When I needed a box of tampons and bar of chocolate from the pharmacy and nothing else, I had no problem making those purchases from a male cashier. When I needed a box of Monistat 3 and ice cream and nothing else, I had no problem purchasing those from a male cashier either. A urinary tract infection and a male doctor at the ER? I could not care less.

Shame is a symptom of postpartum depression, and I was most definitely ashamed of myself. I was ashamed that my vagina had not bounced back from delivery. I was ashamed about the physical pain I felt in a very feminine part of my body, the portal through which my daughter had entered the world. This was not rational shame. This shame did not arise from something I had done wrong. It originated from the very source of my femininity.

There was nothing rational about this shame, but as I would

eventually learn, there is nothing rational about postpartum depression.

THE APPOINTMENT WAS ALMOST OVER.

The doctor asked, "So are you sure you have been feeling well?"

Lovely. We were back on the subject of my mental health.

"Oh yes, I feel fantastic."

"Have you noticed any personality changes?"

"Nope. I feel like me."

Pippa was still crying. Why did the doctor think my mental health was so important? Obviously I was doing fine. I just had a couple of pesky issues I wanted to address before I could stage my escape and comfort my baby.

"I did want to ask you about stool softeners."

"Yes?"

"I've been taking the stool softener that the gastroenterologist recommended ever since I gave birth. Do you think I need to keep taking it?"

"You should keep taking the stool softener for as long as you feel like it is necessary, but at this point, I think you can safely reduce the dose. Does that make sense?"

"Yes, yes it does."

"Do you have any other questions about constipation?"

Six weeks postpartum, I still worried about constipation every day. I did not ask my doctor if my concerns were a problem. Of course, they were a problem. My preoccupation with constipation was a symptom of my increasing anxiety, but I did not see it that way.

With my history of hypochondria, I saw my preoccupation with constipation as proof positive that I was what I had always been: a hypochondriac. I did not want my doctor to think I was a hypochondriac, so I was not about to dwell too long on the subject. I would just have to wean myself off the stool softeners and move on with my life. Besides, I had a question about something even more important than constipation.

"Can I ask you about my wrists?"

"Of course."

"My wrists have been in agony. Could I possibly get a prescription for physical therapy?"

"Let me take a look." My obstetrician gently touched my wrists. "Does this hurt?"

"A little."

"Can you describe the pain?"

"If I move my wrists, it hurts. I've been using cold packs and heating pads but it hurts to even hold a book."

The doctor said that my wrists might be hurting because I had arthritis.

This is where my memory gets murky. I remember clearly that she used the word "arthritis," but I don't remember if she said the arthritis was related to childbirth or not.

Pippa had been crying for ten minutes now. The sound of her cries made me very uncomfortable. I'm not alone in this. Pretty much any mother will tell you that the sound of her baby's cries is impossible to ignore. Scientific studies support this. But since I was at my six-week appointment and needed to lie back on a table for the examination, I felt obligated to ignore Pippa. Besides, if I soothed her and then put her back down to finish the exam, that would just piss her off more.

By the time my doctor mentioned the possibility of arthritis in my wrists, I was so agitated from ignoring Pippa's cries that I could not process any more information. The postpartum depression had also muddled my brain. Sleep deprivation was not helping either. Also, I had already asked Dr. Google about the pain in my wrists, and the internet was happy to provide stories from women who ignored the postpartum pain in their wrists and eventually needed surgery. The word "arthritis," coming from my doctor's mouth, confirmed my worst fears. The pain in my wrists was never going to improve.

My brain started to shut down.

My obstetrician took several minutes to explain what might be happening with my wrists, but this was all I gleaned: it could be arthritis; physical therapy might help; but first, I needed to get a full blood work done at the lab.

"Do you understand?"

The obstetrician had stopped explaining the wrist situation. It was my turn to talk. Apparently I was now in possession of enough information to understand why I needed a blood test for pain in my wrists, but I was too overwhelmed to understand anything. The blood seemed to be rushing extra fast in my arteries; my lungs hurt; the room seemed smaller than ever; Pippa's screams were certainly louder; and my skin seemed to be losing elasticity and having trouble stretching over all my bones.

I did not understand why my wrists hurt. I thought I had just strained some muscles lifting Pippa's infant car seat. It had never occurred to me there might be something more serious at work.

I did not understand why I needed a blood test.

I did not understand why breastfeeding seemed more difficult now than it had the day Pippa was born.

I did not understand why other moms were able to go places with their newborns and I had so much trouble going to one doctor's appointment.

I did not understand why the doctor had asked me so many questions about my mental health.

The doctor was waiting for an answer.

"Yes." I smiled. "Yes, I understand."

7

CHECKING, CHECKING, CHECKING

Two in the morning. I was lying in bed, Nathan sound asleep to my left, Pippa sound asleep in her yellow cradle to my right. The ceiling fan whirred overhead. I was wearing my headphones, and my headphones were plugged into my iPhone, which was playing the sound of a rushing river. Circumstances were perfect for sleep.

Except my wrists were throbbing. Lying in bed, I reprimanded myself. I really needed to stop clutching my smartphone during Pippa's nocturnal feedings. Except scrolling through blogs was the only thing that kept me awake. If I just watched *Frazier* reruns, I fell asleep, and if I fell asleep, I might drop Pippa or, worse, lean forward and suffocate her with my own body.

I tried to put my wrists out of my mind. Thinking about the wrists just made me think about the ultrasound. I had gotten the blood test, and the results had shown elevated enzyme levels in my liver. The nurse said this was probably due to weight gain during pregnancy (you think?), but my obstetrician still wanted me to get an ultrasound of my liver before I could get physical therapy for the wrists.

I flipped from my left side to my right. The blood test had

65

been an ordeal. My parents had watched Pippa, and the entire time I was gone, my anxiety spiked as if I were in the middle of a natural disaster. This made no sense. Pippa was safe and happy with my parents. I had pumped a bottle of breast milk in case she got hungry. The lab was only a few miles from our house so if there was an actual natural disaster, I could still get home.

Nevertheless, I suffered. My heart pounded, my skin crawled as if I were covered by hundreds of bugs, and I generally felt as if the world were about to end. It was not. There was absolutely no reason for the way I felt. At least, there was no logical reason, but there was a biological one.

Postpartum depression.

Anxiety is a symptom of postpartum depression, a symptom I was experiencing with greater intensity and frequency. As I tried to get back to sleep, the thought of the ultrasound made my heart race. There were so many things that could go wrong. What if Nathan had to go to work and I had to bring Pippa to the appointment? What if I could not pump enough milk and Pippa got hungry? What if Nathan was annoyed that he had to go into work a little late because his fat wife needed an ultrasound?

These petty concerns were easier to ponder than the deeper fear: What if I had cancer? Rationally, I knew my doctor was being overly cautious. Just as she had wanted to rule out MS when I was constipated, now she wanted to rule out some serious liver condition when all I had were sore wrists. Yet I could not stop myself from worrying that I might have cancer and leave Pippa to grow up without a mother.

I flipped back to my left side. I could not get comfortable. At least Pippa seemed to be comfortable in her cradle.

Or was she?

I tiptoed over and leaned as close as I could to her face and listened for the sound of her breathing. Her chest moved up and down but the room was dark. Maybe my eyes had tricked me into thinking she was breathing but she was actually in distress.

I gently rested my hand on the soft spot on the top of her head where the skull had not fully closed. For a moment, I felt nothing. Trembling, I inched my hand to the left. My body relaxed as I found it: her pulse.

My baby was still alive.

I got back into bed and closed my eyes. My muscles relaxed, my breathing slowed, and the chatter in my brain faded—

Had I checked Pippa's sleep sack?

At night, Pippa slept in a sleep sack, which was like a sleeping bag with armholes. The sleep sack kept her warm without the risk of smothering her the way a blanket might. Rationally, I knew she was safe and snug in her sleep sack and told myself to go to sleep.

What if I had inadvertently nudged the sleep sack out of place?

What if it was on top of Pippa's mouth?

What if she was suffocating this very moment?

My eyes flew open.

I closed them and urged myself to go to sleep. I knew Pippa was fine. These fears were ridiculous. I needed to get some decent rest before Pippa wanted to breastfeed again.

Just as it seemed as if I could talk some sense into my anxiety, the guilt chimed in: Was I really placing my desire to sleep above my daughter's safety? What sort of mother was I?

I got out of bed, crept toward Pippa, and examined the sleep sack's position. It was several inches away from her mouth.

I went back to bed and closed my eyes. I took several deep breaths.

What if, while walking back to bed, I had caused a disturbance in the air that moved the sleep sack onto Pippa's mouth?

It had not always been this way. In the maternity ward, whenever Pippa was swaddled and in her cradle, I knew she was safe. Or, more precisely, it never occurred to me to worry about her safety.

I do not remember exactly when I started checking Pippa during the night—those first weeks are such a blur—but I do know it was not our first night home from the hospital. That first night, I was too busy figuring out a way to get Pippa to sleep in a place other than my arms. She had slept easily in the hospital cradle but screamed every time we put her in the travel crib in the master bedroom.

Nathan and I took turns holding her. Around 1:00 a.m., out of desperation, I checked a baby book the pediatrician had recommended specifically for sleep issues. The book said newborns could sleep in a car seat. I eased Pippa into her car seat and slowly withdrew my hands. She slept. I rejoiced and went to sleep myself. I was too exhausted to think about her breathing.

But eventually, probably when Pippa was a few weeks old, I started to worry. According to my baby books, sudden infant death syndrome claimed the lives of 1,500 infants every year in the United States. That is not actually that big a number when you consider the fact that in 2013, the year Pippa was born, there were 3.93 million births in the United States. That means for every hundred babies born in 2013, less than 0.04 percent of those babies died of SIDS.

SIDS still terrified me.

It was as if the Grim Reaper were hovering nearby, waiting to snatch Pippa while I had the audacity to slumber. I followed all the advice I could find. We kept the cradle in our bedroom, ran a fan all night, used the sleep sack. Pippa still seemed to be in imminent danger. And so I checked to make sure she was breathing, as if by checking I could ward off evil spirits or, at the very least, reassure my frazzled nerves.

The reassurance, though, never lasted more than a few seconds.

I got out of bed again, the fifth time in as many minutes. This time, after checking Pippa's pulse and watching the fall and rise of her chest, I tucked the sleep sack into her pajamas to make sure it would not get loose during the night.

Now I could sleep.

Except.

Tucking the sleep sack had created a big fabric bulge near Pippa's neck. Could that interfere with her windpipe?

No, I told myself, she was fine. I had pulled the fabric bulge several inches away from her neck.

But. How could I be sure the fabric bulge would stay in place?

I *had* to know.

———

A FEW WEEKS LATER, once again during the middle of the night, I put my hand on the knob of the front door and turned as hard as I could, twisting back and forth until I was sure it was locked. Then, I turned away to go back to bed.

But. Was it really locked or did it just seem to be locked?

I unlocked the door, relocked it, and then rattled the knob back and forth to make sure it was really, really, *really* locked.

I felt calm.

I removed my hand from the doorknob.

My heart immediately started to thump as if I were on the verge of a heart attack.

Was the door really locked?!?

After testing the lock's integrity a dozen more times, I pulled myself away, like a spaceship escaping a tractor beam. At last, I could go back to sleep. I had finished breastfeeding Pippa almost an hour ago, but if I fell asleep right away, I could probably get into a REM cycle before she was awake for the day.

I took a deep breath. Sleep, please, let me sleep.

Was the back door locked?

I had checked the back door just five minutes ago, but maybe something had happened to unlock it.

I chided myself. I was being ridiculous.

But if the door was unlocked, and a kidnapper was prowling the neighborhood . . .

The risk was too high.

After checking the back door, I could not resist the urge to revisit the front door again *because you never know*.

On my way back to bed, I walked through the kitchen.

When was the last time I checked the stovetop burner?

IF YOU PLACE a frog in a pot of boiling water, it will leap to safety.

It is said that if you place the same frog in a pot of room-temperature water and flick on a flame, it will not notice the change in temperature. (This is not actually true. Still, I like the metaphor.) Even when the water has started to boil, the frog will stay in the pot, oblivious that it is being cooked alive.

I was the frog.

I STAGGERED TOWARD BED, half-assured that the doors were locked and stovetop burners lit.

What about the windows?

I started in the kitchen, yanking upward on each window. Then I moved to the living room. I could see with my eyes that the windows were in fact locked.

Or maybe they only looked that way.

I pulled as hard as I could on the first window. It did not budge.

I turned and considered the second. A huge thorny bougainvillea grew in front of that window. Not even Prince Charming could get through those tangles. The window was completely inaccessible.

Yet I could not resist. I *had* to check.

Next I went to the nursery and checked the windows by the changing table. Then it was time to survey the guest room.

But wait.

There was a window in the nursery closet. The old owners had sealed that window shut and it was impossible to open. Besides, it was no bigger than a shoe box. No one could climb through it . . .

I had to know.

I opened the closet door, leaned over diaper boxes, and strained at the window as if the house were on fire and this window were the only way out. Only then could I convince myself to move on and check the guest room windows.

At last. We were safe. I could go back to bed.

I turned and started walking back to bed.

What if an intruder had broken into the house during the day?

My heart beat faster.

What if he was hiding under one of the beds?

My breathing accelerated.

I marched back to the guest room. A small part of me protested. No one could be hiding beneath this bed. The frame was barely six inches off the ground and besides, I had crammed all sorts of junk down there.

What if there was a snake?

My heart started to pound even harder. I knelt down at the edge of the bed convinced that something terrible was hiding just behind the bed skirt. If I looked, it would surely kill me; but if I did not look, it might kill Pippa instead.

I took a deep breath and lifted the bed skirt.

No snakes, no fantastical creatures from horror movies.

I finally crawled back into bed, terrified of waking Pippa or Nathan. Neither stirred. Utterly exhausted, I fell asleep before my thoughts could rouse me out of bed.

FOURTEEN, fifteen, sixteen, oh no, seventeen.

There were seventeen steps.

Not sixteen, a beautiful number that could be divided into two halves of eight steps each or, bliss, four quarters of four steps each.

And not eighteen, which at least had the decency to be an even number.

But seventeen. Seventeen odd-numbered steps.

How could my parents have possibly thought this was a good place to live?

I was nineteen years old, home from college on spring break. My parents had bought a townhouse in a gated community. It was built on top of a hill, so the ground floor was also the top floor. A flight of stairs descended to the second floor, where my siblings and I would sleep.

A flight of stairs with seventeen impossibly odd steps that would torment me every time I needed to go to a different floor.

I experimented with ways to make the seventeen-step stair-case feel like an even number. I tried skipping a step, but no matter what step I skipped, I knew the seventeenth step was there. Stepping on the same stair twice also felt wrong. I tried rushing down the stairs without counting, but not counting felt even worse than counting an odd number.

Counting stairs was one of my quirks. I had a few others—turning jumbles of letters on license plates into words, folding laundry in certain ways, counting how many cars I passed when I was in the faster-moving lane of traffic—but they were just innocuous mind games that made me smile. I freely told friends and family about my little games with a sense of pride. They were proof that I was unique and marching to my own beat.

It never occurred to me that these quirks were more than just games; that they were actually a way of exerting control over my world.

It never occurred to me that I was flirting with obsessive compulsive disorder. Or that my quirks could turn into something sinister if given the right circumstances.

"I'M GOING TO BED."

Nathan glanced up from his laptop. He likes to piddle with various sports-themed games while watching television. "Good night, sweetheart."

It was not even nine o'clock, but at two and a half months postpartum, I felt like a shell of my former self. The sooner I got to bed, the better chance I had of getting a full night's rest and feeling like an actual human being.

I tiptoed into the bedroom, careful not to disturb Pippa. I got into bed and closed my eyes.

Were the doors locked?

My eyes popped back open.

I listened. Nathan was still in the next room watching television and playing games on his computer. I *had* to check the locks, but he would think it was weird if I started locking and unlocking the doors.

I'd have to start with the front door, which was on the other side of the house. The television volume would drown out the sound effects.

It took me a few minutes to convince myself the front door was locked.

Now it was time for the back door.

I sauntered into the den. Nathan's eyes were on the television. I sidled a few steps toward the back door. The back door was technically in the same room as the television, but thanks to the position of the couch, it felt like the back door was part of a separate little mud room. Nathan was not looking at me. I sidled closer and felt a thrill, as if I were riding a bike down a steep hill. I was there, close enough to touch the back door, and he had not noticed me.

I started to lock and relock the doors surreptitiously. Nathan kept watching television. My secret was safe.

Or so I thought.

Long after my postpartum depression was diagnosed and treated, Nathan and I talked about the way I locked and relocked the doors. He'd been aware of what I was doing, but he thought it was a result of normal new-mommy fears. Where he grew up, doors were often left unlocked. No one worried about burglars, and they would have thought you were bonkers if you'd inquired about local serial killers. But I was a city girl. In my world, doors needed to be locked.

At least, that was what he told himself. Maybe he was also in denial. It would have been much easier to think his wife was being a bit silly than to confront the possibility that she was swimming in dark psychological waters.

Besides, Nathan knew only that I was checking the doors before bed. He did not know I was checking Pippa's breathing throughout the night; or that I checked the stovetop burners, windows, closets, under the beds, and sometimes even inside the washing machine; or that I rechecked the doors—and everything else—after every breastfeeding session. Those things happened only when he was fast asleep.

My anxiety sometimes seemed to have a mind of its own. Like, my anxiety knew that it had to be surreptitious and not arouse my husband's suspicion. Otherwise he might have taken me to a doctor, and the doctor might have helped me, and my suffering might not have lasted as long as it did.

8

INSOMNIA

Pippa started crying when the nurse placed a thermometer under her armpit and kept screaming even after she was measured and weighed and the nurse had retreated to the hallway.

I bounced Pippa up and down and sang a lullaby. That did not help, so I sat down on a chair and tried to breastfeed her. That did not help either.

"Why—woo—oooo—meeeee?"

My dad was trying to tell me something but I could not understand what he was saying.

"What?! What?!"

"Why don't you let me take Pippa outside and walk her around?"

"No! No! She has to stay with me!" I thought I was shouting so that he could hear me over the sound of the Pippa siren, but in hindsight, I think I was also screaming to burn off some pent-up anxiety.

I was in an examination room at the pediatrician's office with my dad, mom, and Pippa, waiting for Pippa's three-month wellness visit. In the waiting room, there had been a mom alone with her baby. I could not fathom how she managed the acrobatics of a pediatrician visit without the support of another adult (or, in my case, an entourage who had even chauffeured me to the medical building).

There was more than enough space in the examination room for three adults and a baby, but as Pippa screamed, it seemed too small, as if the walls were inching toward us, just like in the trash compactor scene on the Death Star in the original *Star Wars* movie.

The pediatrician arrived.

"How is everything?"

"Great," I said. Pippa kept screaming.

"Do you have any questions?"

"Yes," I said, but then heat rushed to my face. I had written a list of questions for the pediatrician, but the list was in the diaper backpack. Finding the list meant passing Pippa to someone else and then fumbling through diapers and extra outfits while everyone watched. That was more humiliation than I could handle. I would have to recall the questions from memory, but with Pippa screaming, it was impossible to think.

"She gets like this," I said. "She screams in the late morning and I don't know how to soothe her."

"Have you tried white noise?"

"Yes."

We ran through the list of usual ways to soothe a crying infant. Then the doctor asked, "Are you drinking any caffeine?"

"A few sodas every morning."

"You might want to quit caffeine. It can be transmitted through breast milk and that *might* be agitating Pippa."

The pediatrician said "might"—I remember that clearly—but the guilt saw an opening and pounced. I had started drinking soda and coffee shortly after delivery. (Can you blame me?) The caffeine *must* have been transmitted through the breast milk; it *must* have been harming Pippa; and therefore, I *must* be responsible for every minute of suffering my poor baby had endured in her three months of life.

I was a horrible mother.

By the time Pippa was three months old, I was convinced that something was not quite right. All I had was a premonition that life was a little too difficult.

There was no way I was going to tell that to the pediatrician, my parents, Nathan, or anyone else. If I did that, they would think I was lazy and weak.

As the pediatrician talked about Pippa's development, I resolved to quit caffeine as soon as possible. Thereafter, caffeine became the scapegoat for all my problems. Surely motherhood would be easy as soon as I got it out of my system.

That night, I went to bed shortly after transferring Pippa from my breast to her cradle. It was only nine o'clock, but the wellness visit had drained me. Lying in bed, I kept replaying the visit in my mind, but after a half hour or so, I fell asleep.

Three hours later, my body jolted awake.

I got out of bed and checked everything that might be a security breach, but once I got back into bed, I was still wide awake.

I lay in bed, eyes closed, and willed myself to sleep.

I prayed.

I counted forward and backward.

I took deep breaths.

When Pippa woke at six and cried for breakfast, I was still awake.

The darkness was about to get darker.

"I ONLY HAD ten ounces of soda today. Tomorrow, I'll just drink nine."

"Way to go, babe! How do you feel?"

I paused to consider. "Not too bad right now. I was exhausted all day but that was because I didn't sleep last night. It had nothing to do with caffeine withdrawal."

"I'm sure you'll sleep tonight," Nathan said, making silly faces for Pippa.

I went to bed even earlier than the night before, put on my headphones, and listened to a rainstorm on a white noise app. I inhaled and exhaled, inhaled and exhaled, relaxed, drifted toward sleep, and then my bladder stirred. I had peed less than five minutes ago. Still, I got out of bed and went to the bathroom.

Back in bed, I focused on breathing again but my heart started to pound as if I were in grave danger. It did not matter how I tried to relax. My body refused to sleep.

Nathan tiptoed into our bedroom, careful not to wake me, unaware of the cacophony in my head. I stayed still as a corpse, because if Nathan knew I was awake, he might say something, and then we might talk, and then I might never sleep again. If only I stayed still and quiet, maybe my body would surrender to the sleep I desperately needed.

Nathan started to snore. I got out of bed to pee and checked the time. Eleven o'clock. If I fell asleep now, I could sleep for seven hours. Seven hours was more than enough.

I lay down on my back and started to fall asleep . . . but then felt compelled to shift to my left side. I tried to relax into slumber, but then I felt a crick in my neck and switched to my right side. Now I was wide awake, so I focused on deep calming breaths.

"You okay, babe?" Nathan mumbled, still half-asleep.

"Yes," I whispered, not wanting to wake him.

He reached over and patted my leg. I froze and held my breath. He had to go to work in the morning. He needed his sleep. I had to limit the tossing and turning.

Midnight came. If I fell asleep now, I could sleep for six hours. Six was fine. Six was enough.

Pippa had started sleeping ten hours through the night. I had ten glorious hours in which I could sleep uninterrupted. Between breastfeeding and normal pregnancy discomfort, I had not had this opportunity for almost a year.

Yet I could not sleep. My body had betrayed me.

Thinking about the wasted opportunity only exacerbated my frustration. If only I could just stop thinking, I would sleep.

I peed one more time, a pathetic drop; then, once I was back in bed, my thoughts drifted to the doors. I crept out of the bedroom and started the process of unlocking and relocking.

At one in the morning, I was still tossing from side to side, my thoughts racing. Maybe I was hungry. Breastfeeding burned thousands of calories. If I ate something, I'd be able to sleep.

I crept to the kitchen and ate several spoonfuls of peanut butter straight from the jar. Each time I stabbed my spoon into the jar, my muscles relaxed a little more.

I stopped eating when my stomach felt uncomfortably full. Then I washed the spoon clean because I did not want Nathan to know. He had always loved my body at any weight and never said anything that made me feel self-conscious or ugly, but the postpartum depression had convinced me otherwise.

Besides, I sensed that the frantic eating of peanut butter in the middle of the night was a problem of some sort. A problem that I needed to solve all by myself.

When I finished washing the spoon, I was not ready to go back to bed. First I had to check the pilot lights, in case I had somehow caused a draft that blew one of them out. I hovered my hand over each of the burners, then knelt down to visually confirm that each of the gas burners was flickering and we were not being poisoned in our sleep. Then I had to go check the doors, closets, and windows again because you never know.

Back in bed again, I prayed for sleep. It was 2:00 a.m. Pippa would be awake in four hours—maybe sooner. Please, God, please let me sleep.

Finally, a little before three in the morning, I fell asleep.

Three hours later, Pippa woke up, ravenous and ready to breastfeed. While she nursed, I consulted Dr. Google.

I typed, *baby is three months old and I can't sleep.*

The phrases "postpartum depression" and "postpartum anxiety" showed up in the first page of hits. What? I did not have the baby blues. I loved my baby. Those results could not be right.

I fine-tuned my search, typing, *Can caffeine withdrawal cause insomnia?* Dr. Google unearthed a blog post about caffeine withdrawal. It didn't say anything about insomnia, but buried in the comments section, a few people complained about having insomnia after quitting caffeine.

The internet had obliged and confirmed my hypothesis: the insomnia was a withdrawal symptom. I shoved away any thoughts of postpartum depression. I just had to get the caffeine out of my system and everything would be okay.

"How are you doing? Have you been sleeping better?" My mom sounded concerned. I had called to say hello after Pippa fell asleep in my arms.

"Yes, well, no. But I had my last sip of caffeine yesterday. I'm sure if I wait a few more days and let all the residual caffeine get out of my body, I'll start sleeping better than ever."

"You could call your doctor . . ."

I stroked Pippa's cheek with my free hand. "My doctor can't do anything for me. It's caffeine withdrawal. I just have to be strong for a few more days."

I was trying to convince my mom that the insomnia was on the verge of resolving itself, but really, I was trying to convince myself.

"Maybe if you eased up on the breastfeeding—"

Breastfeeding was still a time consuming affair. I had attended a local breastfeeding support group, and the lactation consultant assured the exhausted mothers that we were making an investment. After six weeks of hard work, our babies would not need to nurse nearly as often as they did during the early weeks. But I had passed the six week mark and then the twelve week mark without any improvements. At just over three months old, Pippa was still feeding like a newborn.

Since I was the woman with all the milk, that meant I was always on call. When I was pregnant, I assumed that pumping would make it easy for me to leave the house to get breaks. My parents could watch Pippa while I got a pedicure or just wandered Target with a big iced coffee from Starbucks. The breastfeeding experts, however, warned that if I went too long without pumping, my milk supply would be compromised. That meant if I went to see a movie, I would have to find a way to pump, but just the thought of pumping in a theater bathroom or my parked car made my adrenaline go crazy.

My mom could see that breastfeeding was not only making my life difficult, but it was also making it difficult for other people to help me relax.

I switched my phone from one shoulder to the other. "Mom, stop it. I'm breastfeeding Pippa for an entire year, and then as long as she wants, end of discussion."

Later that week, when my parents visited, I slunk off to the guest bedroom to nap. I tried listening to a meditation for relaxation but it involved gongs that were like nails on a chalkboard. I switched to a rainstorm, and then a half dozen other sounds on my white noise app. Nothing helped. By the time Pippa was ready to eat again, I felt groggier than ever.

"Do you think it's still caffeine withdrawal?" my mom asked.

"Maybe?"

"You could call your doctor . . ."

"If I don't sleep tonight, I'll call her tomorrow."

I did not sleep that night, but still, I hesitated. I did not want to call my doctor. I had gotten the ultrasound of my liver, prompted by the results of the blood test I got for my wrists, and the ultrasound had revealed: a healthy liver! But the doctor still wanted me to get my blood drawn one more time just to be safe.

I had not yet been to the lab for the second blood test. These days, even the thought of doing laundry made me physically ill with anxiety—what if Pippa cried and needed to breastfeed right when the wash finished? And then I forgot to transfer the wash to the dryer? And mildew started to grow in the washing machine? Or even worse, what if I got the clothes transferred to the dryer but a fire started? What if the smoke detector was faulty?

Compared to laundry, a blood test was a logistical ordeal. I could not take Pippa to the lab—too many germs!—but that meant pumping a bottle so my parents or Nathan could watch Pippa. And pumping?

Pumping was a nightmare.

I had assumed that within a few weeks of Pippa's birth, I would have a freezer stocked with a six-month supply of liquid gold. The reality was much different. The breastfeeding experts advised pumping after a nursing session. That way, you did not risk depleting baby's next meal. After a nursing session, though, my breasts had barely any drops of milk left, never mind the fact that Pippa usually wanted to snuggle or nap in my arms after nursing, and try as I might, I could never figure out a way to hold her safely while keeping the pumping mechanism in place.

On top of all this, pumping itself was not exactly a pleasant experience. It felt a bit like being molested by a robot.

To recap: I was nearly four months postpartum; had quit caffeine and given it enough time to clear my system; was still suffering from insomnia; and had an inkling that now was the time to call my obstetrician, but the last time I had any contact with her office, the nurse told me to get my blood drawn again. If sore wrists had required a blood test, liver ultrasound, and yet another blood test, I could not imagine what hoops my doctor would make me jump through if I told her about the insomnia. She would probably just tell me to get the outstanding blood test already, the prospect of which fried my frazzled mind even more.

Then, for the first time since I'd been pregnant, I got my period.

HALLELUJAH! The insomnia was not a caffeine-withdrawal symptom. It was just a case of a year's worth of PMS. Thank goodness I had not called my doctor over something as trivial as that.

That night, I slept six glorious hours in a row. I had been doing that every three or four days since the insomnia started. Yet another reason I refused to call my doctor. If I scheduled an appointment and then slept six hours the night before, everyone would think I was being a hypochondriac.

When I reported my sleep progress to Nathan, he said, "That's great!" He smiled in a way that said, *I've been worried about you and I'm so happy that you feel better*.

But I could not see that. Instead, I misinterpreted the smile as saying, *Thank God, you have been such a drag with all this insomnia bullshit*.

"I bet I sleep six more hours tonight," I said.

That night, I was awake until three in the morning.

What was wrong with me? It was not caffeine withdrawal. It was not PMS. I could think of no other explanation for the insomnia and anxiety that haunted my days. My body was broken. Something about pregnancy had destroyed my ability to sleep, and I would never sleep well again. I would never have the energy to feel like myself.

I was a zombie.

As Pippa ate breakfast, I stared at the wall, clenching my phone in my free hand. I was too weary for email or reading blog posts about lives far better than my own. I did not even have the energy to press the buttons on the remote control and queue up a television show. I set the phone down on the arm of the chair and closed my eyes. I needed to rest and save up my strength so I could change Pippa's diapers without falling asleep on my feet.

If only I could sleep on my feet.

If only there was a medical reason for the insomnia and anxiety. Then there would be a cure and I might actually get better. Guilt stabbed me in the stomach. I had a healthy, sweet, beautiful baby girl. So many people would kill to have my life. I had to find a way to be content or people would think I was ungrateful and did not love Pippa enough.

If only I had postpartum depression.

I opened my eyes and looked down at my phone. I had never clicked on the links that had shown up when I first started hunting for the cause of my insomnia.

Did I dare hope?

I wondered if I hadn't just been imagining those search results. After all, my brain was fried from insomnia.

Pippa sighed and I switched her to the other breast. I gazed down at her. She was perfect.

It would not hurt to try.

I fired up the browser on my phone and typed *postpartum insomnia*.

A second later, the screen filled with results.

9

MY BREAKING POINT

The more I read, the more it seemed like I might have postpartum depression.

The first thing I learned was that postpartum depression is a spectrum illness. That means there are a bunch of different symptoms, such as feeling irritated, crying, and having scary thoughts, but not every mom experiences the same symptoms.

I had assumed that mothers with postpartum depression spent all day in bed, crying and hating their babies. I was quickly disabused of that notion. Crying in bed was a symptom of postpartum depression but it wasn't a prerequisite to the illness. Moms who loved their babies and never cried could still have postpartum depression.

I bounced between several different blog posts and identified with many symptoms, such as feeling overwhelmed, guilty, and anxious, and, of course, having insomnia. Hope flickered inside me. I was not alone. Maybe it was not just that things were unusually difficult. Maybe there was a diagnosis. Maybe I could get better.

But I kept coming back to the fact that I was not depressed.

Yes, this was a spectrum illness, and yes, I could tick off a lot of the symptom boxes, but how could I have something called depression if I was not depressed?

From what I read, it seemed like not all women with postpartum depression were actually depressed. "Postpartum depression" was more of an umbrella term that included postpartum anxiety and postpartum obsessive compulsive disorder. It was difficult to sift through all the information because, to be honest, my brain was not firing on all cylinders. Rather than try to figure out the nuances and subtleties of postpartum depression, I just focused on the word "depression." It was easier to focus on that part of the illness because it was what I had heard about in passing.

I wasn't depressed.

Which meant I did not have a diagnosis.

Which meant no one could ever help me.

"Pippa's crying! I can't make her stop!"

I had called Nathan at work in the middle of a Tuesday afternoon. I was holding Pippa in my arms while walking laps around the house and cradling my phone between my ear and shoulder.

"What happened? Is she hurt?"

"Nothing happened, she just won't stop crying. She's been crying for a half hour."

"Is she gassy?"

"No. Maybe. I tried burping her. She won't stop crying!"

"She's fine," Nathan said. "Babies just need to cry sometimes."

I wanted to ask him to come home from work. Something felt terribly, horribly wrong, but I could not explain that feeling. So instead of begging Nathan to save me from the undefinable something, I said good-bye and went back to pacing around the house.

Pippa kept wailing.

I switched directions and patted her back, but her cries only seemed to get louder.

I tried a lullaby.

She shrieked and shrieked and shrieked.

I walked through the kitchen, stepped into the nursery, and that was when it happened: I imagined myself raising my arms into the air and throwing Pippa as hard as I could against the floor. I saw her skull crack open and her brains splatter on the floor.

I stopped breathing, pushed the thought away, and clutched Pippa closer to my chest, as if some unseen force were trying to wrench her from my arms.

Except the unseen force was inside my head. How could I guard against that?

I started to shake and sat down on the pink glider my parents had bought us as a gift during the second trimester. I had imagined many serene hours, gently rocking my baby to sleep.

Pippa wailed as if she could read my mind and see the horrible thing I had thought. The thought had lasted barely a second—it was more the flash of an image than a proper idea—but I was horrified.

I patted Pippa's back. She yelled some more. Each holler seemed to vibrate through my body, making the skin ripple off the muscle.

After crying and arching her back for another ten minutes, Pippa wore herself out and fell asleep. My body stayed rigid for hours. I thought about dirty dishes, pump parts that needed sterilizing, unwritten thank you notes for baby gifts, my wrists, insomnia, the parenting book I was reading, the spot where paint had chipped away beneath the windowsill.

Anything but that terrible thought.

No one could ever know.

I must never think about it again.

THE NEXT DAY, it happened again.

Pippa started crying in the late morning, just as she had the day before. I paced and did everything I could to soothe her, but she kept screaming for half an hour. Then, while walking through the nursery, I saw it.

I saw myself raise my arms high above my head.

I saw myself slam my arms down.

I saw Pippa's skull hit the hardwood floor and her brains splatter everywhere.

No, no, no! I did not want to throw my daughter. I pushed the thought away and escaped to the pink chair. I held Pippa closer to keep her safe.

But how could she be safe in a monster's arms?

THOSE FIRST TWO instances were not the only ones. If the dark thoughts had come at random times, like when Pippa and I were happily snuggling, then maybe I could have dismissed them as weird mental hiccups, unpleasant but random. The thoughts, though, only came when Pippa was screaming. I assumed they were my subconscious solution to the problem of my daughter's cries. At least a dead baby was a quiet baby.

After one of these episodes, I blinked away tears and patted Pippa's back, counting to one hundred and then back down to zero.

It must be the insomnia. It had to be the insomnia. If I could be strong and ride out the insomnia, the dark thoughts would surely end.

What choice did I have? If anyone ever knew about these thoughts, I'd lose Pippa.

"Oh look, Pippa, there's Daddy."

A week had passed since the first dark thought. We were outside taking our morning constitutional. It was a beautiful July morning. The sky above was blue with a few puffy white clouds. It was early, so the temperature was still in the low seventies. Overhead, a leafy green canopy kept most of the sidewalk in shade.

Nathan crossed the street and bent over to coo at Pippa. He was near the end of his morning walk (we are a family that loves to walk) and was heading home to get ready for work.

"How'd you sleep, babe?"

"Three hours."

"Sweetheart."

"I could handle the insomnia, but now I feel more and more anxious," I told him. "It's this physical feeling. I'm always afraid."

Nathan frowned. "Of what?"

"Nothing."

Nathan smiled with relief. "Well, if you aren't scared of anything, then you have no reason to be afraid."

That made sense. It really did.

But you can't reason with a mental illness.

"I feel like I'm carrying around a backpack of anxiety and I just want to put it down and walk away. But I don't know how to get it off me. It's like someone welded it onto my back."

Nathan stayed silent. He had helped me through my legal career crises, but this was a little beyond his skill set.

I felt desperate. "I want to figure out how to put down the backpack. I will. I promise, I'll figure it out."

"I know you will."

We hugged, and Nathan headed home, putting his headphones back on for the final block. I watched and wondered how I would ever fulfill the promise I had just made.

Pippa stirred restlessly, so I started walking again. Should I call the doctor? I could. Five weeks of insomnia—surely that deserved medical attention. Plus, there were the dark thoughts, which kept coming every day whenever Pippa cried, but if I told the doctor about those, the authorities might steal Pippa away from me.

Then, there was the possibility the doctor would say I was perfectly healthy. Once that happened, my final slim hope would be extinguished.

And then what?

A FEW DAYS LATER, I stood on the porch with Pippa and watched my parents' car reverse out of the driveway. My parents and sister had been visiting for the past hour. So long as they were in the house, I felt safe. But now I would be alone with Pippa until Nathan got home from work.

My heart beat faster and faster. I took Pippa into the house.

I could not breathe. I held Pippa close and paced the living room.

The air was solidifying and closing in on me and I could not be alone. I did not have the strength to beat the dark thoughts away anymore.

They kept coming, every day, when Pippa started to wail in the late morning. I would walk around the house and try to stay calm, but then I would think about throwing my daughter as hard as I could and I would see her tiny precious skull smashed on the ground and I would think that at least she would stop crying then.

Every time the thought of throwing Pippa came, I pushed it away.

But the insomnia was never-ending. I was getting more tired.

Maybe it was my imagination, but it seemed like the thoughts were getting stronger.

I kissed Pippa on the cheek and tried to sit down on the couch, but I could not stay still. I had to keep moving.

What if the thoughts came again today? I could not do this.

I called Nathan. "Please come home, come home now. I can't be alone. My parents and sister were here and they left, please come home, I can't be alone."

"Oh sweetheart, don't worry." There must have been something scary in my tone of voice. "I'm leaving now."

Then I called my parents. "Please come back. I called Nathan and he's coming home but I can't be alone, I can't, please come back."

"What's wrong? Did something happen?"

"I just can't be alone. I'm so alone." I started to cry. "Please come back."

"We're coming. Right now. Hang on."

I walked outside and stood on the front porch with Pippa, huddled close to the bougainvillea, as if its thorns could keep us safe. I shivered and gasped for air. My hormones had broken the panic button, and although it was a sunny day in a lovely neighborhood, I felt as scared as if our house were surrounded by a pack of wolves and a comet were hurtling toward Pasadena. I had been in situations that actually warranted fear—a major earthquake in the middle of the night, a car accident with a snow plow, the time we thought there was a burglar in the living room—but the physical fear I felt beneath the bougainvillea was a thousand times stronger than the fear I had felt in those instances.

Huge sobs shook my entire body. The emotional release felt good, but I could not stop myself. I had lost control of my senses. That was extra-terrifying.

My parents and sister were back in less than twenty minutes. Nathan arrived soon after. They convinced me to come inside. The crying gradually stopped.

My mom said, "Why don't you guys come and stay at our house so Courtney can get some good rest?" My parents lived about forty miles away on the opposite side of Los Angeles County in a suburb close to the beach.

"I think that's a great idea," Nathan said.

I sat on the couch in our living room, cradling Pippa, while Nathan, my parents, and sister Katherine gathering the things we would need. Occasionally I suggested packing something – a favorite toy, the diaper rash cream, the cradle – but for the most part, I felt too shattered to help.

I had almost reached the bottom of the darkest abyss of my postpartum depression. I was almost ready to ask for help.

But not quite.

I PUT the plates in the bottom rack of my parents' dishwasher and started rinsing the cutlery.

In the living room, I could hear laughter as Pippa babbled. No one else was in the kitchen.

I was alone.

The water got too hot so I adjusted the temperature. As I rinsed suds off the forks, my eyes darted to the left.

The knife drawer.

It was so close. One step to the left, and I would be in front of it.

Time slowed down.

People were still laughing in the living room. I listened—my dad, my mom, Katherine, and there, that was Nathan. All accounted for, two rooms away.

The knives were sharp. In a few minutes, the torture could be over. The insomnia, the anxiety, the panic, the possibility that I might hurt Pippa, all gone and over.

I could hear my heart beat.

I could make it stop beating.

I shuddered and quickly stepped away from the counter. I pushed the thought of knives out of my mind but could not stop wondering: Where had that thought come from? What was wrong with me? Did I really want to die?

There were still dirty dishes in the sink but I immediately joined my family in the living room. I made sure I was always with someone for the rest of the night.

MY OBSTETRICIAN SAT down on a stool at my feet. I towered above her from my seat on the examination table. At my request, my mom sat quietly on a chair a few feet away. I wanted her there, partly for moral support, but mostly because I was worried I might forget to tell the doctor something. My dad was in the waiting room with Pippa.

"So Courtney, what's going on? I understand you are having trouble sleeping?"

"Yes, I've had insomnia for five weeks." I told her about the caffeine, the PMS, and the anxiety.

"Anxiety," she said. "Tell me more about that."

"I just feel scared all the time. I don't know why. But it's like this physical sensation of fear. It's always there . . ."

On the day I summoned everyone home, Nathan suggested I email my friends for moral support. It seemed like a good idea, so I wrote a few people, including my college friend Kendall, about my symptoms and said I thought I might have postpartum depression.

Kendall emailed back within the hour and told me to go to the doctor right away. She had coached me through my hypochondria at Dartmouth many times and had firsthand knowledge about my tendency to overreact to headaches and stomach cramps. But this time, she thought my experiences required medical intervention. She even told me to keep seeing doctors until someone helped me. My mom and Nathan had been urging me to call the doctor, but Kendall's email gave me the final nudge I needed to actually get help.

I called the doctor's office and spoke to the receptionist. It was Monday afternoon. The first appointment available was Thursday.

Thursday. That meant three more days of suffering. I asked the receptionist if I could talk to the doctor.

"Only if it's an emergency."

I hesitated. Something told me that I fit the criteria for an emergency, but I also worried the doctor would tell me to go to the emergency room. That seemed excessive. I took the Thursday appointment.

For three nights, we had slept at my parents' house. I had slept almost six hours each of those nights—not great, since Pippa was sleeping ten hours each night, but nothing to whine about either.

The guilt of inconveniencing my parents and Nathan was like an anvil on my shoulders. So Thursday morning, I announced that I was feeling much better and was ready to move back home to Pasadena. I believe I was experiencing something called "denial." I thought I was doing so well, I even told my mom that I wanted to cancel my doctor's appointment.

"Don't!" She looked appalled.

"But I'm doing so much better. She's probably just going to tell me to take some vitamins."

"Maybe, but if that's the case, at least we'll have the information. If you cancel, who knows how long it will take to get another appointment? Just go to the doctor. Please."

So here I was. Judgment day. I wanted to keep talking about my anxiety, because once I stopped, it would be the doctor's turn to speak. Then she would tell me that there was nothing wrong with me and scold me for not getting the extra blood test after the liver ultrasound.

I searched for more words to say but my head felt so muddled, it was difficult to string words together. I stammered into silence.

"Courtney."

I held my breath.

"You have postpartum depression."

The anvil on my shoulders disappeared. I had a diagnosis—a medical diagnosis. I still could not believe I had postpartum *depression*, but all that mattered was that the doctor saw that I needed help.

My mom piped up from the corner of the room. "Courtney, was there something else you wanted to tell the doctor?"

She was referring to something that had happened the day before. Pippa had started her late morning crying jag. Neither of us could console her. My anxiety increased until I looked my mom in the eyes and said, "I want to die." Now, in the examination room, my mom was reminding me to tell the doctor about that moment. She still had no idea about the dark thoughts.

Was there something else I wanted to tell the doctor?

I was so tired of keeping secrets.

I took a deep breath.

"I have thought about throwing Pippa. So that she would die and stop crying."

Saying it out loud, the admission did not sound as terrible as I thought it would.

"I pushed those thoughts away but they were very scary," I continued. "And I have thought about going to the hospital and being put in a coma. And last night, I was alone in the kitchen, and I thought about how close the knives were and how easy it would be to slit my wrists and end all this suffering."

My obstetrician scooted her stool closer to me and looked me in the eyes. "I'm glad you are telling me this. I think you need to get some help at the hospital. Will you voluntarily admit yourself for psychiatric care?"

Terror flared in my chest. I turned toward my mom and cried, "You promised they would not take Pippa away!"

And then, as quickly as it had flared up, the terror whooshed away and was replaced by relief. My parents were here. I realized I was inventing an unreasonable fear of some government authority snatching Pippa away to avoid getting help. That was not going to happen. There were too many lawyers in my family.

I turned back to my doctor. "Yes. I will voluntarily admit myself to the hospital for psychiatric care."

10

COMMITMENT ISSUES

"Have you had any thoughts of hurting yourself?"

"Yes." It felt like such an intimate moment, but the triage nurse just tapped away furiously at her keyboard. She did not seem interested in eye contact, so I stared at the novelty dancing flower on her desk. Those things had seemed so cool when I was thirteen.

I was taken to a comfortable armchair and someone drew several vials of my blood. Almost a year ago to the day, I had been in my general physician's office for a wonky back, and the phlebotomist had drawn my blood to confirm the plus sign on the yellow sticky note. I had imagined all the things I would do with my baby. We would meet friends for lunch, go to museums, take long walks in shady gardens . . .

Now my baby was miles away, at a baby store with my parents so they could stock up on formula, while I was being admitted to the hospital for psychiatric care.

A nurse ushered me and Nathan to a private room in the emergency ward. It had been only twenty minutes since our arrival. After several months of a slow unraveling, things were happening quickly.

"So." I picked at the paper gown I was wearing over my clothes. "This is weird."

"Very weird," he agreed.

Sitting in the emergency room waiting for my admission to the psych wing, I assumed Nathan hated me for dragging him through the humiliation of having a mentally ill wife. At the obstetrician's office, I had not even been able to call him with the news. I had begged my mom to tell him. (That must have been a fun conversation.)

In truth, Nathan did not hate me for having postpartum depression, but he was a bit blindsided. For weeks, I had been insisting that the insomnia was a symptom of caffeine withdrawal and that I was fine. Just that morning, as he left my parents' house for work, I had hugged him and told him I was feeling so much better. My symptoms mostly occurred beneath the surface. He could not read the thoughts in my head or see the way that my stomach churned. When my adrenaline raced so hard it seemed my heart would burst, I forced my face to stay calm and in control.

We were silent. Nathan looked at his phone. I looked at my phone. The minutes dragged.

I should have cancelled the appointment with my obstetrician, I thought. Maybe I would get better, but I feared that Nathan would never forgive me for inflicting this ordeal on our family.

AFTER WE'D WAITED for about an hour, my new psychiatrist whirled into the room, introduced himself, and kicked Nathan out.

"I want you to know that everything we talk about will remain confidential and I'm going to do everything possible to keep your admission voluntary," he said. He was about ten years older than me and had hair that looked a bit like Einstein's but shorter. "If your admission is involuntary, then it becomes a matter of public record and that information is available to future employers."

"Thanks." I could not care less. The idea of "future employers" seemed inconsequential in my current state.

"So what's going on?"

"Well, I think I have postpartum depression except I'm not depressed. I'm anxious and I've had insomnia for five weeks, but I'm happy. So I'm not depressed."

"But why are you here?"

"Because I'm really anxious."

"Anything else? Lots of people get anxious. Any particular reason why you need to spend the night in the hospital?"

How many times was I going to have to say out loud that I had thought about hurting myself and my daughter?

"Yesterday I thought about how easy it would be to reach over to the knife drawer and end all of this."

"That's it!" The psychiatrist actually seemed pleased by my suicidal thoughts. "So tell me more about the anxiety."

"It's physical."

"What does that mean?"

"Like, um . . ." I felt pressured to answer quickly as if I were taking a timed examination. "There's no logical reason for the anxiety. I just feel scared. I feel like something terrible is going to happen but I don't know what. I feel like there's a comet hurtling toward my house, and even though I know there isn't, I have that sort of adrenaline all the time. I can't talk myself out of the fear."

"Don't worry, we can help you with the anxiety and the depression."

"I'm not depressed."

"Have you been having fun?"

"Yes." The question felt like both a trick and an accusation.

"How?"

"How?"

"How have you been having fun?"

I felt a flicker of anger toward the psychiatrist. I'd said I was happy, I'd said I was having fun, why didn't this guy believe me? Except nothing came to mind.

"Well it's not like I can go to Disneyland every day. I just had a baby. But Nathan and I have been watching a lot of television."

The psychiatrist lifted an eyebrow and typed something on his laptop. What the hell? I'd said I was anxious, not depressed— wasn't anyone listening to me? I stayed silent, though. It did not seem like a good idea to fight with my psychiatrist.

"How long will I need to stay in the hospital?"

"About a week."

A week? Seven days? I could not spend an entire week away from Pippa. I wanted to throw up.

"I can tell you are smart." The psychiatrist looked straight into my eyes. "I can tell you are trying to understand the meaning behind my questions and give me the answers you think I want to hear."

My brain whirled back through the tape of the past few minutes. I could not remember saying anything that could be interpreted as me giving answers the psychiatrist wanted to hear. I was giving honest answers. My heart beat a little faster. The room seemed to be spinning. Why did the psychiatrist think I was playing mind games? Was he playing mind games? Was I losing? Why had he turned a conversation into a chess match?

The psychiatrist leaned back in his chair until the chair's front legs were several inches in the air. "Let's talk about medication."

"I'm breastfeeding and I am going to continue breastfeeding when I go home. So I need to take something safe for that."

"Why don't you quit?"

"Breastfeeding has a lot of health benefits for the baby."

"All the health benefits are front-loaded in the first three months."

"Nathan has bad allergies and I'm hoping to keep Pippa from inheriting them."

"Get a dog. That's more effective if you are worried about allergies."

A dog? A *dog*?

"But if you insist on breastfeeding, there are safe options." The psychiatrist pulled out his iPhone and started showing me information about medications. I could not process what he was saying as he read meaningless medical terms out loud in a rapid voice.

I was relieved when he finally left. His questions had been exhausting. *He* had been exhausting.

———

THE HOSPITAL HAD four psychiatric units: the A Ward was for patients in no danger of hurting themselves or others; the B Ward was for patients in danger of hurting themselves but not others; the C Ward was for patients who needed to be restrained in their beds because they were a danger to themselves and others; and no one talked about the D Ward.

"In the A Ward, you get a private room and a little extra freedom." A tall nurse with long hair—she seemed like an angel—was explaining my options while Nathan held my hand. He had been by my side since the psychiatrist left. The A Ward was clearly the place for me. "But tonight, there are no beds available in the A Ward."

Damnit.

"Tomorrow, someone is being discharged and you can take her bed. But tonight, you need to stay in the B Ward."

"In my own room?"

My angel winced apologetically. "You will have a roommate."

"Like her?" I nodded toward a patient in the hallway who was being guarded by an orderly who looked like a Norse god. She was built like a linebacker and had eyes that were portals to hell. Nathan and I had nicknamed her the horror movie patient.

"No, no, no!" My angel laughed. "The patients in the B Ward are mostly older people with Alzheimer's. They are gentle, kind souls. *She* is going to the C Ward. You will not have to share a room with anyone like that."

Somewhat reassured, I agreed to spend the night in the B Ward.

An orderly brought a wheelchair, and I sat down. The hospital's psychiatric wing was in an entirely different building from the ER. I assumed we would have to go outside. After hours in a windowless room with harsh fluorescent lights, the promise of fresh air was thrilling.

But I was not going to feel any fresh air on my face.

We were not going outside for a pleasant stroll past the flower beds.

We were going underground.

A security guard led the way and Nathan took up the rear. I sat quietly as the orderly pushed my wheelchair down one hallway and then another. The security guard stopped by a door and fumbled with his keychain. It opened with a groan and we entered a tunnel.

There were exposed pipes, dirty puddles, and metal lockers. I expected a rat to scurry across our path. We might as well have been traversing an abandoned subway tunnel.

We walked/rolled in silence but for the echo of our footsteps. I thought about asking the orderly if he had ever read *One Flew over the Cuckoo's Nest* but decided against it.

This could not be happening to me. An actress was sitting in this wheelchair being rolled through a dark, damp tunnel; an actress was about to spend the night in the psych ward. I was not the sort of person who was about to discover what was on the other end of this secret subterranean passage.

11

WELCOME TO THE B WARD

After a two-minute journey, we emerged from the tunnel and stopped before a door. The guard waved a card in front of a security pad and pushed the door open. It looked heavy. This was not the sort of door you could buy at Home Depot. You had to special order it from the contractors who built prisons.

As the orderly wheeled me into the hospital's psychiatric wing, I noticed this place was not like the other parts of the hospital. In the maternity ward, where I had stayed not too long ago, there had been lots of activity—happy visitors, nurses checking charts, orderlies delivering diapers, babies crying, and all sorts of hospital personnel passing through with birth certificates and hearing test equipment as the newborns were ushered through their first days of life. Doors were propped open so that you could overhear the chatter of new grandparents and catch glimpses of tiny hands and feet.

There was no activity in the psychiatric wing. The doors we passed were closed. No one loitered in the halls.

The halls of the maternity ward were decorated with posters, paintings, plants, and even a mural. The carpet had a geometric pattern. The nurses and orderlies wore brightly colored scrubs, often with patterns involving Disney characters or cats.

In the psychiatric wing, everything was beige. The only thing of note was a large room with transparent walls. It looked like it might once have been a cafeteria. There were several folding tables pushed together, lots of chairs, a vending machine, and a piano. When I saw the piano, my spirits brightened. Maybe there was an eccentric composer taking a break from reality in the B Ward and I would get to hear him compose his next masterpiece. That was the sort of thing that usually happened in movies.

The security guard buzzed us through another heavy door.

"You can get up now."

I stood. The guard and the orderly left without saying another word. As if they might catch whatever I had if they acknowledged my existence.

A nurse asked Nathan and me to sit on a bench while she sorted out an insurance issue. Apparently the insurance company wanted to transfer me to another hospital, otherwise we might need to pay the entire bill. That was too much for me to wrap my mind around—would I need a different psychiatrist? Would I have to go through the admission process again? When would Nathan be reunited with Pippa?—so I studied my surroundings instead.

It quickly became evident that I would not be meeting an eccentric composer in the B Ward.

I was sitting a few feet away from a windowless common room crowded with chairs and tables that must have been found in an alleyway after a rainstorm. Instead of my composer, there was a man with a full head of silver hair sprawled in front of a television. I would soon learn that the television was always on, and Silver Hair was always parked in front of it. He was the mayor of the B Ward. He talked loudly to the nurses about his money problems and lived in sweatpants and stained T-shirts but nevertheless managed to maintain an air of respectability. I could easily imagine him in a slightly disheveled linen suit sipping bourbon with Mark Twain.

Moments after Nathan and I arrived, a man in his seventies sat down on a chair a few feet away from our bench and stared at us. Nathan and I scooted several feet down the bench. The old man scraped his chair across the floor until he was once again staring straight at us.

"Babe?" Nathan whispered.

"Yeah?"

"The only crazy thing you have ever done is let yourself be admitted here."

An older nurse looked through the things I had with me. Most of my possessions—including my iPhone—were considered contraband and had to be surrendered.

I did not want to give up my phone. No phone meant no photos or videos of Pippa. Nathan whispered again. "Don't worry, babe, you can sneak the phone in."

The nurse, though, had X-ray vision and made me relinquish my iPhone to Nathan. Inside, I seethed. No one had said anything about giving up my phone. I did not get cell phone service in this dungeon, so it was not like I could use the phone to stage my escape. How could I hurt anyone by looking at photos of my baby?

It was 8:00 p.m. Who knew what sort of trouble Pippa was causing my parents? "Nathan, you should go."

"That's okay. I'll stay until your admission is finalized."

"I want you to go. Pippa needs you. I'll be fine."

"Are you sure? I can stay. I should stay."

"No, please go, please take care of Pippa."

We hugged and kissed good-bye, but even as he held me in his arms, Nathan seemed to be millions of miles away. He was living on Earth. I was trapped on Planet Postpartum Depression. Would I ever find my way home?

I watched Nathan walk to the end of the hallway. A nurse

buzzed him through the door. He turned back, waved, and then he was gone.

I was alone.

THE OLD MAN was still watching me, except now he was methodically demolishing a three-inch stack of deli turkey slices. He would remove a single slice from the stack, jam it into his mouth, and stuff in another slice before he could finish chewing the first. As he gobbled up the turkey, he muttered to himself in gibberish. After a few minutes of this systematic deli stack attack, the meat was nearly gone.

Silver Hair turned away from the television. "Albert! Knock that off! You are going to make yourself sick."

Albert pretended he did not hear Silver Hair—or maybe he actually did not hear him. He was in the middle of a feeding frenzy.

Silver Hair shouted to the nurses. "Do you see what Albert is doing? He is eating all the turkey. He is going to make himself sick. He is going to make himself sick!"

Albert kept eating and muttering, stuffing slice after slice of turkey into his mouth. I politely looked away.

About fifteen minutes after Nathan left, my admission was finally complete and a nurse fetched me.

"Can I have some dinner?" I asked.

"No." She had a thick Russian accent. "Dinner was served at five. But you can have whatever is in the common room fridge."

The nurse showed me the fridge, a miniature model stocked with a stack of deli ham slices, some packets of grape jelly, and a half-used pint of milk.

"Do you want some ham?"

"No, thank you." I made a mental note to thank Nathan for giving me a bag of cashews from the cafeteria before he left.

The nurse escorted me to the door of my room, handed me the saddest towel I had ever seen, and left. It was not yet 9:00 p.m. but my new roommate had already gone to bed and turned off the lights.

I crept inside and investigated. It was spacious, with at least eight feet of open floor between the two beds. The beds were beige, as was the tile floor. There were also two plastic chairs (beige) and two sets of shelves (you guessed it: beige). The walls were painted beige and were otherwise undecorated. There was a window next to my bed. It had a view of a concrete wall.

My roommate was a woman in her late eighties—the benign Alzheimer's patient my ER nurse had promised. I felt an enormous weight lift off my chest when I saw her. She looked gentle, sweet, and frail. If she snapped and tried to hurt me, I could easily bat her away with one hand.

I quietly stowed the few things I had with me on an empty shelf and drifted back into the hallway.

I needed to pump. The hospital's lactation department had brought me a breast pump in the ER. It resembled a large toaster oven, except it was yellow, sat atop a pedestal with wheels, and did not make toast. Nathan had wheeled it through the damp tunnel to the B Ward, but a nurse had confiscated it and locked it away.

I stood at the window for the nurses' station and waited for someone to say hello. The nurses noticed me but kept chatting among themselves.

"Excuse me?"

A nurse rolled her eyes and slowly rotated her chair toward the window. "Yes?"

"Can I please have my breast pump?"

"Do you need to pump already?"

"Yes, it's been several hours and I have to pump before I go to bed."

"Fine." The nurse fetched the pump, acting the entire time as if I had asked her for a spare kidney. I had to summon all my courage to ask her where I could pump.

"In your room."

Stupendous.

My roommate was still in her bed, and I did not want to pump in front of a stranger, so I rolled the pump into the bathroom. However, the bathroom did not have an outlet, and the pump's cord was only a few feet long. I would have to pump in the bedroom, less than ten feet away from my roommate.

Fantastic.

My roommate decided this was an excellent time to wake up and chat.

"Hi," she said. "I'm Edna. Are you my new roommate?"

"Yes."

"What's your name?"

I hesitated. Nathan had told me to lie about my name to the other patients so they could not track me down later, but adopting an alter ego in a mental ward did not seem like the best idea. The doctor might think I was crazier than I really was.

"I'm Courtney."

I debated how to sit: facing the wall or the center of the room. If I faced the room, Edna would have an unobstructed view of my boobs. If I faced the wall, she would see only the profile of my breasts, but if someone opened the door to our room, they would see everything. I decided on the lesser of two evils and angled myself away from Edna's gaze. Hopefully no one would open the bedroom door for the next twenty minutes.

I started to set up the pump.

"What is that? Is it an oxygen tank?"

"No, it's a breast pump."

"What's that for?"

"For pumping milk."

"Why do you need to pump your milk?"

"Because I have a baby at home and I'm breastfeeding her."

"What are you here for?"

I turned on the breast pump. "Postpartum depression."

"I'm here because the new supervisor at my nursing home is awful and if I stay there, I will die. I tell you, I will die."

"Oh no."

"No one listens to me . . ."

Edna detailed all the evils of her nursing home while I pumped. I tried to relax so that my milk would let down, but this was not exactly a day at the spa. I did not like pumping in front of anyone—not Nathan, not my mom, not my sister—and now I had to pump in the presence of a chatty stranger.

This was not helping my anxiety.

"I told my doctor but no one listens to me . . ." Edna prattled on.

The door to our room opened. I fumbled the cup that I was holding to my chest as a male nurse apologized.

That was how I learned the nurses checked our rooms every fifteen minutes.

Edna was unfazed by the interruption. "I tell you, everyone has been dying since the new director took over the nursing home. Why did you say you were here?"

I mustered my sweetest, most patient voice. "I'm so sorry, but it's difficult for me to talk while pumping."

Edna, who had been sitting up in bed and waving her arms around like a conductor, put her head back on her pillow and watched me quietly.

My stomach churned. This woman was old and lonely. I should have entertained her questions. Why was I such a horrible person? I wanted to crawl under my hospital bed and cry.

BY THE TIME I finished pumping, it was nearly 10:00 p.m. I wandered to the nurses' station, and they gave me my medicine:

one hundred milligrams of sertraline and thirty milligrams of mirtazapine. Both drugs are used to treat depression and anxiety. Once again, I felt like a character in a movie, taking my little paper cup from the nurses and swallowing my pills as they watched. I doubted the pills would help—at least not right away. Surely it would take months of experimentation to find the magical dose (if any such dose existed).

There was nothing else to do except go to bed and wait for dawn. I lay down, took some deep breaths, and tried to relax. From my bed, I could watch a clock on the wall. The psychiatrist had warned me that I would probably need sixty milligrams of mirtazapine to sleep. The nurses would give me more if I had trouble falling asleep. I promised myself that when the little hand reached eleven, I would ask the nurses for an extra dose of mirtazapine.

My brain raced.

My heart thumped.

The little hand marched toward eleven.

In five minutes, I would ask the nurses for that extra dose. I braced myself for another visit to the nurses' station and an eternity of insomnia. I closed my eyes. Maybe I could trick myself into sleeping.

I OPENED my eyes and looked at the clock. It was three in the morning.

Had I read that right? Had I really slept for four hours?

I tiptoed to the bathroom, peed, got back into bed, and waited. Having already slept four hours, I assumed the sleeping part of my night was over.

At 3:15 a.m., someone opened the door. My entire body tensed. The door closed. It was just a nurse doing a room check.

At 3:30 a.m., the door opened again and then loudly clicked

shut. How was I supposed to fall asleep if nurses kept opening and closing my bedroom door? How could anyone sleep under these conditions? I was here because I had insomnia. Let me sleep, oh please, let me sleep!

An endless ticker tape of trepidation ran through my head. My adrenaline increased while little phantom bugs crawled up and down my arms.

But beneath the adrenaline and phantom bugs, things were happening. The medications were sorting through my hormones and neurons and putting them back in order. When a nurse opened and closed my door at 3:45 a.m., I was not awake to hear it.

AM I WEARING A SWEATSHIRT?

"Is that an oxygen tank?"

"No. It's a breast pump."

"What's that for?"

It was a little after six in the morning.

"It's for pumping my milk."

"Why?"

I did not have the heart to ask Edna to be quiet again, so I fielded all of her questions while pumping. The interrogation made me feel even more naked and vulnerable than I already was.

I returned the pump to the nurses' station and lingered, hoping for some conversation. The nurses ignored me. Breakfast was over an hour away. I would have to find a way to pass the time.

Then I remembered the room with the piano and vending machines. A pre-breakfast soda sounded delightful. Clearly caffeine had not been the cause of my insomnia.

I walked toward the big door at the end of the hallway. This felt almost normal, like I was back in college, walking to the soda machine in the dormitory basement for a study break.

I reached the door and leaned against the big metal bar across the middle. I pushed. The door did not open. I pushed again, with all my might. The door did not budge. It was almost as if it were locked . . .

I jumped back several steps. Mother of God. I had unintentionally been trying to escape the mental ward.

I twirled around and darted into the common room. The hall monitor had not been watching.

I collapsed on a chair and took a few deep breaths. Yesterday, I had not realized the full extent of what it meant to admit myself for psychiatric care at the hospital. Since it was voluntary, I assumed it was a bit like checking into a spa for a chance to rest and recover my health. I would be able to leave whenever I was ready. Reality, though, was a little different. My surroundings made me even more anxious than I had been at home, and I was not free to go whenever I liked.

I was a prisoner.

IN THE COMMON ROOM, Silver Hair was bogarting the television. I riffled through a stack of celebrity gossip magazines that were at least six months old. Despairing of having anything to do, I went back to my room to relax before breakfast.

"What's your name?"

"Courtney."

"I'm Edna. I'm here because if I stay at my nursing home any longer, I'll die, I tell you, I'll die."

What I would have done for a book.

When I reached my Edna limit (which did not take long), I went back to the hallway. A dozen patients were awake and milling around the corridor outside the common room, waiting for breakfast. A few sat on the benches where Nathan and I had sat last night, waiting for my admission to be finalized. Most were standing, tapping their feet and jiggling away nervous energy.

Against the wall in the hallway, there was a small desk—nothing fancy, just an elevated platform for a desktop computer—and an office chair. A nurse sat there. The main nurse's station was about twenty feet away, so the nurses took turns manning this outpost to monitor the patients. In addition to the nurse at the desk, another orderly and nurse stood amongst the patients, like police officers making their presence known at a protest.

A month ago, on Father's Day, my parents, brother, and sister-in-law had visited our house. Their presence had felt like a barbarian invasion. I had retreated to my breastfeeding throne and cowered with Pippa in my arms. So my nerves were not exactly ready to mingle with a bunch of strangers waiting for breakfast in the mental ward. I stopped about eight feet away from the crowd and leaned against the wall.

"You need to go wait with everyone outside the common room." A nurse frowned as if I were the unruliest patient in the ward. I shuffled down the hallway. This did not seem like the time or place for civil disobedience.

"It's so hot in here. Turn on the air conditioner!"

"It's not hot, Gertrude." The nurse at the small desk did not even look up from the chart in her lap.

"It's hot! Too hot! Turn on the air conditioner!"

Another nurse sighed. "Gertrude, take off your sweatshirt."

"I'm not wearing a sweatshirt."

Gertrude was a five-foot-tall waif in her forties with long brown hair that looked like it had been styled by a hurricane. The sweatshirt in question was at least five sizes too large for her emaciated body, and to be clear: she was most definitely wearing it.

By now, the hallway was packed with patients and nurses. The patients wore comfortable clothes they had brought from home.

Except Albert.

Albert was wearing a kimono-style hospital gown. In theory, the gown covered all his important bits and pieces, but only if it was properly adjusted and carefully tied in place. There was no margin for error. Albert had casually put on his hospital gown like a bathrobe over pajamas—except he was not wearing pajamas.

Or any other article of clothing.

He slouched belligerently on a chair while muttering Albertish. The gown's top half flapped open so that everyone could see his hairy chest. The bottom half covered his private parts—barely. If Albert shifted his position or breathed too deeply, that gown was going to flap open and expose things that no woman with postpartum depression should ever have to see.

At first, I stayed in the hallway outside the common room but directed my gaze away from Albert. Then Albert shifted positions and my instinct to NOT SEE ALBERT'S PENIS overrode my desire to obey the nurses. I retreated down the hallway.

Two young nurses, male and female, argued about who should handle the situation. (By "situation," I mean "Albert's dick.")

The male nurse said, "C'mon, it's your turn to deal with Albert."

The female nurse rebutted, "This situation requires a man's touch. You tell him to cover up."

It did not seem like an ideal time for debate club. A man was indecently exposing himself. Could someone at least throw a towel over that shit?

After several minutes, the male nurse reluctantly sidled up to Albert and told him to fix his gown.

Albert refused.

The male nurse said, "Albert, fix your gown."

"No. Kabble noble."

"C'mon."

"No! Finkle va boom NO!"

"Albert, I'm going to have to take you to solitary again."

"No, va boom, NO."

"Albert, stand up *now*. To your room!"

Albert grunted and huffed as the nurse made him stand and walk back to his room. I kept my eyes averted until I heard a door slam shut.

The slamming door should have made me feel safe, but I was not going to feel safe so long as I was a patient in the B Ward.

BY THE TIME BREAKFAST ARRIVED, I was woozy with hunger. In the past eighteen hours, I had eaten only a handful of cashews. A nurse shoved a tray at me and told me to eat in the common room.

There was an empty armchair next to a small table. It was the perfect place to eat my bowl of sludge and flip through a magazine, but I worried the nurses were observing my every move. If I ate alone, I might be classified as an unsociable loner.

Would that go in my chart?

Did I have a chart?

Would the psychiatrist make me stay in the B Ward forever if I ate breakfast alone?

Was I overthinking everything?

Did the psychiatrist know I was overthinking everything?

I joined my fellow patients at the communal table.

Did I belong here?

I looked at my bare arms. Was I actually wearing a sweatshirt? HOLY FUCK WAS I WEARING A SWEATSHIRT?

I was a patient in the B Ward; the patients in the B Ward had some serious psychiatric issues; ipso facto *I* must have some serious psychiatric issues. After all, if I was delusional and hallucinating, I wouldn't know that I was delusional and hallucinating.

What was happening to me?

My psychiatrist arrived halfway through breakfast.

"Just leave your tray and follow me." He walked down the hallway and gestured me into a conference room.

I sat down and started to ask a question, but he held up his hand. "Hang on, hang on, hang on." He thumped down into his chair and yawned dramatically, not bothering to cover his mouth. He sighed noisily, flipped through the folders in his hand, and yawned again. He started to read my chart. I thought about my half-eaten breakfast and hoped none of the patients were having their way with it.

After several minutes, my psychiatrist leaned back in his chair. "So, how did you sleep?"

"Okay. I slept about four hours, woke up, and then slept for another two."

"That's great!"

"Can I be transferred to the A Ward?"

The psychiatrist studied me for a long moment. "Why? The beds here are the same as in the A Ward."

That was not my understanding. The friendly nurse in the emergency room had assured me that in the A Ward, I would have a private bedroom and a little more freedom. It would make this voluntary admission feel a lot more voluntary.

I stuttered, "I have a roommate and I'd rather have my own room and I feel like I don't belong here. It's tough. I don't know how to interact with the patients."

The psychiatrist glanced at his watch. "What do you mean?"

"Well, it's just that . . . some of the people here . . ."

"What?" The psychiatrist yawned again.

"I think some of the patients are schizophrenic."

"So? Just talk to them like you would anyone else."

By the time the psychiatrist left, my pulse was pounding. How could he think that sharing a room with a stranger was the same thing as having a private room? Did he think I belonged here? With Albert and Gertrude and Edna? Was I losing my mind?

I went back to the common room to finish my breakfast, but an orderly had already thrown my meal away. Now I would be scared *and* hungry.

It was as if the psychiatrist and nurses wanted to exacerbate my illness.

"Is THERE a way that I can call home to check in with my family? I didn't see a phone in my room."

"No phones in patient rooms, but here, you can make calls with this." The nurse handed me a cell phone so large and old, a clown could use it as a circus prop. I walked a few steps away and called my parents' house.

"Hello?"

"It's me!" My body shivered with joy. I had never been so happy to hear the sound of my dad's voice.

"How are you?"

"Much better. I slept last night. Not a ton but I did sleep."

After a while, he passed the phone to Nathan.

"Hey, babe, how are you?"

"Good!" I said. "Well, you know, as good as I can be. How's Pippa?"

"She's good. She misses you but she's drinking formula just fine. I'm going to take a shower and head over there to visit you this morning."

For the first time since my admission to the B Ward, I felt like an actual human being and not just a problem that needed to be ignored.

LATE MORNING, a petite man with glasses stopped me in the hallway. "Are you Courtney? I'm Howard, your social worker."

Apparently everyone in the B Ward was assigned a social worker.

"Sorry it took me so long to catch up with you," he said. "Why don't we go talk in your room?"

Edna was in bed but vacated the room at Howard's request. I sat on my bed. Howard dragged a chair closer and sat a few feet away from me, one leg crossed over the other.

"So Courtney, how are you doing?" The social worker seemed genuinely interested in my answer.

"Okay." (Translation: I miss my baby; I'm afraid my husband hates me; I'm such an inconvenience to everyone; I hate pumping in front of Edna; I'm bored; I'm scared.)

"So you are here for postpartum depression?"

I nodded.

"We had a patient here with postpartum depression but she was discharged yesterday. That's such a shame. It would have been great for you to meet her."

I sat up taller. "I'm glad she was discharged. I'd be worried if there were a ton of long-term patients here with postpartum depression."

At the end of our meeting, Howard leaned a little closer. "You know you don't belong here, right? The patients here have much more serious issues than you."

I nearly wept from relief.

"THERE'S GOING to be a social activity in the common room in a few minutes."

From the nurse's tone of voice, I deduced that healthy, improving patients attended group activities. Crazy patients stayed in their rooms.

I walked as quickly as possible to the common room.

When I got there, I sat down at the main table with a handful of patients. Silver Hair and Gertrude were both in attendance. Albert and Edna were not.

We played a trivia game. A social worker asked, "What's the name of a state that starts with the letter *I*?"

Gertrude said, "Omaha!"

Silver Hair slapped the table. "Gertrude! Don't be such a dumb ass! Omaha doesn't start with the letter *I*. Iowa and Illinois."

I silently listened, not mentioning Indiana or Idaho. No one likes a show-off.

The social worker asked us to name a president.

Gertrude said, "Thomas Edison!"

I suppressed a chuckle. I felt a twinge of guilt from the gods of political correctness, but shoved it away. *I* was a patient here. That meant I could laugh inside my head at Gertrude's responses to the trivia questions.

If only I weren't so alone. Laughter is so much more cathartic when it's shared with another person.

NATHAN ARRIVED with a bag of clean clothes, snacks, toiletries, and books—my husband, my hero, he brought books. A nurse immediately confiscated the bag, including the books, and told me she would inspect it later.

I scanned the B Ward for a place to sit. The common room was crowded with patients, and Edna was lying pathetically in bed. I was not going to ask her to leave the room, not when I had a visitor and she seemed to be all alone. Nathan and I wandered down the hallway.

Albert wandered after us.

While Albert watched, Nathan showed me recent photos of Pippa on his phone. "She's been crying a lot, but she's eating. And she slept fine last night. How are you?"

"Ready for the A Ward."

"How's your roommate? Do you feel safe?"

"Oh yes, totally safe. She wouldn't try to hurt me. Though if she did, I could take her."

"Good."

Down the hall, a patient started shouting loudly for water.

"That's Gertrude . . ." I told Nathan about my morning but could not relax. It was all too awkward, standing in the hallway of the psychiatric wing with Albert lurking a few feet away.

I knew I was broken and needed to be in the hospital to get better, but at the same time, I felt guilty about needing hospitalization. Everyone was being inconvenienced by my weakness: Nathan, living with his in-laws and missing work to visit his wife in the psych ward; my parents, rearranging their lives to watch Pippa; and even my psychiatrist, who had to wake up early to check my status.

I felt tense around Nathan, as if anything I said might be the last straw. Anything might make him decide I was not worth all this drama, and he would leave me and take Pippa with him.

I wanted desperately to feel like Nathan-and-Courtney, so in sync that a single word could make us laugh until our faces hurt. But we were not: I was Courtney, a patient in the psychiatric wing, and he was Nathan, the husband of a woman destroyed by postpartum depression.

Standing there in the hallway of the B Ward, I felt as if our marriage was over. Our vows had included "in sickness and in health," but surely there was an exception for this. I thought I had found my soul mate. The odds had been against us: a boy from rural Nebraska and a girl from Los Angeles. We had been in sync for six years now, which was six years more than most people got. There was no way we could ever get back to the magic of those six years, but at least we had had them.

Then Albert tried to escape.

13

THE GREAT ESCAPE

I t was the most pathetic escape attempt in the history of escape attempts. Still dressed only in his hospital gown, Albert raced toward the exit. It took him about thirty seconds to "run" fifteen feet, but his face was grim with determination. He was going to batter the door down with the force of his mighty speed.

"I'm busting out!" he shouted, English breaking through the gibberish, and he pushed madly against the exit. The door was not going to open unless a nurse buzzed him through, but Albert pushed and kept shuffling his feet for extra momentum.

A nurse meandered after him, looking amused but annoyed. "Albert, knock it off."

"Va boom! Kipkip la vola!"

Nathan and I retreated to the other side of the hallway. It felt wrong to laugh at an escape attempt since I myself had accidentally done the same thing a few hours ago.

We laughed anyway.

Albert's escape attempt was so feeble, it seemed as if he were doing it to break up the day's monotony. He was the class clown of the B Ward, and when the class clown does something hilarious, you laugh.

We laughed together and no longer seemed like strangers. We were Nathan-and-Courtney, Courtney-and-Nathan, and maybe I was in the psych ward and he was exiled to my parents' house, but at least we had a new in-joke.

I leaned against Nathan and said, "I don't belong here."

Nathan kissed the top of my head. "Of course you don't."

If only there was a way to convince the psychiatrist that I would recover much better in the A Ward.

Long after Nathan left, the nurses still had my bag of toiletries and clean clothes. I walked by their station several times and ascertained that they were busy gossiping and pretending the patients did not exist.

Finally, my desire to feel clean outweighed my fear of the nurses. I stopped at their station. "Excuse me, could I please have the things my husband brought?"

A nurse, not bothering to look away from her magazine, said, "No, we haven't had a chance to look through them yet."

I shuffled away, still wearing yesterday's underwear, shirt, and pants. I felt grimy and gross and just wanted to take a shower, put on some fresh clothes, and reclaim a tiny scrap of dignity before that scrap got cut to shreds during my next pumping session in front of Edna.

This was ridiculous.

Something inside me roared, just as something had roared to life when I thought I was going to need a C-section after three hours of active labor, and I went back to the nurses' station. I waited for their attention and said, "I need at least a clean set of clothes and my bathroom supplies."

The nurses glared at me, but I did not care. I was doing everything I needed to do. I was the model patient. I was not exposing my genitals. I was not complaining about the thermostat setting. *I just wanted some clean underwear.*

A nurse sighed and dragged over my bag as if it were a two-ton shipping container. She watched as I rummaged through the bag and pulled out some shampoo and clean clothes.

"Can I have one of the books?"

The nurse dumped the bag back on the floor. "No, we have to inspect it first."

I don't know if this was a power play by the nurses—break the patient's spirit so she does not start a riot—or if the nurses were really that lazy. But this I know: by not letting me take one lousy book, the nurses were compromising my mental health. Of course, they had been doing that ever since I arrived and was offered a stack of deli meat for dinner, so I should not have been surprised. But after being treated like royalty in the maternity ward, I found it shocking to be dehumanized when the whole point of my admission was to feel like myself again.

I retreated to my room. Edna was talking to her social worker and sounding very agitated—"I hate it there, they are monsters, the new director is a devil"—but nothing was getting in the way of my shower.

During our honeymoon, Nathan and I had stayed at the Four Seasons in Maui. Our bathroom had a separate shower and bathtub. The shower stall was about the size of our entire bathroom at home; the water pressure was adjusted to perfection; and bathroom speakers played several different radio stations. The complimentary products were nicer than anything I used at home, and the towels were too plush for words. Of all the highlights of our honeymoon, from zip-lining to tropical drinks served in actual pineapples, the thing we had talked about the most since then was the Four Seasons shower.

This shower felt better.

The stall itself had all the ambience of a prison cell. The

showerhead was flush against the wall, because an inch of exposed pipe could have been used to hang oneself. This meant the water's trajectory was barely a trajectory at all—more of a trickling down the tiles. To get properly wet, I had to lean against the wall. Gertrude's hurricane hairstyle was starting to make sense. It did not matter. It was still the best shower of my life.

In the maternity ward, the day after Pippa was born, a nurse had helped me into the shower stall and set up a chair so I could sit and untangle the elaborate knots in my hair. For a minute, I had let the water wash away the salty residue of labor. Then the guilt and anxiety had started. What if Pippa needed to breast-feed? What if Nathan had to go to the bathroom? What if my doctor stopped by and needed to examine my battle wounds? It was easier to rush out of the shower and leave the knots for another day.

Once Nathan returned to work, showers became a necessary evil. I had to shower to wash germs off my body and keep Pippa healthy, but the minute I stepped inside, Pippa always seemed to wake up and start screaming. The times she kept napping, my body still tensed, haunted by the echoes of yesterday's howls.

But Pippa was not here. I could shower for as long as I wanted and never hear my daughter's wail. For the first time in four months, a shower did not feel like a form of torture.

I shampooed my hair, working it into a rich lather before washing the suds away. Then I poured more shampoo into the palm of my hand and did it all again, carefully massaging every inch of my scalp. I anointed my hair with conditioner and combed it, tenderly untangling knots. The trickle of water was almost comical, but I felt as if I had stumbled upon some hidden cove and was showering beneath the crystal-clear waters of a magical waterfall.

The shower was not just washing away the grime of the past twenty-four hours. It was purifying my body and dissolving the postpartum guilt and stress—only for a few minutes, but that was a few minutes more than I had had in months.

I could do this. I did not want to linger in the B Ward, but if I had to stay another night, I could get better here.

DRESSED AND FEELING CIVILIZED, I opened the bathroom door, thinking I would lie down on my bed and enjoy a reprieve from the hubbub of the common room.

Edna was shouting at her social worker and a psychiatrist who had arrived during my shower. "I will kill myself! I just know I will! I can't go back, I can't go back. I will kill myself!"

I mumbled, "Excuse me," and slipped out into the hallway. I walked to the common room. Silver Hair was at his post by the television (did the man never pee?), Gertrude was riffling through the gossip magazines, and Albert was muttering to himself. I turned around and wandered back down the hall. In lieu of a rest, maybe I could get some exercise by pacing the hallway.

Gertrude followed.

She got closer and closer until our arms were touching. Then she asked, "Can you get me some water?"

"Um, the water fountain is over there."

"Won't you get me some water?"

"I'm sorry, I don't have a cup."

I tried to walk away but Gertrude remained glued to my side. She said, "I will be your boon companion. Can we be roommates?"

"I'm sorry, I already have a roommate."

A nurse/hall monitor was sitting nearby. Gertrude stopped and said, "I want this one to be my roommate."

When Gertrude was not looking, I made eye contact with the

nurse and mouthed "NO!" as dramatically as possible. I felt like the nurse and I were sharing a moment.

Then I realized the nurse was ignoring me just as she was ignoring Gertrude. The nurse did not know or care that in college I wrote a thesis about Benjamin Franklin's autobiography; that I dreamed of writing novels someday; or that I once knit myself a pink sweater. She knew only that I was a mental patient, and as far as she was concerned, that was all she needed to know.

My identity had been reduced to a mental illness. No matter how many showers I took, the nurses would always see me as a diagnosis on a chart.

I felt so, so alone.

THE NEXT TIME I went to my room, Edna's bed was empty. Someone had stripped away the sheets and blankets.

A nurse told me Edna had been sent to the C Ward.

All of a sudden, it seemed very possible that I might become Gertrude's boon companion. Would I wake up with her stroking my hair, whispering about the thermostat?

I took a deep breath and tried to return to my post-shower serenity. There was a handwritten sign on Gertrude's door that said "This Room – Gertrude Only." We were not going to be roommates no matter how little the nurses thought of me.

Maybe I would not get a new roommate. Maybe I would get to sleep alone tonight after all.

After lunch, the nurses finally let me take one book and one extra set of clean clothes to my room. Everything else needed to stay locked in a safe.

No matter, at least I had a book.

I walked back to my room, feeling almost giddy. The nurses might think I was being antisocial, but this was what I needed. A break from Gertrude and Albert. A room to myself. A chance to relax and read and restore my energy. This was what would help me recover and get me back to my baby.

I stepped into my sanctuary and walked toward my bed on the far side of the room. Out of the corner of my eye, I saw something. My entire body tensed.

Edna's bed was no longer empty.

It was occupied.

By a very large person.

Who seemed familiar.

I looked toward my new roommate.

Her eyes were wide open.

No.

She was staring at me.

No!

Her eyes were so blank, they might as well have been empty sockets.

No, no, no!

It was the horror movie patient.

Not knowing what to do, I kept walking and sat down on my bed. The horror movie patient stared at me. I looked at the floor. She kept staring. I gulped and tried to say hello, but words would not come out of my throat. I grabbed my book and fled.

I went to the nurses' station and asked, "Do you know when I'm going to be transferred to the A Ward? I'm supposed to be transferred today."

"I don't know." A nurse with big hair flashed a smile at me. "You'll just have to wait and see."

"I have a new roommate and I don't want to share a room with her. She was in the ER last night with me and she was being guarded by an orderly and I don't think she's safe. Can I be transferred now?"

"Oh, don't worry about that. We can't transfer you until we have the doctor's approval."

I went to the common room, read the same paragraph in my book a dozen times, and went back to the nurses' station.

"Excuse me, I want to request a roommate transfer. Also, I'm waiting to get moved to the A Ward . . ."

And so it went for an hour. Every five or ten minutes, I would go to the nurses' station and request a transfer. One time, I even volunteered to share a room with Gertrude.

At first, the nurses were unusually kind and friendly. I thought this meant they were on my side and working behind the scenes to improve my situation. It was all a façade. The nurses were trying to subdue me with smiles and concerned expressions. They were not actually interested in helping me.

After an hour of this dance, the nurses returned to their usual bitchy selves. As soon as they saw me coming, any sign of humanity disappeared from their eyes. They did not want to listen to me.

How could this be happening? Less than twenty-four hours ago, a muscular orderly had been guarding the horror movie patient. My friendly ER nurse had insisted—insisted!—I would not share a room with her. Where was my gentle Alzheimer's sidekick?

I was being treated for anxiety and insomnia and now the nurses wanted me to sleep with a sociopath? Sure, the nurses did room checks every fifteen minutes, but the horror movie patient could snap my neck in three seconds. She could be eating my face by the time the nurses found me.

There was no way I could sleep in the same room as her. I would refuse to take my meds. I would stay in the common room all night. I would do something drastic to get sent to the C Ward —at least those patients were restrained.

After six or seven trips to their station, I realized there was nothing I could do or say to convince the nurses that I needed a new assignment. It was time to play my trump card. I asked the nurses for the phone and called Nathan.

"I have a new roommate," I told him. "It's the horror movie patient from the emergency room. I told the nurses I need to be moved to the A Ward but they won't listen to me because I'm a crazy patient."

"I will take care of this. I love you."

"I love you."

I did not know what Nathan would do, but I knew he would rescue me, even if he had to batter down the door to the B Ward himself.

In a twisted way, the horror movie patient was helping me break through the postpartum depression. For months, I had been refusing the help of others, insisting that I had to get better on my own. Now I was admitting I needed someone else's help, and not just anyone's help, but Nathan's help. I had not even stopped to worry if I was inconveniencing him.

The horror movie patient was terrifying, but maybe a little terror was the jumpstart I needed to get out of the depression.

IN THE LATE AFTERNOON, a nurse pulled me aside and whispered, "Do you want to hurt yourself?"

"No, I do not." I hoped my voice sounded sane and reasonable. Since checking myself into the hospital, I had not had a single dark thought, but since my psychiatrist thought I was in the business of playing mind games, I did not know if anyone would believe me.

The nurse walked away, leaving my fate unknown. Bedtime was hours away. Nathan would find a way to fix this. Until then, I would just have to avoid my bedroom.

Except I needed to pump.

I procrastinated as long as possible and then went to the nurses' station, shivering with fear. This time, a young nurse who seemed less jaded than the others fetched my pump. She actually looked in my eyes when I spoke. When she saw me wheeling the pump toward my room, she asked where I had been pumping.

"My room."

"I'm sure we can find somewhere more private for you."

A doctor was using the conference room, and the nurses' station was off-limits, but no one was in the solitary confinement room. There were no outlets in the room itself, but there was one in the alcove between the room and the hallway. It was not totally private—there was a small window in the door between hallway and nook—but anything was better than pumping in front of my new roommate.

I pumped and dumped and continued the waiting game, slowly walking past the nurses' station for any clues as to my fate. I tried to read but could not concentrate on the words.

Soon it would be dinner. Then medications time, when Nurse Ratched would watch me place my pills on my tongue and check to make sure I had swallowed them. The pills would make me sleep. I would never know the horror movie patient was coming until it was too late.

I thought about calling home but waited. I did not want to hear Nathan say, "I'm sorry, babe, but there's nothing I can do. Good luck tonight."

The minutes ticked closer to bedtime.

I asked to pump again. In the alcove, I could at least forget about my impending doom.

The friendly nurse helped me wheel the pump to the alcove. I plugged it in and washed the bits and pieces. Just as I was taking off my shirt, someone knocked at the door.

It was the nurse with the heavy Russian accent. The one who

had offered me a stack of deli meat from the communal fridge and made me give my iPhone to Nathan.

I opened the door an inch. "Yes?"

"You are being transferred to the A Ward. Go get your stuff."

Yesterday, my transfer from the emergency room to the B Ward had taken four hours.

"Can I pump first?"

My least favorite nurse shrugged and walked away.

I closed the door and turned back to the pump.

What if the powers that be changed their mind while I was pumping?

I burst out of the alcove. "Wait! I'll be ready in thirty seconds!"

As I followed my new favorite nurse down the hall, we passed a man crouching in a puddle. A nurse was saying, "You are going to have to clean that up and wash your clothes. Why can't you urinate in the toilet?"

I held my breath, terrified that this, or some other diversion, would interfere with my escape. A moment later, though, the nurse buzzed us through the exit and I stepped into freedom.

Or, at least, a better version of hell.

14

THE EEYORE WARD

"Should we stay here for group therapy? Or do you want to go outside to the courtyard?"

"I don't care," a blonde woman in her late fifties said. She had been struggling with depression ever since menopause.

"Doesn't matter," a brunette said. She, too, was in her late fifties and had been struggling with depression since menopause.

A voice inside of me was clamoring to go outside, but I shrugged when the social worker looked at me.

"Well, someone needs to choose," the social worker said.

"Courtyard is fine," the brunette said.

"Great, let's go."

Our group of six walked down a corridor and entered the large dining room with soda machines. The morning before, this very room had been the inspiration behind my accidental escape attempt. Now, I was freely walking across its floor toward a courtyard.

My psychiatrist was wrong. The mattresses might have been made by the same company, but the A Ward and B Ward were as different as the Ritz-Carlton and the Bates Motel.

My bedroom was mine—all mine! The head nurse had decreed I could keep my belongings, including the pump and all its accoutrements, in my room. It had a window with a view of a little courtyard, the sky, flowers, and green leaves. Before breakfast, I had even spied on some nurses taking a cigarette break.

The common room was significantly larger and decorated with new, comfortable furniture. There was yogurt and fruit in the fridge. The lighting was more cheerful, and unlike the dingy beige walls of the B Ward, the walls here had been freshly painted bright white. There was a bouquet of flowers at the nurses' station.

The social worker needed to use her security card to buzz open the door to the courtyard, so there were still some limits on our liberty. But I was happy to see that the courtyard was surrounded by walls that, with a boost from my husband, I could easily vault.

The social worker leading group therapy introduced herself as Maureen. She had short hair, glasses, and according to the schedule in my room, was thirty minutes late for our session. "Why don't we go around the table and introduce ourselves and tell everyone why we are here," she suggested.

The blonde woman started. "Well, I've been here for a week now. I'm getting my next shock therapy treatment tomorrow. They don't seem to be helping, but I'll try anything. My mom killed herself when I was sixteen, and I found her body after school. That was awful. It nearly destroyed me. I want to die now. I really do. But I don't want to do that to my kids."

I shifted uneasily on my chair. Shock therapy was still being used in 2013? That sounded way too much like something from *One Flew over the Cuckoo's Nest* for my comfort.

"What about you, John?" Maureen looked hopefully at a man who might have been in his late twenties or early forties. It was difficult to tell because he was always looking at his feet.

John shrugged and whispered, "No."

Maureen nodded and turned toward the menopausal brunette.

"And what's your name?"

"Robyn. I've been here four days now. I've had insomnia for fifteen years. I can only sleep an hour or two at night."

Fifteen years? An hour or two? I wanted to vomit.

"Have you been sleeping here?" Maureen seemed unimpressed with these numbers.

"Yes, because my doctor prescribed Ambien, but my husband will not let me take Ambien when I go home because I took it before, and I was sleepwalking and went outside."

When it was my turn, I told the group, "I'm here because I have postpartum depression that has manifested itself through anxiety and insomnia."

"What does that mean?" Maureen asked.

"It means I feel physically scared all the time, and I haven't been sleeping, but I'm not depressed. I'm not depressed at all."

I had met with my psychiatrist three times now, and every time, he told me that I was depressed. And every time, I had to keep myself from clenching my fists under the table, because he seemed to have superhuman vision and I did not want him adding anger management issues to my diagnosis. But still, I was livid with his insistence that I was depressed, because I knew I was not. I had never been depressed, was never going to be depressed, and was certainly not depressed now, during the happiest time of my life.

No one could say anything to convince me otherwise.

———

"THIS PLACE FEELS SO MUCH BETTER than the B Ward. Thank God you got transferred. Oh hey, I grabbed you some quarters so you can use the vending machines."

Nathan gave me a ziplock bag filled with loose change. This was his second visit of the day. First, he had visited during the interval between therapy and lunch. Then he had gone home to take care of "life bureaucracy." Now he was back. I think he needed to see me as much as I needed to see him.

"Can I watch that video of Pippa again?"

"Of course."

Nathan had taken the video when Pippa woke up that morning. The sun had not yet risen, and Nathan had turned a lamp on to its lowest setting, but I could still make out my baby's features: her little feet, constantly moving as if she were riding a bicycle; the length of her torso; the sweet expanse of her cheeks. But I did not care about the visual. I just wanted to hear her voice. She was hoarse from crying too much but still babbling to her daddy. Her coos made me smile while breaking my heart at the same time.

I watched the video a few times before handing the phone back to Nathan.

"So what have you been up to since I left?" he asked.

"We had gym time and I got my heart rate up to 160 just like the doctor asked."

"Does that help with the postpartum depression?"

"The doctor said it will. Apparently it doesn't matter how long my heart rate stays at 160, I just need to hit that number. Then I showered and read a little."

"I hope the novels are okay. Your sister picked them out."

"They're great."

"So is there anything else this afternoon?"

"Occupational therapy."

"What's that?"

"I have no idea. I always thought occupational therapy was for people who had a stroke and needed help learning how to use a fork again."

"Me too."

"I'll call and tell you about it later today."

We kissed and I rested my head on Nathan's shoulder. We were sitting outside in the little courtyard where we had had group therapy.

"You okay staying here another night?"

"Oh, yes." I tried to downplay my enthusiasm, but the A Ward felt right. This was where I needed to be.

"Because I can totally get you over that wall if you want to go home."

I laughed. "That's exactly what I thought when we came out here for group therapy."

"So what do you want to do today?"

The menopausal women shrugged; the old man in his eighties grunted; the man who never made eye contact was hiding in his bedroom.

We were standing in the hallway outside the mysterious occupational therapy headquarters. I recognized the therapist from a group therapy session in the B Ward. She had asked each patient to identify a hobby and then a way to pursue that hobby in the B Ward. One patient had said he liked jogging, so we spent most of the session discussing ways for him to jog in the hallway without hurting other patients. I braced myself for another rousing discussion about jogging strategies.

"This is your guys' time, so you need to decide how you want to use it."

The brunette shrugged. "What is there to do?"

"I can get out a plastic bowling set that we can play with outside."

Bowling? That would never have been allowed in the B Ward, even if the pins and ball were plastic.

"Or we could play some board games."

Board games? I *loved* board games.

"Or we can do arts and crafts again."

Arts and crafts? Holy shit, I wanted to do arts and crafts! But I stayed silent, feeling like I should not have a vote since I was the newest member of the A Ward.

"That all sounds good," the woman receiving shock treatment said.

"David, aren't you still working on that stool? Would you like to finish that?"

The man in his eighties made some noncommittal sounds.

After a few more "whatevers" and "it doesn't matter," we decided on arts and crafts and followed the occupational therapist into a large and spacious room that looked like the art room at my elementary school. The therapist started unlocking cabinets and said we could do any project that our hearts desired.

I hunted through the cabinets for about five minutes. I wanted to grab everything off the shelves, run back to my room, and spend the rest of the day gluing Popsicle sticks together. After much deliberation and agonizing, I decided to decorate a white cardboard box with precut tissue paper squares. I squeezed some glue onto a paper plate, dipped a paintbrush into the glue puddle, and quickly lost track of time.

After I had decorated half the box, the occupational therapist said, "I like the colors that you are choosing."

I paused and admired my creation. The bag of tissue paper squares included a full range of colors and hues, but I had chosen a bright spectrum of pink, blue, and green.

"These are my favorite colors," I said.

"Most patients prefer blacks and browns and navy blues."

I looked at the menopausal women's projects. The blonde was painting a ceramic flip-flop for her granddaughter in some dark colors that had mixed into a brown mess. The brunette was also decorating a box with tissue paper squares, but she had gravitated toward black and navy-blue.

"I wish I had chosen bright colors like you," the brunette lamented.

"Why don't you start over?"

She shrugged and kept sticking her dark squares onto the box. It looked terrible.

We had an entire hour for occupational therapy, but the other patients left early. I kept gluing on tissue paper squares and chatting with the occupational therapist.

"How old is your daughter?"

"Four months."

"My kids are in preschool. It was such a big transition when they were born."

"I'm struggling to make mom friends. Everyone keeps telling me I need friends with babies close in age to Pippa, but I don't know how."

"Mom friends are important. I live in Pasadena now, but grew up on the Westside, so I didn't have any close friends in the area when I had kids."

"I'm a Westside transplant, too. I grew up in the Palisades."

"Me too!"

We quickly established that we had gone to different schools, and the therapist was a few years older than me, but we had grown up with all the same haunts and traditions: same Fourth of July parade; same YMCA Christmas tree lot; and the same deli with sandwiches named after local celebrities. The more we talked, the more I wanted to talk and share stories, but the hour was soon over.

"I'll be here tomorrow," the therapist said as I cleaned my paintbrushes at the sink. "I'll bring some information for the parenting class where I met all my mom friends. I think you'll like it."

As I walked back to my room in the A Ward, I suddenly felt

relieved that my psychiatrist wanted me to spend a week in the hospital. Another day in the hospital meant another day of arts and crafts. Though I could not articulate why, I knew arts and crafts was helping me, maybe even more than the medications.

LATER THAT AFTERNOON, I turned the page of one of the novels my sister had sent. It was good, but I felt like I should be doing something else.

I checked the schedule. Nothing until dinnertime.

Back to the book. I shifted positions on the bed but could not get rid of the feeling that I should be doing something else.

But what?

Then it came to me. I put the book back on my nightstand and walked as fast as I could to the nurses' station.

"Could I have a pen and some paper for writing?"

"Let me see what we have." A moment later, the nurse returned with a blunt pencil and some blank paper from the printer. "Will this work?"

"Yes. Thank you." I resisted the urge to speak with exclamation points, not wanting to raise any alarm bells. All the other patients were subdued and bored. I thought that was how I was supposed to act.

I sat down on my bed cross-legged, used the paperback as an impromptu desk, and started writing whatever thoughts popped into my head. Within seconds, I entered the flow of writing. I did not look up from the paper for at least a half hour.

When I stopped writing, it was not because I had run out of things to write but because my hand needed a break. I looked out at the courtyard and let my thoughts wander.

How could I have forgotten about writing?

I had finished the first draft of a novel and vowed to return to it as soon as possible. I had even worked on it during Pippa's naps for a few days. What had happened? Why had I stopped?

My hand still hurt but I picked up the pencil and started writing again. It did not matter what I wrote just so long as I let the words spill out of me onto the paper. So long as I was writing, I was no longer just going through the motions of living. I was truly and totally alive.

And damn, that felt good.

I HAD an uncontrollable urge to get out of bed and *move*. I had to exercise *right now*, but gym time was several hours away. I told myself to lie still and get a little more sleep but that felt impossible.

It was Sunday morning. My third full day in the hospital. Something was happening to my body.

I lay down on the floor and did stomach crunches. Then I stood up and did jumping jacks and lunges. My skin was tingling with energy and I was itching to sing and dance. Was I having a manic episode? Was I bipolar?

This had happened to a friend. Shortly after she gave birth, she was diagnosed with postpartum depression and prescribed an antidepressant. The antidepressant triggered her first manic episode. New diagnosis: my friend was bipolar. For several months, the doctors scrambled to find the right medication and dosage. My friend even had to spend a week in a psychiatric hospital.

Just like me.

Oh God, I was bipolar.

Except this energy was too much even for a manic episode. Whatever I had must be really, really terrible. If the psychiatrist knew I was vibrating with this much energy, he would lock me away forever.

During my second round of crunches, the head nurse opened my bedroom door and popped inside for a room check. I froze.

"Great idea!" she said. "That looks like excellent exercise. I need to work on my abs."

After she closed the door, I lay still for a few more seconds. If the staff did not restrain me, I would end up knocking down a wall—COURTNEY SMASH! Yet the nurse did not seem concerned, so I resumed the crunches.

When gym time finally arrived, I climbed floor after floor on the stepping machine. My muscles started to burn, and the burn felt good. Every fiber of every muscle was singing and twirling like Julie Andrews in the opening sequence of *The Sound of Music*.

What was happening to my body? This energy was delightful, but what would the psychiatrist think?

And then it hit me, right in the middle of gym time, as I wiped sweat off my brow.

Nothing was wrong.

Everything was right.

This abundance of energy? This desire to move and craft and yodel and write? This was me. For the first time in four months, I actually felt like myself.

"You're right, I'm depressed. I couldn't see it though until I felt my energy return. Today I woke up with so much energy that I thought something was wrong but then in the gym I remembered this is the way I feel when I'm healthy."

"That's great." My psychiatrist flipped through a notebook.

Nathan squeezed my hand. I had felt ecstatic when the psychiatrist arrived during Nathan's visit. The psychiatrist often felt like a hostile enemy force. Partly because he yawned and thought the A Ward were exactly like the B Ward, but mostly because he controlled my discharge. It was nice to have Nathan's moral support.

I took a deep breath. "I'm ready to go home. I need to be with Pippa and Nathan and my parents so I can get better. I don't belong here anymore."

The psychiatrist frowned. "I think you should stay for the full week. All you patients are the same. You start to get better and then you want to be discharged before the week is up. What's the rush? I want to believe this epiphany of yours, but it sure is coming at a convenient time, isn't it?"

Now it was my turn to frown. "What do you mean?"

"You insisted you were not depressed. And then, conveniently, as soon as you want to be discharged, you tell me you suddenly realize you are depressed. Seems fishy to me. But whatever, I'm not going to stop you. If you think you are ready to be discharged, it's your life. Let's see how you are doing tomorrow."

As the psychiatrist talked, the palms of my hands got sweaty. The psychiatrist had seen that I was depressed before I could. Maybe now he was seeing something else. Did I still not know the state of my own mind?

After the psychiatrist left, I turned to Nathan. "Do you think I'm making up this epiphany?"

"Not at all, babe. You seem changed. On the phone, when you called after occupational therapy, you sounded genuinely excited. You seem a lot more like yourself. I don't think I realized how badly you were doing until I saw you getting better."

"I don't want to go home if I'm just going to end up back here in a week, but I don't feel like I belong here," I said. "This is the Eeyore ward. Everyone is talking about their insomnia, which just makes me worry that my insomnia is going to come back. I can feel myself improving when I'm in my room writing, but then when I start talking to the other patients, I can feel the anxiety increasing. I need to get out of here."

AFTER NATHAN LEFT, I went back to my room to rest. Sitting on my bed with a novel, fatigue claimed my body, starting with my feet and then spreading through my limbs until every muscle seemed to be falling toward the floor. My body was telling me to take a nap. I was powerless to resist.

I put my head on the pillow and closed my eyes. For an hour, I tried to nap but could not fall asleep. When I had insomnia, my brain would not stop chattering. Lying in the hospital, the issue was not incessant noise in my mind. My brain just wasn't tired. My muscles felt as if I had been running all day, but my brain was well rested and ready to live.

Weird.

Even weirder: the longer I lay in bed with my eyes closed, the more exhausted my muscles felt. I opened my eyes. If I was tired, resting was the solution—right? Except resting seemed to be exacerbating the fatigue.

I don't know where it came from, but an idea presented itself: I should go to the common room and color. Earlier that day, during occupational therapy, I had finished my tissue paper box. Not wanting to start a project that I might not have time to finish, I had started coloring. When the hour was up, the occupational therapist let me take some supplies back to the common room.

Coloring did not require much energy and was far more entertaining than waiting for a nap that would not come. I shuffled to the common room, looked through a stack of pages copied from a children's coloring book, selected one with a butterfly and started coloring. As the wings and background flowers filled with shades of pink and yellow and green, I lost track of time and the fact that I was a patient in the A Ward.

By the time I finished the picture, my muscles felt fine. Doing something creative had been more restorative than lying prone in bed.

Except that made no sense. My body was adjusting to new medications. The fatigue must have been related to that. Coloring a butterfly had no effect on my energy.

I may have been ready to leave the A Ward, but I still had a lot to learn about beating depression.

15

BREASTFEEDING BLUES

The next morning, while awaiting my discharge, I attended my final group therapy session. When it was my turn to talk, I launched into my usual spiel: "I have postpartum depression that has manifested itself through anxiety and insomnia—"

A new patient raised her hand. "I'm so sorry to interrupt, but I have a friend. She breastfed her firstborn and had postpartum depression. When she had her second baby, she did not breastfeed and she did not get postpartum depression that time. Are you breastfeeding? Maybe there's something about breastfeeding that is causing your depression."

"I'll keep that in mind." I smiled but inside, I was seething. Clearly this patient was a devil trying to cast me out of the Garden of Breastfeeding with the temptation of formula and bottles. *I*, however, was strong. *I* was a good mother. *I* would keep breastfeeding Pippa until she was at least a one-year-old.

Yet deep inside, underneath the layers of guilt and anxiety, I felt a flutter of a traitorous thought. My milk production was so, so low. Plus breastfeeding was so time-consuming. It kept me trapped in a chair for hours every day, and even if someone volunteered to watch Pippa, I could not go very far because I would still have to pump. Maybe breastfeeding was not the best thing for me and Pippa . . .

And I was a wicked mother for even having these thoughts. I would keep breastfeeding Pippa until she was at least a one-year-old in accordance with the prevailing advice of the World Health Organization and the American Pediatric Society.

End of discussion.

MY DAD WALKED into the A Ward, totally nonchalant, as if he were picking me up from soccer practice.

I waved to the head nurse. "I guess I'm going. Good-bye."

"Good-bye, Courtney!"

Fireworks seemed appropriate. Or, at the very least, a lecture about taking my medications. The nurse, though, just buzzed us through one door, and another, and then we were outside.

I got into my dad's car. My home was east of the hospital, but we were headed west. Nathan, Pippa, and I would be staying at my parents' house indefinitely while I was in mental health limbo —not sick enough for the hospital, but not well enough to spend my days alone with my baby. Nathan was at court, so I would not see him until dinnertime. I had seen him every day I was in the hospital, so I was not too worried about our reunion.

Pippa was an entirely different matter.

After I agreed to admit myself to the hospital for psychiatric care, my mom summoned my dad from the obstetrician's waiting room where he was watching Pippa. I held Pippa in the examination room while a flurry of activity happened in the background. I did not realize it at the time, but my obstetrician needed to find a psychiatrist to oversee my admission. (The psychiatrist who usually handled her postpartum depression cases was unavailable.) My parents and Nathan were busy figuring out logistics for taking care of Pippa. But I felt too exhausted and broken to participate in those conversations. Instead, I sat and held Pippa.

When it was time to go, I carried my baby from the doctor's office to the elevator, kissing the top of her head as we rode down to the ground floor and then hugging her tight as I walked across a small courtyard to the parking garage. Nathan had parked next to my parents' car, so I kept holding Pippa, supporting the back of her head with my hand, until we reached the vehicles.

I did not want to let my baby go. I bent my head close to hers and whispered promises into her ear. "Mama loves Pippa. So much. I have to go away, baby girl, but I'm coming back. I promise, Pippa, I'm coming back. I love you. Mama loves Pippa."

Then I handed her to my dad and got into Nathan's car. A few tears clouded my eyes. That was the only time I cried the day I was hospitalized. In the following days, when Nathan came to visit me, I told him to leave Pippa at home with my parents. The hospital was at least forty-five minutes away from their house. I did not want Pippa being schlepped back and forth on my account.

Also, I could not bear the idea of saying good-bye to her again.

Now, after four days apart, we would finally be together.

Would she remember me?

Would she be happy to see me?

Would she hate me forever?

My stomach started to churn. Why hadn't I done a better job of fighting off the postpartum depression alone? How could I have let this happen?

I willed my dad to drive faster but wanted the car ride to last forever.

My mom was walking down the stairs when I stepped over the threshold into my parents' house. She greeted me and said that Pippa was in the nursery with Laura.

The nursery? Oh right, someone had mentioned during one of my many phone calls home that the guest room was now the nursery. I walked there as fast as I could.

I saw her as soon as I entered the room: my baby, my precious baby, lying on the changing table, having her butt wiped by a stranger.

As I rushed toward her, Pippa twisted to see who was there. As soon as she saw me, her face lit up with the biggest smile she had ever smiled.

I wanted to snatch her up and cover her with kisses, but Laura, the doula, was snapping the buttons on a purple velour onesie that I had never seen before. So instead, I stood by Pippa's head and stroked her hair. "Hi, Pippa! It's Mommy! I'm back. I missed you so much. You got so big. Wow, such a big girl."

She was not just big. She was tremendous. Her cheeks were chubbier, her limbs were longer, and the circumference of her torso—well, she looked like the strongman in an old-fashioned circus, chest puffed out in a tight suit. She must have gained at least a pound while I was gone (which is a lot when you weigh only twelve or so pounds). My mom had mentioned a trip to the mall for baby clothes. That suddenly made sense.

I wanted to bump the doula to the side and snatch Pippa into my arms, but I waited. I felt intimidated by the doula's authority.

The day I was admitted to the hospital, Pippa had cried for hours on end. My mom had summoned a friend who already had several grandchildren, but she could not soothe Pippa either. That's when my parents decided they needed a Mary Poppins to intervene.

While I was still in the hospital, my mom had gushed about Laura the doula. "Oh, Courtney, she's wonderful. It's like she knows magic. Your father and I could not comfort Pippa, but

Laura knew exactly what to do. *And* she got Pippa to nap in her crib."

"Wow, that's great, naps in the crib." I was mortified that a stranger was taking better care of my baby than I was, on top of the guilt I was feeling that my parents had to pay someone to do my job.

At last, Laura finished dressing Pippa. I scooped her into my arms and sat down on a nearby chair. "Pippa! Hi, sweetie. It's me, Mama."

Pippa turned to watch Laura, who was busy tidying baby stuff on the dresser. I kissed my daughter on both her cheeks. "Mommy missed Pippa. So much. I'm so glad to be back."

Pippa squawked and kept her eyes on Laura.

I unbuttoned my shirt and offered a breast to Pippa. She closed her lips tightly and turned her head from my body. She made more fussy sounds. My entire body ached.

I silently shouted death threats at the doula, but she stayed in the nursery. My heart raced. If she lingered much longer, Pippa would never love me again and why oh why had I gone to the hospital, why had I not been stronger—

I stopped myself mid-thought and carried Pippa out of the nursery. I walked upstairs, took her into an empty room, and closed the door.

I sat down on the floor. "Hi, sweet girl, it's Mama. Mama's back. I'm so sorry I had to leave. But I'm back now and I feel a lot better. I missed you so much! Oh I love you, my precious girl."

Pippa turned away from me yet again and looked at the wall. She was ignoring me.

A panic attack was breathing against my neck, threatening to pull me into a spiral of darker and darker thoughts, but I took a deep breath and resisted. No one at the hospital had taught me how to deal with anxiety—the focus there had been on sleeping enough and doing things we enjoyed—but I knew, in the marrow of my bones, that I had to find a way to stay calm for my baby even as she rejected me.

So I sang.

"You Are My Sunshine," while tickling her toes.

"Candle on the Water," while nuzzling her cheeks and stroking her soft baby hair.

I counted her fingers and recited nursery rhymes.

Then I talked and talked and talked. "Mama loves you. Mama missed you so much. Oh, Pippa, I love you so much. And my goodness, you are so big. You are busting out of your clothes! Baby girl, we have to take you shopping. Mama is back now, and she's not leaving again. We will take long walks and go to the park and we are going to have so much fun."

Through all of this, Pippa let me hold her but refused to look at my face. She looked at the wall, her lap, the ceiling, the other wall, anywhere but at me.

Then, twenty minutes after I started serenading her with Mama's Greatest Hits, Pippa turned her head toward me and looked into my eyes. For a moment, she hesitated. Then her lips stretched into a big grin, her blue eyes sparkled, and she leaned her head closer to mine. If she could have talked, she would have said, *Oh, Mama, I can't stay mad at you.*

I continued singing and tickling Pippa, and now she smiled and babbled back at me. We clicked back together, mother and daughter.

It was as if I had never left.

AFTER WE HAD PLAYED and cuddled for a half hour, Pippa seemed hungry, so I tried to breastfeed her again. This time, she latched on and enjoyed a quick snack, but she kept unlatching so she could smile and make eye contact with me with both of her eyes. (She could only sort of see me with one eye when my breast was mashed up against her face.) After only a few minutes, she pushed my breast away and wanted to play.

I had no idea that was the last time I would ever breastfeed Pippa.

An hour later, before her bath, I tried to feed her. As soon as she saw my breast, she pursed her lips tightly and turned her head away. Once the breast was safely back in my bra, she smiled and leaned toward me again. She was making hungry sounds, but I told myself she was not ready to eat.

After her bath, she kept making sounds that said *I am ravenous!* Every few minutes, I offered my breast, and every time, she pursed her lips as if I were offering poison.

For the next hour, we continued this dance. The breastfeeding authorities had taught me to feed on demand, but they had not told me what to do when the baby demanded formula. With every failed attempt to reestablish breastfeeding, my shoulders slumped lower and lower.

I could no longer ignore the concerns that had started in the psych ward. I had pumped religiously, but no matter how long I extended each session, I barely produced any milk. Maybe pumping produced less milk than an actual baby at the breast—but why did my breasts feel empty when I woke up in the morning? They should have been full and ready for breakfast. Was I really making enough milk for Pippa?

My prenatal yoga teacher would be so disappointed. I thought back to the class, about six months ago, that she had talked about breastfeeding.

"Breathe in . . . breathe out." My teacher's voice was very soothing. "Imagine a light is emanating from your uterus. What color is that light?"

I sat on my yoga mat and imagined a gold light sparkling out of my torso for about ten seconds. Then I thought about the pain in my lower back.

"Open your eyes," the teacher said. "How do you feel?"

A chorus of pregnant women nodded and murmured "good."

"I like to start our classes with a question. Today, I want to ask if you are going to breastfeed your baby."

The first five moms answered the same way: "Yes, I'm breast-feeding."

Then it was my turn. "I'm going to breastfeed so long as it works for me and the baby."

The yoga teacher frowned. "That's the wrong attitude. If you allow yourself to keep open the possibility that breastfeeding won't work, then it won't. In my years as a doula, I have helped countless women with breastfeeding. The attitude they bring to the table is *always* the deciding factor. You have to tell yourself, *I am breastfeeding!* and be firm in your resolve, or else you will fail."

My cheeks burned. "I had no idea. Okay. I am breastfeeding. I am breastfeeding!"

Now, hours after my release from the psychiatric unit, I thought of the prenatal yoga teacher. If she were here, she would urge me to keep repeating that mantra: *I am breastfeeding, I am breastfeeding, I am breastfeeding!* She would tell me to pump and then feed Pippa breast milk from a bottle. After all, Pippa might be able to refuse my breast, but she could not get up and pour herself a bottle of formula from the fridge.

I do believe in the power of positive thinking. When I expect things to go wrong, I lose my temper over the slightest mishap. When I expect things to go well, I handle disasters with grace and serenity. There was something to the yoga teacher's advice. One's mentality really can affect the success of an enterprise.

But sometimes, a mantra is no match for the way one's body works. Some mamas are made to breastfeed their children. Others are not. In a different time and place, I would most certainly have been employing the services of the village wet nurse.

Pippa was moving from "slightly miffed" to "uber-cranky."

The poor girl was hungry. Surely the breast strike could not last much longer.

My mom stood nearby. "I could call a lactation expert . . ."

I sighed. "No, that's okay."

I stroked Pippa's cheek.

Pippa looked into my eyes and smiled.

I smiled back.

I turned to my mom. "There's no need for a lactation expert. Can you please get me a bottle?"

THAT NIGHT, I sobbed in the shower.

I had decided to breastfeed even before I got pregnant. Most of my friends breastfed their babies. The ones who didn't had medical reasons like Lyme disease or bipolar disorder. Since I did not have a medical exemption, I would of course join the ranks of my breastfeeding friends.

All the reading I had done after I got pregnant had convinced me that breastfeeding was critical to my daughter's health and well-being. My favorite bloggers posted photos and stories about breastfeeding, and they looked so hip and confident—and thin. Everyone who breastfed seemed to shed all the pregnancy weight that I desperately wanted to lose.

Freshly discharged from the psych ward, taking a shower at my parents' house, I was a hot mess. Breastfeeding had to end—I knew that in my stomach, my bones, my heart. It aggravated the depression and anxiety. I constantly worried about the logistics of nursing—was Pippa hungry? When would she be hungry? Where would I feed her? Were my breasts clean enough? The thought of breastfeeding in public made me want to throw up. It became my excuse to stay at home. Even during my morning walk, when I was never more than a few blocks from home, my stomach churned over the thought of Pippa whimpering for milk.

Knowing all that did not make the end of breastfeeding any easier.

Not so long ago, breastfeeding fell out of favor. Women were shamed for nursing in public. Workplaces did not accommodate moms who needed to pump. Breastfeeding advocacy was necessary so that women could be women and feed their babies however they pleased, whether by bottle or breast, and damn the old man at the restaurant who thought this was unappetizing and would banish the new mother to breastfeed while sitting on a toilet in a less-than-clean bathroom.

However, as with other parenting matters, the pendulum swung to the extreme. Take the breastfeeding class that I attended at my hospital during the third trimester. Everyone in the class was there to learn the nuts and bolts of nursing. The teacher, though, dedicated the first hour to spreading propaganda about why breastfeeding was vastly superior to formula. The message was clear: formula was poison; good mothers breastfed their babies.

Of course I wanted to be a good mother. Between that breastfeeding class, my prenatal yoga instructor, and the books I read, I became brainwashed into believing that breastfeeding was a matter of life or death. No one bothered defending formula. During the time I was pregnant, I was never offered a formula sample, never saw an advertisement for formula, and never read a single positive sentence about formula. The first time we considered formula was when Pippa had jaundice and required supplementation, but as soon as her bilirubin levels improved, getting her off formula became imperative.

At the time I started breastfeeding, I was in the most vulnerable phase of my life. I was getting sucked into a whirlpool of guilt and anxiety. With every week, I became more and more convinced that I was unfit to be Pippa's mother. That I was lazy, incompetent, and weak. Breastfeeding became my lifeline of sorts. So long as I could cling to breastfeeding, I could feel like a decent mom.

Except the lifeline was actually a noose. I could not get enough sleep, sleep that I needed to physically recover from childbirth. I could not take the time to bathe and eat healthy meals because I spent so many hours trapped in a chair, clutching a nursing baby. I could not even leave the house for a few hours and feel like my old self for fear of having to pump in public.

The night that Pippa and I stopped breastfeeding, I cried in the shower because I was losing a part of myself that made me feel like a good mother and I did not yet know what would replace that part. I was grieving for the death of my idealized maternal self.

Then I cried to unclog the other emotions that had been building up in my cells: the fear I had felt in the B Ward; the pressure from constant guilt and anxiety; and the self-consciousness of being the sort of person who got postpartum depression.

All my life, I had forced myself to be stoic, even after my cousin Kim died unexpectedly. I had prided myself on being stronger than tears. But now I was taking a shower at my parents' house, after four days in the hospital, and my daughter did not want to breastfeed, and my heart was broken, and it hurt, and I let myself cry and cry and feel the pain until I had cried it all away. And then, when I had cried until I could cry no more, I felt something new.

Relief and lightness.

My heart, broken by the end of breastfeeding, was already mending itself.

16

CELEBRITY CAMEO

"Let's go sit by the fountain."

Pippa smiled up at me and kicked her feet.

"You really like kicking, don't you? I think you might like soccer." I pushed her stroller into the crosswalk. We were still staying at my parents' house in my childhood neighborhood. I had walked across this crosswalk at least a thousand times. "But only if that's what you want to do. You don't have to play soccer just because Mama did. Here we go. This bench looks perfect. It's shady and you can look at the cars."

It was early August now. In Pasadena, it would be oppressively hot, but here, the ocean breeze kept the temperature at an idyllic seventy-two degrees. I had picked a bench by a dolphin fountain on a little grassy green that looked a lot like the classic small town America you see in the movies. That's probably because I was sitting in a spot regularly used for filming movies and television shows that take place in small town America. (Yes, it is weird to watch a movie and spot your favorite café. No, you don't ever get over that thrill.)

I kept talking as I unbuckled Pippa's straps and lifted her onto my lap. "There goes a white car. That car is black."

Pippa cooed. I sipped my iced coffee.

"That's the mail truck."

Pippa drooled a bit.

"Baby girl, are you already teething?"

A man wearing shorts, sunglasses, and Ugg boots walked into a smoothie shop across the street. I smiled when I recognized him.

"That was Adam Sandler."

Pippa gnawed on her teether. She was not impressed by movie star sightings. To be honest, neither was I. Growing up in this neighborhood, I was used to seeing celebrities running errands.

It had been a week since my discharge from the hospital. I was sleeping seven or eight hours every night, and the anxiety had dropped down to a much more manageable level. Instead of constantly feeling like we were under attack by vampire zombie aliens, my body merely hummed with tension comparable to what I had felt when I was studying for the bar exam.

"Baby girl, should we walk over to the drugstore?"

Pippa babbled, "Ahh goo ahh."

"I'll take that as a yes."

Our morning walks had become much more adventurous. During the darkest days of my postpartum depression, I had kept pushing Pippa's stroller around the neighborhood in the hopes that some exercise and fresh air would help me sleep, but I had never ventured more than a few blocks from home. I needed to be able to get home quickly in case Pippa wanted to breastfeed.

I was still pumping a few times each day, but that was just to prevent mastitis. Pippa was now exclusively drinking formula, and we loved it. If she got hungry during our walk, I just picked a shady spot, cracked open a bottle, and let her guzzle to her heart's content.

I bumped the stroller into the store. After fawning over the stationery aisle, I steered the stroller toward the children's section.

"This is a rattle."

Pippa's eyes widened.

"You don't need it. Don't give me that look. You have enough rattles." The rattle went back on the shelf.

"Here's a book about Monet's garden." I showed Pippa the cover, and she smiled. "Do you need a new picture book? Okay, you can never have too many books."

I lingered for a moment in front of the art supplies. Recently, I had done a lot of lingering in this very spot. Nathan had bought me crayons and a few coloring books so I could continue the art therapy I started in the A Ward. For the past week, every night after Pippa went to sleep, I hung out with Nathan and colored. The routine relaxed and soothed me.

I itched for something more.

I grabbed a blank art pad off the shelf and headed for the cashier before I could change my mind.

———

LATER THAT MORNING after my shower, I reached for a shirt and started to put it on but something caught my eye. I looked closer at the shirt. It was stained, and not in a decent spot on the hem or sleeve, but right in the boob region.

I tossed the shirt on the floor. Back when I was breastfeeding, I had almost never bothered with a bra. The clasps were too much work. (Depression made everything seem like too much work.) Milk must have leaked onto this shirt.

I picked up another shirt and checked for stains. It was filthier than the first.

"MOM!"

"What? Why are all your shirts on the floor?"

"They are all disgusting."

My mom had spotted the milk stains long before I was admitted to the hospital for psychiatric care. At the time, she had gently suggested I order more shirts online but I snapped at her to mind her own business. I could not handle the idea of buying new shirts. Also, when I looked in the mirror, the shirts looked good enough. Depression lowered the bar for what constituted a clean shirt.

My medication, however, had boosted the bar back to its usual place. I no longer wanted to wear the rags from my post-partum depression days.

My mom hesitated before speaking. Postpartum depression can make a woman more irritable and quick to anger. My mom had borne the brunt of that symptom and was struggling to find the words that were least likely to elicit a verbal assault. Just the day before, she had asked if I wanted to go to the mall for new clothes while Laura watched Pippa. It was an innocent suggestion, but I had lashed out at her. The mall? Did she really think I would leave my baby for that long? And I did not need new clothes, thank you very much. (It was not my finest moment.)

Yet I was improving quickly. I could finally see the stains that had been invisible twenty-four hours ago, *and* I had enough interest in my appearance to want new shirts, *and* I could fathom taking a few hours to go the mall without my baby.

After a long pause, my mom spoke. "Do you want to go online to order more shirts?"

"Or maybe we could just go to the mall today?"

"I can be ready in two minutes."

"How was your day?"

"So good!"

"Yeah?" Nathan was hunched over a piece of paper, using a

brown crayon to color what appeared to be a shield which was being carried by . . . a troll? A minotaur?

I filled him in on our trip to the mall. "I don't think I've bought anything except online since Pippa was born. It was so nice to walk around and actually try things on."

"Cool. Do you have blue over there?"

"Light or dark?"

"Dark."

When I colored, Nathan usually worked on his laptop. (By "work," I mean played around with his Rotisserie baseball team.) Tonight, though, he had pushed the laptop to the side and was drawing with me. I had pulled one of my mom's art history books off the shelf and was copying a Van Gogh with extravagant swirls and flourishes into my new blank notebook. Nathan was drawing something inspired by Dungeons & Dragons.

Nathan looked at my work in progress. "Hey, that's pretty good."

"Thanks." In high school, we'd had to copy Van Goghs with pastels. I remembered it being stressful because I was worried about getting an A. This was much more fun. "Oh, I got Pippa some new clothes today."

"She's so cute."

"She's a sweetheart. And my mom got me a new diaper bag."

I said this casually, but it was a big deal. During my darkest days, I had fixated on different purchases that I thought would make life easier. I dreamed of what I thought of as the One True Sling, the baby carrier that would turn me into a happy mom. Then there was the Ultimate Nursing Wardrobe, which would make breastfeeding in public a breeze while making me look sophisticated but sassy. But I would have gladly sacrificed the One True Sling and Ultimate Nursing Wardrobe in order to secure the Magical Diaper Bag.

The Magical Diaper Bag would turn me into an all-star mom. It would be waterproof, urine-proof, and poop-repellant, have ample pockets for all the sundry items that motherhood required, and above all, it would announce to all potential mom friends, "Courtney is awesome."

I had spent hours reading descriptions of diaper bags and agonizing over the Optimal Pocket Situation. This was not a mere numbers game. There was also the question of size and placement. Were there pockets on the outside of the bag? Did they have zippers? Was there a special pocket with a hook for my keys? And another pocket to sequester the unused pacifiers that Pippa shunned at home but might decide to use as soon as we left the house?

I added multiple bags to my Amazon Wish List and looked at them several times a day. I spent more time debating which diaper bag I should buy than I had spent choosing a law school to attend. (This probably seems like an exaggeration. Let me assure you: it is not.)

My favorite diaper bags were totes meant to be carried over the shoulder, but my back still ached from pregnancy. An over-the-shoulder bag might aggravate the back pain, whereas a back-pack would distribute the weight of sundry baby items more evenly.

What to do?

After much agonizing, I finally ordered a diaper backpack with a pink pattern.

It was hideous, cumbersome, and all-around awful. The thought of returning it, though, was too much for my depression-addled brain to fathom. I nicknamed it the Pink Monstrosity and forced myself to take it everywhere I went. Which did not actually mean much, seeing as I was largely a recluse.

I finished my Van Gogh drawing and flipped through the art history tome. A Gauguin caught my eye, but I decided to close the book and draw whatever came to mind.

"What's that?"

I laughed. "It's a haunted house. I used to draw these whenever I could in the second grade. I don't know why this popped into my head."

"Is that a crocodile in a moat?"

"It is."

"That's pretty messed-up for a second grader."

I feigned indignation. "It was in a Berenstain Bears book that I loved."

"I do not remember any crocodiles in the Berenstain Bears books that I read."

"It was something about a spooky old tree and the bear cubs were on an adventure. We had a cassette tape so we could read along and there were sound effects. I loved it."

Before we went to bed, I sneaked another peek at my new diaper bag. It was my favorite color, apple green, and had a built-in changing pad. My mom knew how much I hated the diaper backpack and had asked, on the drive to the mall, if she could buy me a new diaper bag.

"No, Mom, I already have the backpack."

"But you hate it."

"Doesn't matter. I bought it. I have to use it."

"Please, Courtney, let me buy you a diaper bag."

"Stop it, Mom." She didn't understand how guilty I would feel if I got a new diaper bag. Then again, I still didn't understand that irrational guilt is a symptom of postpartum depression.

At the mall, my mom conveniently parked by Nordstrom. To enter the mall, we *had* to walk past the Nordstrom baby department. And if we were going to walk past the baby department, we might as well check if there were any cute clothes on sale . . .

Fifteen minutes after our arrival, I relented and let my mom buy me the apple-green diaper bag.

I took my medications and got into bed.

"Good night, Nathan."

"Good night, sweetheart. Remember, don't get up if you hear Pippa. I can handle the nighttime shift."

"Thanks, babe."

I turned off the lamp and closed my eyes. Tomorrow, my parents were taking me to my favorite Greek restaurant for lunch. That was exciting, but I was even more excited to use my new diaper bag.

It was only a new diaper bag.

Then again, it was my way of giving the middle finger to the postpartum guilt. I had felt that mothers were supposed to be martyrs. Having a nice diaper bag was my way of saying that I did not have to immolate myself on the altar of motherhood.

During the first four postpartum months, I had spent my days in maternity sweats that I had cut off at the knees. I thought they gave me the swagger of a sexy pirate. They actually made me look like a castaway.

I forgot to brush my hair. I almost never washed my face. I stopped caring about my appearance.

Compared to my other issues—anxiety, obsessive compulsive rituals, insomnia—my appearance might seem like a superficial concern. I can see how someone would think I should have been focusing on my spirit and mind and doing something like yoga instead of hitting the mall. Mental health, however, cannot be isolated from the other parts of your life, including your wardrobe.

So long as I was wearing milk-stained shirts, I would think of myself as the woman who had slunk around the house in cutoff sweats. So long as I used the Pink Monstrosity, I would be reminded of the way I had obsessed over that purchase and still got it wrong.

I had to get those shirts and that bag out of my life if I wanted to make a full recovery.

Sometimes a diaper bag is more than a diaper bag.

A few days passed. I felt myself getting stronger and stronger. Then it happened.

It was morning. I had just woke up but kept my eyes closed. Pippa had not yet stirred and I wanted a little more rest.

When my insomnia started, Pippa was sleeping ten hours every night. Now that I was sleeping better, she had started teething and was waking up twice for a bottle. (I believe Alanis Morissette would call this "ironic.") Nathan had been taking both nocturnal shifts, but the night before, I had volunteered to take the second.

"Babe, are you sure? I don't want you to push yourself too hard."

"I'm sure. I can't take the first shift because my medicine makes me too drowsy, but I can handle the second one. You need your sleep, too. I'd like to help."

In hindsight, I was probably pushing myself too hard. It had been only two weeks since I was discharged from the hospital. I needed my sleep.

But I also needed and wanted to feel like I was taking an active part in my life. Above all, I wanted to be Pippa's mom, but during the day, Laura was in charge. At least, that was how it felt in my head. In actuality, Laura was a total sweetheart who wanted to make my life easier. But in my head, she was the professional and I was the amateur, so I let her make all the decisions about when and how Pippa ate, napped, was bathed, and so on. Getting up for that second shift helped me feel like I was reclaiming my maternal jurisdiction.

Which is not to say I had enjoyed waking up at 4:00 a.m. to feed Pippa a bottle, but I liked the idea that I had the ability to partake in all parts of mothering, even the ones that took place before sunrise.

After a few minutes of extra rest, I opened my eyes.

Where the hell was I?

Why was the window over there?

What was wrong with our bedspread?

I blinked and looked at the window.

The blinds were wrong. And the curtains. We didn't have curtains.

Oh! We were at my parents' house.

For a moment, I felt so silly. We had been staying here for two weeks. A few days ago, while I was taking Pippa on a walk, I had wished we could stay here forever. Pasadena seemed so far away. It would be so much easier to start over and live with my parents.

Overnight, something had shifted.

It was time to go home.

MOMENTUM

"**A**re you looking for anything special?" The store owner looked down at the skeins I had lined up on a table.

"I want to knit a blanket for my niece. My sister-in-law is due next month and her favorite color is purple."

"Do you have a pattern in mind?"

"I'm going to do seven stripes—"

"Oh, the pattern from Purl Bee? That's my favorite way to make a baby blanket."

Pippa was at home with Laura. We had been back in Pasadena for a few days, and my parents had enlisted Laura's help for the next six weeks. (Although we actually parted ways after two weeks. Laura was doing the night shift with twins, and I was feeling so much better, I wanted to fly solo.) Our first day back in Pasadena, I had reclaimed the house. When I had been feeling overwhelmed by everything, the idea of trying to tidy seemed impossible. Surely it would take days of uninterrupted effort.

It actually took about three hours.

The most time-consuming task had been sorting through "the boxes." When I was on my quest to buy my way out of postpartum depression, I had purchased dozens of items that, upon their arrival, I rejected and put back in their respective boxes, to be returned at some later date. My parents had returned as many as they could, but there were still many that needed my attention.

Sorting through the boxes felt a bit like an archaeological dig, except instead of the remains of an ancient civilization, I was finding artifacts from the postpartum depression months: industrial-sized bags of banana chips, boxes of granola bars, and red cowboy boots.

Yes, you read that right: red cowboy boots.

No, I don't have an explanation for the boots. I don't even remember ordering them. The banana chips and granola bars were snacks that I could keep on either side of the breastfeeding throne. Maybe I thought the boots would pair well with my castaway sweats.

Our second day back in Pasadena, I procured Pippa's birth certificate and got a TB test for the class the occupational therapist had recommended. I had assumed it was a mommy and me class, but it was actually a non-credit class called "Parent Education" offered by Pasadena City College. I could not have comprehended tackling these tasks or taking a class offered by a college before my stay in the psych ward.

Our third day back in Pasadena, I consulted my to-do list and realized there was nothing left to do. I practically rubbed my hands together when I realized I had the time to visit the yarn store.

My grandma taught me to knit when I was in law school, and that hobby had satisfied a deep, primal ache to make things with my hands when my days were mostly spent in libraries, grappling with things like the rule against perpetuities and the *Burford* Abstention Doctrine. (Full disclosure: I asked Nathan to suggest some "pompous things we learned in law school" and this is what he remembered. I think I missed the chapter on *Burford*. Actually, I think I skipped that entire class.)

Ever since my first scarf, I had kept my hands busy with craft projects, mostly knitting but also cross-stitch and crochet. While pregnant, I knit Pippa a rainbow-striped blanket and pink cardigan and cross-stitched several small creatures to hang in the nursery.

The postpartum depression had put an end to the knitting.

It wasn't like I didn't have time. When my parents visited, or when Nathan was home, they held Pippa as much as possible. I could have grabbed my needles and yarn and clacked away on a new scarf. But I didn't. I just sat on a chair feeling awkward and hollow.

The depression waters had now receded enough that I remembered that knitting was something that made me feel like a better person. Now I admired the skeins of yarn I had laid out on the oak table: four different purples and a few neutral shades.

"Do you need needles?"

"No, I'm all set."

As the owner tallied up the bill, I caressed my wrists. The pain was gone. When was the last time I had even thought about my wrists? When had they stopped hurting? Had the postpartum depression amplified the pain? Had I been fixating on the wrists because that was easier than sorting through the issues racing through my head? Or had the wrists been hurting not from overuse but from neglect? I had thought my wrists needed as much rest as possible, but maybe they had been craving activity and movement.

Maybe it was the momentum I had learned about in the hospital that had melted the pain in my hands.

"MOMENTUM IS CRITICAL. If you got off your chair yesterday, it will be easier to get off it today, and even easier to get off it tomorrow. The first time is the hardest. You have to make yourself get up so you can rebuild momentum."

I looked down at my lap and suppressed an eye roll. Three days of group therapy in the A Ward; three different social workers; three lectures about the power of momentum. The social workers were all women in their forties with short hair and glasses, as if they had been manufactured by a factory.

"Depression destroys momentum. So even when your medications are working, you still have to fight to rebuild your momentum."

I nodded. It was the day of my discharge from the A Ward. The psychiatrist had assured me just an hour ago that I would be going home. I was not going to argue with this social worker and jeopardize my escape.

"Can you guys think of any ways to build momentum?"

Everyone stared at the table.

The social worker pivoted toward the old man who hated talking. "Bill, what things do you enjoy doing at home?"

This was another thing I had learned during group therapy: to build momentum, it was important to do things you enjoyed.

"I collect stamps."

"Stamps." She sounded hesitant. Was the social worker actually stumped by this one? "So . . . what sorts of activities do you do with stamps?"

"When I get a new one, I put it in an album."

"Anything else?"

"No."

For the next several minutes, the social worker searched for ways to build Bill's momentum, and Bill kept shrugging and insisting there was nothing else to do. His daughter had his car and besides, he could not drive anymore; his wife was dead; the only activity he enjoyed was stamp collecting.

I raised my hand.

"Courtney? Yes?" The social worker looked like she wanted to hug me.

"Bill could start a blog."

Bill frowned. "A blog?"

"Yes, a blog about stamps. That will give you something else to do with your collection and writing about it will be fun." I sat up straighter. "You can take photographs of your collection and share everything you have learned."

As I talked, Bill nodded. He actually seemed interested in the blog. *I* was interested in the blog. There were so many things he could write about, so much knowledge he could share—

"I don't know anything about computers."

The menopausal patients grunted their agreement.

"Blogging isn't that tough. I'm sure your daughter could—"

"She's too busy driving around town in my car to help me out."

The social worker chimed in to help salvage the blog, but Bill was obstinate. He did not seem interested in this momentum business.

I leaned back in my chair and looked up at the sky. Just yesterday, sitting at this very table, I had felt a sense of belonging and community with my fellow patients. But since our last group therapy session, so much had happened: I had gone to the gym and realized my energy was back, spent the afternoon writing, decided it was time for my discharge, and colored all evening in the common room. I no longer belonged here.

I had to leave so I could continue building my own momentum.

"This is better than I remembered." I dunked another chip into the guacamole. "So delicious."

It was a Sunday in late August, about five days since my trip to the yarn shop. We had been back home in Pasadena for a week and a half. Pippa, sitting next to Nathan, was examining the menu as if she could actually read what it said and was trying to decide between a burrito and an enchilada.

When she got bored, Nathan passed her to my side of the booth. I let her practice standing on the tabletop. She proudly surveyed the restaurant.

She looked so big in her dark pink dress, a gift from my freshman roommate. The dark hair she had at birth had fallen out. Her new hair was blonde, but there was not much of it. Pippa was bald and beautiful.

"When does she start solids?"

"Next month. She doesn't seem interested yet."

"That's because Pippa loves her bottles." Nathan reached over and tickled Pippa's neck. "Look at those fat folds!"

When she got hungry, Nathan made a bottle. The breast-feeding experts had made formula sound so complicated. Bottles required sterilizing, formula needed to be heated to baby's exacting demands, and if you were traveling, everything had to be prepared in advance and schlepped around in a cooler.

Reality was quite different. The bottles went in the top rack of the dishwasher and presto, they were good to go. Pippa was happy to drink her bottles either at room temperature or straight from the fridge. When we were on the go, it took all of eight seconds to prepare a bottle—screw off the lid, tap formula inside, shake, and serve.

I did not miss breastfeeding. Neither, for that matter, did Pippa.

She snuggled into my arms and I let her bottom rest on top of the table. Pippa alternated between gazing into my eyes and turning to watch waiters carry sizzling platters of fajitas. Nathan reached across the table and squeezed my hand. We both smiled at Pippa.

To think, less than a month ago, I had been a patient in the psych ward.

Life could not possibly get any better than this moment. I assumed I had fully recovered from postpartum depression. I had all the momentum any person could ever need.

I SET up camp next to some shelves crammed with toys and immediately regretted my decision. The two moms seated to my right already knew each other. They were not going to be interested in talking to me.

I spread a blanket on the floor and lay Pippa on her back. She hated tummy time, and I was not about to demonstrate her screaming prowess during the first minutes of our first Parent Education class.

"Hi! How old is your daughter?"

I looked around in confusion and then realized the mom to my right was talking to me. "Oh, hi, Pippa is five months old."

"Pippa? I love her name!" the woman exclaimed. "My daughter is almost five months too. I'm Veronica. This is Andrea. We live in the same apartment building and are both new to Pasadena."

During the first postpartum months, I had been overwhelmed by the sight of my best friend's name in my email inbox. I complained to Nathan that she had forgotten what it was like to have a newborn and was harassing me. I simply did not have the time for email. Never mind the fact that I spent hours every day on the same chair, imprisoned by breastfeeding, refreshing the same blogs incessantly, hoping for a new post.

Later, when I was fully recovered, I looked through my email history. My best friend had emailed only every three or four days —hardly the stuff of harassment. Postpartum depression, however, had turned me into a hermit. Any social contact felt like an attack.

Ever since my discharge from the hospital, I had been emailing my best friend more frequently, but she still lived thousands of miles away. With the postpartum depression on the wane, I ached for connection with people within my zip code. I did not realize just how deep that ache was until I found myself in the company of women with babies the same age as Pippa, navigating the same murky waters of teething and diaper rashes. As we talked, I felt as if I were soaking up some vital nutrient that had been missing from my diet.

All too soon, the teacher started class. I checked the clock. I had been talking to Veronica and Andrea for nearly forty-five minutes. How had the time passed so quickly?

To think that a week ago, while eating lunch at a Mexican restaurant, I had thought I felt as healthy as I could ever feel. Yet now, I found myself glowing with a new vibrancy.

And the momentum was just getting started.

"WHERE SHOULD WE GO TODAY?"

Pippa cooed as I adjusted a clean diaper.

"Let's see, we've been to Target . . . it's too hot for the park . . . what about the mall?"

Pippa stuffed her fist into her mouth.

"Okay, the mall it is."

A month ago, leaving the house had required a monumental effort. I'd spent days preparing myself for a simple trip to a breastfeeding support group, where everything was designed to accommodate nervous moms. After the excursion, I'd spent days at home, exhausted and regathering my emotional strength.

The social workers were right. The more time I spent at home, the more difficult it was to leave. Yesterday, I had gone to the Parent Education class for the first time. Today, I was raring to attack the mall.

"Baby girl, look at all the lights."

Pippa could not stop smiling as I strolled through a department store and into an inner courtyard with a carousel. Neither could I.

We stopped at an indoor playground and stood by the wall so Pippa could watch the big kids playing. "Don't worry, sweetie, you'll be able to play here before you know it." When I put her back in the stroller, Pippa started to bawl. I took her out for another look, and she was immediately calm.

"We can watch some more."

Eventually, though, there was a smell coming from Pippa's diaper that could not be ignored. It was time to locate a changing table.

I strolled leisurely toward my favorite department store, my breathing and heart rate remaining normal. Very recently, a poopy diaper at the mall would have been a catastrophe. Today, though, it did not even register as an inconvenience.

I felt like a climber who had reached the pinnacle of a mountain, victorious, alive, and ready for more adventures.

I had no idea that as far as my recovery was concerned, I was still at the base of the mountain.

18

COGNITIVE BEHAVIORAL THERAPY

My psychologist—I was now the sort of person who had a psychiatrist *and* a psychologist—shook my hand and showed me into his office. It was early August, about one week since my discharge from the hospital. Nathan, Pippa and I were still staying at my parents' house. While I was still in the hospital, the psychiatrist had suggested I meet with this psychologist, promising he would help me become the master of my anxiety.

The psychologist sat down on a chair next to a desk with a computer and told me to sit wherever I liked. There was a pair of chairs by the window, but I chose an armchair closer to the psychologist.

This would be my first experience with cognitive behavioral therapy (or "CBT"). The psychologist explained that our sessions would involve lots of talking but he would also give me homework assignments.

"To start, why don't you tell me why you are here?" The psychologist spoke perfect English but had a lilting accent. I eventually learned that he was from a small village in Spain and that I could always depend on him to be running at least twenty minutes behind schedule.

"I'm here because I have a lot of anxiety and my psychiatrist thought this would help me manage that. I've always been an anxious person. When I was young, before I was even in preschool, I had this thing about doors. I always wanted the door to be closed . . ."

For the next fifty minutes, I relayed my life story to the psychologist. Near the end of the hour-long session, I finally started to describe the past few months of my life. With hardly any time left, I said, "I thought about throwing Pippa as hard as I could against the floor. And I thought about taking a knife and slitting my wrists to end my suffering."

"Let me stop you there." The psychologist had been listening attentively and taking notes. This was the first interruption. "These dark thoughts—are these the reason you are here?"

My brow crinkled. "No. I had those thoughts and I went to the hospital and I got better. I'm here because I want to be less anxious."

"So you do not want to talk about the dark thoughts you had about hurting yourself and your daughter Pippa?"

"I do not."

"Okay. Well, we are out of time, so let's continue next week."

Relieved, I paid the receptionist and hurried to my car. When the psychiatrist had suggested I try cognitive behavioral therapy, he had only mentioned it in the context of my anxiety. He had not indicated there would be any need for me to rehash the worst moments of postpartum depression. There must have been a communication error between the psychiatrist and psychologist.

I shuddered as I turned the key in the ignition. If the psychologist expected me to talk about the dark thoughts, this CBT thing was not going to work.

"So last week, at the end of our session, you mentioned that you had dark thoughts about hurting yourself and Pippa."

"Yes."

"Are you still having these thoughts?"

"No, no, not at all. I haven't had any dark thoughts since before I admitted myself to the hospital."

"How do you feel about having had those thoughts?"

"What do you mean?"

"Do you have any feelings about the fact that you thought about hurting yourself and Pippa?"

"Oh." I took a quick emotional inventory. "No. I feel fine."

"I want to tell you something important."

I nodded.

"You do not own your thoughts."

I frowned.

The psychologist said it again, slowly and forcefully. "You do not own your thoughts."

I frowned a little more deeply.

He said it again. "You do not own your thoughts."

My brain recoiled. What was he suggesting? When I thought about hurting Pippa, those terrible thoughts originated within me. It wasn't like they had been whispered by a demon. Of course they were mine.

"You do not own your thoughts."

"I don't understand."

"Let me give you an example. Do *not* think about an elephant."

An image of an elephant popped into my head. I smiled. "You put that thought into my head by saying 'elephant.'"

"That's right. And the dark thoughts you had about hurting Pippa and yourself came from a chemical imbalance. They did not come from you."

I nodded slowly.

"You are not your thoughts. You are your actions. Did you act upon the thoughts you had of hurting Pippa?"

"No, never. I shoved them away."

"That was you. The thoughts were just thoughts. The act of pushing the thoughts away—*that* was you."

I smiled. The psychologist was making sense . . . sort of. Although I still did not understand why we were wasting our time talking about this.

"Would you like to talk some more about your experiences with postpartum depression?"

"No."

"No?"

"I had postpartum depression but I recovered from that in the hospital. I'm better now. There's no need to talk about what happened. I'd rather just deal with all this anxiety I'm still feeling."

"So let me make sure I understand you correctly. You do not want to talk about the postpartum depression anymore?"

"Correct. I don't want to talk about the postpartum depression."

Case closed.

Or so I thought.

"I never knew there were so many teethers."

"This place has *everything*."

It was mid-September, about six weeks since I had been discharged from the hospital and four weeks since I returned home to Pasadena. Except now Pippa and I were staying with my parents again. Nathan was working on a trial in downtown Los Angeles and staying at a hotel near the courthouse. (More on the experience of being a pseudo-single mom with postpartum depression later.)

On this lovely September day, I was at buybuy BABY, a massive store devoted to all things baby, with my parents and

Pippa. There were aisles upon aisles of toys, clothes, strollers, sippy cups, first aid supplies, and everything else that a twenty-first-century parent might covet.

It did not take me long to find the books.

I focused on the baby books. There were parenting books as well, but I had burned out on parenting books during the first months of Pippa's life. They had exacerbated my anxiety. It was safer to admire the selection of Dr. Seuss and Sandra Boynton. I added several to the cart before heading back to my parents.

I paused mid-aisle.

A self-help book had caught my eye. The cover said something about secrets to being a happy mom.

I wanted that book.

I started to reach for it but stopped myself. This was silly. I knew everything I needed to know about happiness. Besides, we had made a pilgrimage to buybuy *BABY*, not buybuy *Mom*.

But I adored self-help books. I grabbed the book off the shelf: *The Happiest Mom: Ten Secrets to Enjoying Motherhood* by Meagan Francis. I started to skim through the chapters and did not want to put it down.

My mom called for me to look at something. I dropped the book into the cart and strolled back to the toys. I needed some new bathroom reading anyway.

WITHIN HOURS of our return from buybuy BABY, I had inhaled *The Happiest Mom*. It gave me a lot of great ideas, but more importantly, it got the wheels in my head turning. Since Pippa's birth, I had been reading a lot of books about raising a happy, healthy child.

But what about me?

I started looking for books about motherhood on Amazon.

My searches returned lots of results. Clearly I was not the first woman to seek a little guidance on the subject.

As I skimmed synopses and reviews, a thought tickled the back of my mind. I ignored it at first and kept looking at memoirs and self-help books that addressed the art of motherhood in general. The thought, though, persisted.

What about books on postpartum depression?

I shoved the thought away. I did not need books about postpartum depression. My experience of the illness was in the past tense, thank you very much. All I had to do was keep taking my medications. I did not need to learn about symptoms or alternative treatments.

Or did I?

I put my phone away and played pat-a-cake with Pippa. She burbled and giggled.

Hadn't Brooke Shields written a memoir about postpartum depression?

I typed her name into the Amazon search bar and clicked on *Down Came the Rain*, her memoir about maternal mental illness. I felt as if I were doing something dangerous and forbidden. I needed to put as much distance between myself and the diagnosis as I possibly could. Reading a memoir about postpartum depression would place the illness front and center on the stage of my life. How could I linger on a subject that had landed me in the mental ward?

Below *Down Came the Rain*, Amazon suggested some other books I might like to read, including *Postpartum Depression for Dummies* by Dr. Shoshana Bennett. This was a revelation. I had read *Dummies* books on topics as diverse as California wine, American history, sewing, and football. If the *For Dummies* series had published a book about postpartum depression, that meant there was a market for it.

I hesitated.

To get the most out of the book, I would have to order a physical copy. That meant there would be a book about postpartum depression in my house. Which meant that a visitor could stumble upon the book *and then they would know.*

I clicked order anyway. I would have to keep the book somewhere safe. That ought to be easy enough. It wasn't like I was going to read any more books on the subject. One was enough.

ONE WAS NOT ENOUGH.

Postpartum Depression for Dummies was enlightening and empowering. I learned about so many important things, like the risk factors for postpartum depression and how my new medications worked. Surely that was all I needed to know about my illness.

Except I couldn't stop thinking about Brooke Shields's memoir.

I added the book to my virtual shopping cart.

What was I doing? I had to stop associating with the subject matter. What would people think if they found out? I'd be exiled to the island of depressed mommies.

But no matter what I did—wash dishes, change diapers, answer emails—my thoughts wandered toward *Down Came the Rain.* What had postpartum depression been like for Brooke? Had her experience been anything like my own? How had she recovered?

I had to know.

"HOW DOES the book make you feel?" the psychologist asked.

"Awful." I was a fast reader and *Down Came the Rain* was short. Technically speaking, I should have been able to read it cover to cover in one sitting. But I could not finish it in one sitting, or two or five or ten. Whenever I started to read it, chills crawled all over my body. Then my stomach churned until I thought I would puke. It was too difficult for me to read for more than ten minutes in a row.

"Why do you think that is?"

"Well." I inhaled slowly. "It makes me remember the way I felt when I had postpartum depression."

"You said before that you did not have any issues to discuss in regards to your postpartum depression."

"Can I change my mind about that?"

"Of course." The psychologist kept a neutral expression on his face.

"I think I have some issues from the postpartum depression, but I don't understand why. I *had* postpartum depression. I went to the hospital. I'm taking sertraline. Shouldn't I be better?"

"No, no, no. You have been through a traumatizing experience. It is natural to have a lot of thoughts and feelings about it. Would you like to talk some more about having postpartum depression?"

I sat and thought. "Yes. I would."

"Here's what I think you should do. Before our next session, read *Down Came the Rain* very quickly, over the course of two or three days at the most. Write down any thoughts or questions you have. Then we can talk about your experience reading the book together."

A few days later, I picked up the book, this time with pen in hand, and started reading. I followed the psychologist's advice and underlined the passages that resonated with me. For example, Brooke wrote about her despair of ever feeling better. I easily related to that. Just like my mom, Brooke's mom suggested she stop breastfeeding to give herself a break. Brooke also thought she should be able to handle motherhood all by herself. It was almost as if Brooke had access to my innermost thoughts.

I did a lot of underlining.

At our next session, we had a book club for two. "I struggled a lot with Brooke's descriptions of wanting to throw her baby."

"Why?"

"Well." I paused. "I thought about throwing Pippa. So it made me flash back to those moments."

The psychologist nodded.

"I don't understand why I'm having so many feelings about stuff that happened a month ago."

"You have been through a traumatic experience." The week before, he had said the exact same thing. The psychologist rarely repeated himself, so I knew this was important stuff. "You needed some time to distance yourself from the event before you could acknowledge and consider your feelings."

"I do feel better now. I felt so shitty while reading *Down Came the Rain*, but now that we have talked about it, I feel lighter."

"It's like you are a pressure cooker. You needed to let off some steam."

"That makes sense."

"And maybe, some more steam will build up and you will need to let it out again."

Externally, I nodded in agreement; inwardly, I registered my vehement protest. Surely I had felt enough crappy feelings. Surely I had released enough steam for one lifetime. Surely I was done with the subject of postpartum depression.

As we wrapped up our discussion of *Down Came the Rain*, the psychologist said, "I know you love writing." As part of my homework assignments, he had me write about the things that made me anxious. I usually had at least twenty pages for him. This was apparently a bit more prolific than his other patients.

"You could write a book about your experiences with postpartum depression, just like Brooke Shields did. That would be very good for you. It would help you understand and release your feelings. And it would help so many other moms, too. Just like Brooke Shields's book has helped you."

"Maaaaaybe." I did not want to hurt the psychologist's feelings, but all I wanted to do was move on with my life and forget that this dark chapter had ever happened.

Besides, a memoir would advertise to the world that I was the sort of mom who got postpartum depression. There was no way I would ever be able to do something like that.

19

LOSING MY RITUALS

"What sort of things do you do to keep Pippa safe?"
It was the beginning of my fourth session of cognitive behavioral therapy. Before I continue this part of my story, I would like to hit the brakes and apologize for any chronological whiplash you might be experiencing. In Chapter 17, I took you through experiences that happened a month after my discharge from the hospital. Then in Chapter 18, I backtracked to my first appointment with the psychologist. By the end of Chapter 18, we were at my ninth session of cognitive behavioral therapy. Now we have to jump back to the fourth session.

Sorry about that!

My recovery from postpartum depression involved multiple and simultaneous fronts. While I was busy building momentum and learning how to take better care of myself, I was also addressing different issues in therapy. It was a bit like juggling. While roller skating. For the first time ever.

Cognitive behavioral therapy was not a tidy and orderly experience. It was messy and organic. In terms of writing a memoir, it would have been fantastic if I could have discussed all my issues related to having dark thoughts during my first two sessions and then moved on to entirely different subjects, but that's not what happened. I could not have a productive conversation about dark thoughts until I was ready, which meant the conversation started during the second session but then happened in earnest during sessions eight and nine. I guess I could have taken some artistic license and jiggered with the timeline to make this memoir tidier, but I did not want to misrepresent what cognitive behavioral therapy was like. It was a dynamic experience that depended on *me* and what *I* was ready to do. It was not a college course with a syllabus and predictable lectures.

And now, back to our regularly scheduled programming.

It was the beginning of my fourth session of cognitive behavioral therapy, and the psychologist had just asked what sort of things I did to keep Pippa safe.

"Oh, let's see," I thought out loud. "I do a lot of different things to keep her safe. I put her in her car seat and make sure she is buckled securely. I never leave her unattended on the changing table. I make sure there aren't things within reach that she could choke on. Normal things."

"Anything else?"

"Well." I tried to take a sip of coffee. The cup, though, was long empty. "I make sure the doors are locked at night. I check the burners on our stovetop. I check her breathing during the night to make sure she is okay."

These "personality quirks" had vanished while I was in the hospital because there was no baby, closets, burners, or locks to check. (Although I did peek often under my bed which, to this day, I believe was fully justified. Gertrude could have been there.)

After my discharge, while we stayed with my parents, the quirks started to reestablish themselves. I did not have to check the burners (electric stove) or the locks (security system), but I did check Pippa's breathing and peek inside closets when no one was looking.

A month had passed since my discharge. We had been back home in Pasadena for two weeks. All my quirks were back, in their full force and glory, as if I had never been hospitalized.

My psychologist jotted some notes. "So you check the locks and burners and make sure Pippa is breathing. Anything else?"

"I look under the bed and check the closets."

"Anything else?"

"I check the windows. And the washer and dryer sometimes."

"Anything else?"

"I don't think so."

"Why do you do these things?"

"To keep Pippa safe."

"What would happen if you did not do these things? If you did not check the locks or under the beds or if you did not check on Pippa's breathing?"

"Something bad."

"Like what?"

I tried again to extract a sip from the empty coffee cup. "Pippa might die. Or someone might kidnap her."

"These things that you do—checking the locks, looking under the beds, checking Pippa's breathing during the night—they are rituals."

"Rituals?"

"Yes. You do them to alleviate your anxiety."

"I guess."

"The rituals actually increase your anxiety."

"What? No. I have to do them. They make me *less* anxious. They keep us safe."

"They do not. Pippa is breathing whether or not you check that she is breathing. The door is locked whether you check it or not."

"But maybe the door is unlocked."

"So what if it is? The odds of a kidnapper checking your front

189

door the night you forget to lock it are minuscule, practically nonexistent."

My entire face crumpled into a massive frown.

"When you lock and relock the door, you feel better, but only for a brief moment. When you check the lock, the act of checking confirms that there is something for you to be scared of. That reinforces your anxiety. So although you feel better for a brief moment, your anxiety quickly returns, stronger than ever."

I thought about the previous night. While Nathan was getting ready for bed, I had scurried to the front of the house to check the door. I had felt a surge of relief as I locked the door. I forced myself to push the memory a little further . . . and crap, the psychologist was right. After the surge of relief, I had quickly crashed back into anxiety.

Even though I was sitting in my psychologist's office, far away from my house and its doors, my adrenaline spiked as if I were stuck in the endless cycle of checking the locks.

"I think you're right. My rituals increase my anxiety."

The psychologist nodded.

"So what do I do?"

"In order to reduce your anxiety, we have to turn your rituals to dust. This week, for your homework, I want you to stop checking the doors. You are not allowed to check if they are locked. And then I want you to write about how that makes you feel."

I lodged a formal protest. "That's crazy."

"By checking the locks, you are only increasing your anxiety," he repeated. "To decrease your anxiety, we have to turn the ritual to dust."

"But how will I know if the door is locked?"

"You lock the door when you come home, right?"

"Yes."

"You have to trust yourself."

"But if I don't check the locks, I'll feel anxious."

"At first, yes. But you have become stuck in a ritual that is only increasing your anxiety. After a few days, I promise, you will begin to feel better."

"What if I only check the doors once before bedtime?"

"No. In order to eliminate your anxiety, you have to extinguish the ritual entirely. If you had been obsessively washing your hands, you would not be allowed to shower or wash your hands for several days, maybe even a week or a month. When the obsession was conquered, *then* you could wash your hands a reasonable number of times during the day."

Now did not seem like the right time to mention the hand washing. Shortly before my hospitalization, during the insomnia weeks, I had started washing my hands excessively. For example, after running to the bathroom to pee, I would rinse my hands with liquid foaming soap. Then, while drying my hands, I would start to wonder if the towel was actually clean. I would throw the towel in the hamper, grab a new one, and wash my hands again. Except now I would question whether the foaming soap—which we had been using for years—was actually ridding my hands of all the bacteria and germs that might hurt Pippa. I would squirt antibacterial goo on to the palms of my hands, only to wonder if there were any toxins in the goo. Back to the soap I would go, and this was all for just one visit to the bathroom.

The hand washing habit had quickly snowballed into breast washing. The first time I washed my breasts was after a quick swim in our backyard pool. I showered before Pippa needed to breastfeed, but then I worried whether I had washed all the chlorine off my body. I soaped down my breasts again just to be sure. By the time I was hospitalized, I felt compelled to wash my breasts clean before every nursing session. At least the end of breastfeeding had also meant the end of boob washing.

The psychologist was still talking. "For now, we have to turn your ritual with checking the locks to dust. Once we have done that, then you can check the locks when you have good reason to do so."

"But Nathan's from small-town Nebraska. They leave doors unlocked all the time. Sometimes he forgets to lock the door. I have to check the locks to make sure we are safe."

"I have a friend who lives in Los Angeles, and he never locks his front door."

"That's crazy."

The psychologist shrugged. "He has never been robbed."

"But he might be. A lunatic might decide to come in and kill him."

"The odds of that happening are very, very low."

I was beginning to feel desperate. "Can I visually check that the locks are in the locked position?"

"No."

"Can I tell Nathan to check the locks?"

"No."

"What if I tell Nathan that I am going to bed and, per my homework assignment, I will not be checking the locks?"

The psychologist paused and considered. "That would be fine."

I hated this homework assignment. If I did not check the doors before bed, they might be unlocked, and if they were unlocked, we would be vulnerable to all sorts of attacks. My psychologist might as well have asked me to throw Pippa into a tank of starving sharks.

But no matter how crazy it seemed, it was a homework assignment, and I had always been the sort of girl who not only did her homework but got excited about it.

That night, as I retired to the bedroom, I said, "Babe, I'm going to bed. I'm not checking the locks."

That was it.

I did not ask Nathan to make sure the locks were locked.

I did not visually confirm our fortress's security.

And I most certainly did not lock and relock the front and back doors two dozen times each.

I got into bed and felt as if I were being tortured. My heart pounded. My stomach heaved. My skin tingled.

When Nathan joined me in the bedroom, I studied his face to see if he had checked the locks. I could discern nothing.

My heart was beating so fast, surely Nathan would hear it. If only I could remind him to check the locks, I would feel better. How was I going to fall asleep? How could this possibly improve my anxiety?

"Good night, Nathan."

"Good night, sweetheart."

Was that the voice of a man who was 100 percent certain that the front and back doors were locked? I could not tell.

"I love you," I whispered.

"I love you."

Was that an "I love you, and I triple-checked all the locks," or an "I love you, the front door is slightly ajar and there's a maniac prowling the neighborhood"?

My body trembled with fear. If only I could get out of bed and check the front door . . .

THE NEXT FEW nights were agony, but my inner A+ student started to prevail. I denied my rituals and wrote about my feelings, which ranged from terror to rage at my psychologist.

After a few days, the homework was still challenging but it did not feel like torture. When I wrote, my chief feelings were still fear and anxiety but I also discerned a flutter of calm. That calm feeling grew and grew until by week's end, I actually felt better. I had stopped wanting to check the locks.

Over the next few weeks, my psychologist dialed up the intensity on my homework assignments. One week, I had to stop inspecting Pippa while she slept. The first night, I felt certain she would die before dawn. By the end of the week, though, when I put her down for bed, I was confident in her safety.

Another week, I had to stop looking under the beds and checking the closets for intruders. This took a lot of self-control and determination, but not as much self-control and determination as I had needed to stop checking the locks on the doors. My overall anxiety was decreasing every time I turned a ritual to dust, and as my anxiety decreased, it became easier and easier to eliminate the next ritual.

I had been clinging desperately to my bedtime rituals because I thought they made me feel better, but the psychologist was right. They were chains dragging me deeper into the hell of my anxiety. Now I was eager to break all the chains.

Except for one.

I was still repeatedly checking the gas burners on our stovetop every night before bed. My psychologist and I argued about this ritual for at least twenty minutes.

"You have to stop checking the burners. They are making you anxious."

"But they actually go out from time to time, and when they go out, gas is leaking into the air."

"Then fix the stovetop."

"I already had the repairman over a few months ago. He did what he could. It's a 1950s stove and sometimes the pilot light just gets snuffed out and needs to be relit."

"Then you have to buy a new oven. Get an electric one."

"What? No. No, no, no."

"If you don't turn this ritual to dust, you will not get better."

"But we have looked into getting a new oven. The modern ovens are not the same size. So we would either have to remodel the entire kitchen or buy an oven that is too small for the space and then we'd have a big gap between the oven and cabinets. And that will affect the house's resale value when we move."

After lots of arguing, my psychologist reluctantly agreed that I could check the pilot lights once every night if I reasonably thought they might have been snuffed out. At our next session, I reported my success on the homework assignment. The psychologist still thought I should get a new oven, but we agreed to disagree and move on to the next ritual.

IT WAS the middle of the night. I had just gotten back into bed after peeing.

Pippa, now seven months old, had recently started sleeping in her bedroom.

Was she okay?

I turned over to my side and squeezed my eyes shut.

The house was so quiet. How could I be sure that she was fine?

I rolled over and grabbed the video monitor off my nightstand. I stared at the fuzzy image. There she was, safe in her crib. Her head was turned to the side, in a position that looked comfortable. I put the video monitor back on the nightstand and closed my eyes.

Was she *really* okay?

I reached for the monitor and took another look. She had shifted positions. Good, I thought, she's alive.

Then it hit me: a new ritual had snuck into my life by way of the video monitor.

During the past few months, the psychologist had helped me dismantle my rituals. I no longer felt compelled to check the doors, burners, windows, or other household "dangers." I also no longer felt the need to bathe my hands in antibacterial goo several times a day or wash my hands repeatedly after a diaper change. Honestly, I do not remember when or how that ritual stopped. It just did. If I had to guess, I think that as I turned my primary rituals to dust, the secondary ones lost their power over me and slipped away.

Cognitive behavioral therapy was working.

My anxiety, though, was a slippery sneaky snake trying to find a chink in my newfound calm. Sure, I had dismantled the obvious rituals, but maybe it could gain a foothold with a new ritual that could masquerade as something any rational, thoughtful mother would do. Surely any mother would feel the need to check and recheck the video monitor to keep her baby safe.

The act of checking the monitor, though, was not keeping Pippa safe. It was only increasing my anxiety.

The urge to take a third look at the video monitor was like a physical itch, but I realized I was on a slippery slope. If I checked a third time tonight, I would let myself check four times tomorrow. Before I knew it, I would have an elaborate ritual of tiptoeing into the nursery and reaching an arm into the crib to check for Pippa's pulse. As the ritual became more complicated, my anxiety would deepen and seep into other areas of my life. It would not be enough to make sure Pippa was alive. I would need to double-triple-quadruple-check the locks to make sure she was not endangered by sexual predators roaming the streets of Pasadena. Then I would be back to looking under beds, checking the stovetop burners—

I unplugged the video monitor and put it in a drawer. After all the progress I had made, I was not about to let OCD back into my life. Even if the video monitor cost as much as the crib.

I was just like they said in one of my favorite commercials. Video monitor: $300. Mama's sanity?

Priceless.

20

SENSORY OVERLOAD

"Shall we do 'The Grand Old Duke of York'?"

A few moms groaned at the teacher's suggestion while I suppressed a grin and scooped Pippa into my arms, ready to work my triceps.

"And when you're up, you're up!" I lifted Pippa several feet into the air.

"And when you're down, you're down!" Back to my lap she went.

"And when you're only halfway up, you're neither up nor down." A little up, then all the way up, and back down to my lap. Then, for good measure, I lifted Pippa up one more time and gave her kisses on each cheek. She laughed, and I tickled her neck to make her giggle a little more. I could spend all day listening to that laugh.

It was late autumn in Pasadena, which meant it was about eighty degrees outside and a few trees had yellow leaves. Even better, it was Monday morning, my new favorite day of the week. Monday was the day I attended the Parent Education class offered by Pasadena City College.

"Are there any songs you would like to include in our music

time today?" Our teacher looked around the room and waited. The moms were suddenly busy adjusting bibs and blankies.

I sat quietly, too shy to raise my hand. What if I stuttered? What if the moms were annoyed with my song request? What if they shunned me?

The teacher smiled and waited.

Oh, what the hell. I lifted my arm into the air.

"Courtney! Yes?"

"Could we do 'Row, Row, Row Your Boat'?"

"We most certainly can. For this one, it works best if you lie your baby on top of your legs and then take their hands into yours for the motions. Beautiful. Row, row, row . . ."

This was so much better than the mommy and me class I had tried when I was in the throes of postpartum depression. On the surface, the classes did not seem that different, but thanks to postpartum depression, my reaction to the classes could not have been more different. My maternal mood disorder tampered with my senses so deeply, it even affected the way I experienced a children's song.

———

To HELP you appreciate the way postpartum depression affected my sensory perceptions, I'd like to jump back in time to a weekday morning in June, about five weeks before my hospitalization. Pippa was nearly three months old, and I was sinking faster and faster into the darkness of depression. But at the time, I did not know or even suspect what the next month of my life had in store for me. All I knew was that the Authorities kept telling me to make mommy friends who had babies close in age to Pippa, and my lack of mommy friends was starting to feel like a matter of life or death. Hence, this class for moms and their non-crawling babies.

We were in a room at a local hospital that was normally used for community classes. Nathan and I had sat in this room together for an all-day labor and delivery class; I had also come here for a crash course in breastfeeding. The tables and chairs had been cleared away for the mommy and me group.

A teacher paced the room. "Let's sit with our knees up and put our babies in our laps. Your knees are the candle and at the end of the rhyme, you can jump your baby over your knees."

She could not be serious. Couldn't we just sing "Old MacDonald" and make some animal sounds?

I had barely carried Pippa over my knees before the teacher launched into the next song. All the other moms had already put their babies back on the floor and were clapping along. The clapping was thunderous. Surely this cacophony was too much for tiny baby ears.

"All right, mommies, everyone on your backs!"

The other moms started to do some Pilates-type choreography. I tried to follow along but felt like a porpoise doing stomach crunches. Pippa made a noise that I decided was fussy, so I scooted away from the circle and started breastfeeding. After a half-hearted suckle, Pippa pushed away my breast. I reluctantly rejoined the circle. If only there were not so many women jam-packed into this room. Also, earmuffs would have been nice. The other moms seemed to be shouting the lyrics.

"Everyone, it's time to dance! We are going to march like ants!"

A conga line quickly formed. This was too much. Why had the teachers turned mommy and me class into boot camp? Before the song was over, I whisked Pippa away from the chaos and retreated to a far corner to feed her again. As she latched on, my body relaxed and I felt more centered—as if bits of myself had flown around the room, and by breastfeeding, I was pulling them back together.

After twenty minutes of music, the teacher announced it was time for a break and then small-group discussion. At last, I would get to talk to some of the other moms. I scanned the room. Who would be my friend?

As I sat with Pippa, the other moms scooted into clusters. Apparently everyone already knew each other. I was the new kid at school, and no one wanted me at their lunch table.

The teachers started to walk a slow circuit around the room. They each had a small plastic bottle and wand and were blowing bubbles. I felt like I was going to jump out of my skin. The bubbles seemed to be sucking the oxygen out of the room. The lights were too bright. The other moms were talking more and more loudly and bubbles were filling the air and—

Pippa whimpered. I scooped her up, grabbed my diaper bag, and retreated to the car. I could not believe I had subjected Pippa to such a noisy environment.

ABOUT TWELVE MONTHS after I was diagnosed with postpartum depression, I made a photo album documenting that crazy year. When the album arrived in the mail, I curled up with it on the couch to admire my handiwork. Flipping through the pages, I marveled at how much Pippa had grown.

There she was, on the scale, moments after birth, eyes scrunched shut in outrage. And there she was, cuddled close to Nathan. I brought the book closer. Yes, that *was* a fresh spit-up stain on Nathan's T-shirt. At least the photographs captured the authentic experience.

I smiled at the first selfie I took with Pippa on the day Nathan went back to work. Had she ever been that small and helpless?

No one would suspect just from these photos that I had had postpartum depression, anxiety, and OCD. My heart, though, beat a little faster with each page that I turned. March, April, May ... I was getting closer to the day I thought all was lost.

Then my heart skipped a beat.

I stared at the photo. Pippa was lying on her back, craning her neck to get a better look at a rainbow parachute.

I must have taken that photo during our first attempt at a mommy and me class, the class that had been too stimulating for a little baby. Toward the end, the teachers had brought out a rainbow parachute and told us to place our babies beneath it. I had opted to place Pippa on a blanket ten feet away from the parachute so that she would not get overwhelmed. I remembered that moment so well, especially how scared Pippa had been of the parachute.

Except in the photograph, Pippa did not look the slightest bit scared or overwhelmed. She looked curious, like she would have been very willing to get into the middle of the action and sit beneath the parachute with the other babies.

It had been me.

I leaned back on the couch.

Those feelings of the class being too noisy and crowded. At the time, I had thought that was how Pippa felt, but it had been me. I had projected my misery on Pippa because that was easier than accepting the truth: that I had been undone by a parachute and some bubbles.

I wiped away a few tears.

Oh my God, the bubbles. When the teachers blew bubbles and they popped in the air near the babies, my adrenaline had started to race as if fireworks were exploding in the classroom. That probably sounds like an exaggeration, but that was what post-partum depression did to my body. It made something innocent, like bubbles, feel like a vampire attack. The stress I felt was as acute as if the danger had been real.

Depression altered my experience of the world, as if it had crept in during the night and fiddled with the dials of my central computing system. Everything—noises, sights, smells—seemed amplified exponentially. I was easily overwhelmed by things that would never have even annoyed me before.

That's why a few innocent bubbles felt like fireworks. But I could not see what was happening to me. After all, I had grown up in one of the biggest cities in the world. I had gone zip-lining in Maui, attended a playoff game at Dodger Stadium, and celebrated New Year's Eve in Manhattan. I was not claustrophobic. I was not unusually sensitive to noises. Why would childbirth have changed that?

That was why I had spent so much time at home during those early months. If the depression made a mommy and me class feel like a war zone, anywhere else would have been unbearable.

I never addressed the symptom of "sensory overload" with my psychologist or psychiatrist. Nonetheless, the symptom resolved itself.

Maybe it was the sertraline resetting my hormones and brain chemistry.

Maybe I just needed more sleep.

Maybe the work we did to address my anxiety helped bring everything back into perspective and normalize my experience of the world. I don't know, but in the end, it doesn't matter.

All that matters is that within two months of my diagnosis, I could easily attend a Parent Education class with twenty other women and their babies and experience it for what it was: a chance to make new mama friends and bond with my daughter. Once my recovery started, the momentum made all sorts of good things happen.

But I could not leave well enough alone. I had to get in the way of my own recovery to keep things as interesting as possible.

21

THE MINI RELAPSE

The psychiatrist took a bite of his salad. "Talk to me. How are you doing?"

I was at the psychiatrist's office for my monthly appointment. It had been two months since I was discharged from the hospital.

"Pretty good."

"How much are you sleeping?"

"Seven or eight hours every night."

"That's fantastic!" He leaned forward and gave me a high five. "Since you are sleeping so well, maybe you want to try going to bed without the mirtazapine and see what happens. What are you taking, thirty milligrams before bed?"

"Yes."

"That dose is so small, it's probably just having a placebo effect."

At bedtime that night, I took my sertraline but skipped the mirtazapine. Then I crawled into the guest bed at my parents' house and turned off the light.

Three hours later, Pippa woke up. Nathan was about twenty miles away, asleep in his hotel bed in downtown Los Angeles. He had a case at trial and was so busy, it was easier for him to stay in a hotel near the courthouse. I had decamped to my parents' house for the duration of trial. For over two weeks now, Nathan had been gone and I had been solely responsible for all of Pippa's nocturnal meals.

(Whiplash alert: I previously mentioned this trial in Chapter 18, when I was reading Shields's memoir and processing the experience of having postpartum depression. During my recovery, Nathan only had to leave for one long trial. As you will shortly see, that was more than enough.)

Pippa quickly guzzled her bottle and fell asleep in my arms. I held her for ten minutes just to be sure I could safely transfer her back to her cradle. Then I put myself back to bed.

Except I could not fall asleep again.

The mirtazapine was inches away in a bottle in a drawer of the nightstand. All I had to do was reach over. I did not even have to get out of bed. But the doctor had said to see what happened without the medicine. He said it might just be having a placebo effect.

Be strong, I told myself.

After about ninety minutes of tossing and turning, I fell back to sleep, but Pippa wanted another bottle at four in the morning. Then, after another hour of dozing, she was awake for the day. I had slept five hours in three different stretches—nothing close to the six uninterrupted hours experts recommend. My dad came downstairs and took charge of Pippa. I stayed in bed for the next two hours, half-awake, half-dreaming, but never diving into the deep restorative sleep that my body could get only in the middle of the night.

Before bed that night, I gulped down my sertraline and then contemplated the bottle of mirtazapine. I heard the psychiatrist's voice in my head: "That dose is so small, it's probably just having a placebo effect."

I was not the sort of person who needed a sugar pill to fall asleep. I returned the mirtazapine to the nightstand drawer and went to bed. I quickly fell asleep, but Pippa woke up twice during the night to feed; and after both feedings, it took me more than an hour to fall back to sleep. The longest stretch I slept all night was two hours.

I was exhausted. I should probably have waited until Nathan's trial was over to experiment with my mirtazapine dose, but since I had already skipped two nights, I figured I might as well keep going. Maybe my body just needed to adjust to life without a bedtime placebo.

I turned off the light and laid my head on the pillow. I closed my eyes and took a deep breath. Then the inner monologue started.

I'm so tired.

I need to sleep.

I'm going to be so tired tomorrow.

Why can't I sleep?

I'm never going to sleep again.

My body is broken.

This time no one will be able to fix me.

A dozen times, I considered the mirtazapine; a dozen times, I told myself I did not need a silly placebo to fall asleep. I just had to be strong.

"DAD, CAN YOU WATCH PIPPA?"

"No problem." Pippa was already sitting on his lap, keenly watching my sister's miniature dachshund, Rowan. She did not even notice when I left the kitchen.

Over the past three nights, I had slept less than fifteen hours. My brain was tired; my muscles were tired; even my skin seemed tired. Tears filled my eyes. By the time I walked into my parents' room, I was sobbing. My mom was on the phone, so I started to turn away.

"Courtney! What's the matter? What's wrong?"

I cried harder.

"Just a second. Sara, I'll call you back later."

"It's okay, talk to Sara."

"Courtney, don't be silly, come here. What's wrong?"

I curled up on my mom's bed. "I'm so tired. Pippa keeps waking up every night. And I stopped taking one of my medications because my doctor said it was probably just having a placebo effect. And last night I could not get to sleep. It was just like the insomnia. It's back. I've ruined everything."

"Courtney. Pull yourself together. You haven't ruined anything. You are just going through a tough patch. Your husband's busy with work. Let's get some extra help. Let's call Laura and see if she can come tonight."

"She can't." I sniffed. "She's been working with twins and she'll be too tired to help."

"Maybe she can recommend someone else."

I rubbed snot away with my arm. "No one will be able to help."

"Courtney, stop this death spiral. Call Laura."

"I can't. Will you?"

I felt as if I were back in the darkest moments of my postpartum depression. Then, I had been too afraid to call my husband to let him know about my admission to the psychiatric ward. Now, I was too afraid to call one of the sweetest doulas on earth.

In July, I had at least been able to get better.

Now, in September, less than two months after my discharge, I had destroyed all my progress. This time, no one would be able to help me. I had destroyed any chance of reclaiming my life.

Why had I ever thought I could get my life back?

"I skipped my mirtazapine dose the past three nights and have not been sleeping well."

"Have you told your psychiatrist?"

"No." I yawned. "Apparently my dose is so low, it might just be having a placebo effect. He told me I might want to try skipping it to see what happens."

The psychologist frowned. "It sounds like you tried skipping it, and your body did not respond well. Maybe it is having more than a placebo effect."

"I don't want to be dependent on medication if I don't need it."

"Say a little more about that."

"It's been eight weeks since I was discharged from the hospital. Most moms can sleep without mirtazapine. Why me?"

"Ah, yes, *why me?* You can think that—*why me?* But there is a flip side to that."

"There is?"

"Of course. Instead of *why me?*, you can ask, *why not me?* Plenty of women get postpartum depression. Someone had to get it. Why not you?"

"Why not me?"

"Why not you?"

I crossed and recrossed my legs to buy a little time. "Why not me? Why not me? I like that! *Why not me?* It makes it seem more like the luck of the draw instead of something I did to incur the universe's wrath."

"Do you think you did something to deserve postpartum depression?"

"No. Of course not. The more I think about it, the more I think I was already an anxious person going into childbirth, but then my hormones went bonkers and here I am."

"Here you are. So, the mirtazapine. What do you think you will do tonight?"

"I don't know. I called my psychiatrist's office yesterday and they never called back."

The psychologist scowled.

"But the psychiatrist didn't order me to stop the mirtazapine immediately. He said just to experiment."

"And having experimented for three nights?"

"I'll take the mirtazapine tonight. Why should I suffer unnecessarily?"

"You shouldn't. Pregnancy is a huge event. It might take months for your hormones to settle. You've only been taking mirtazapine for six weeks. There's no need for you to rush your recovery. By the way, what does Nathan think of all this?"

"You mean stopping the mirtazapine? He doesn't know."

"He doesn't know?"

"His trial is still going on. I've barely seen him since it started. He doesn't have time to hear about my medications. I miss him but I have to be strong and get through this."

"When was the last time you saw him?"

"A week ago. He visited for a few hours on Saturday and left after dinner." I paused. "And we're not seeing him this weekend. He's too busy."

"How does that make you feel?"

"I don't know. Bad. Awful. I miss him. I wish we could just talk on the phone for a little bit. But I told him I understand he's busy and we don't have to talk on the phone. I told him it's okay to just email."

"Maybe you should ask Nathan to talk on the phone and tell him how hard this has been for you."

"No. I have to be able to do this on my own."

"Courtney, you have to stop being so hard on yourself. Babies are a lot of work, and parents need as much help as they can get. It takes a village. You need to get help from family, from friends, or pay for it. And Nathan needs to know that you are having a tough time."

"But he's so busy."

"So what? You only have to talk for two minutes."

"But I've been there. I know what it is like to be working on a trial. I know how time-consuming trials can be."

"Let me ask you this. If the roles were reversed, and you were working on a trial, and Nathan was at home with Pippa, would you want him to pretend that everything was okay?"

"Nooooo."

"Why not?"

"Because I'm his wife. Even if I'm busy, I want to know what is happening with him so that I can be as supportive as possible."

"And if you were away at trial, would you be able to take two minutes every day to stop what you were doing and talk to Nathan?"

"Of course."

The psychologist suppressed a grin.

I conceded. "It doesn't matter how busy Nathan is, I'm still his wife, and he can still take a two-minute break to talk to me. But email is so much easier. Why should I expect a phone call?"

"Why is email easier?"

"Because he can read my emails and respond whenever it is convenient for him."

The psychologist nodded.

"But it's not the same. I haven't heard his voice in a week and I might not see him for another week."

"There is something very powerful about hearing your loved one's voice."

After the session, I sent Nathan a quick message: *Hey you! I hope you are doing as well as possible. At some point today, I'd like for us to talk on the phone. Just two minutes, I know you are busy. But I still need to hear your voice. Love you!*

Then I waited and worried. I had made lots of progress with

my nightly rituals, and that had reduced my anxiety levels, but I still felt a little skittish about my relationship with Nathan. I worried that if I said or did the wrong thing, he would lose his patience with me forever.

This was also a classic case of communication failure. When I told Nathan that he did not have to call, I was trying to be accommodating and helpful, but I still hoped he would want to call. Nathan had not read my mind and jumped at the offer. It was the biggest trial of his career. He had been preparing for it since before Pippa's conception. Trials are intense and can make a lawyer go into survival mode: poop, pee, eat, sleep, and kick ass at trial.

All of that was true, but I think Nathan was also emotionally exhausted after the past two months (not to mention the four months that preceded my hospitalization). No one had ever prepared him for what to do in the event that his wife ended up in the psychiatric ward after giving birth. He was expected to jump into the fire and figure it out. By the time trial started, eighteen-hour workdays were probably a bit of a reprieve from worrying about his soul mate's sanity.

Nathan called after dinner. "Yeah? You wanted me to call?"

"Yes, thank you for calling. I . . . I just . . . I wanted to tell you . . . I just wanted you to know that this trial has been very difficult for me. It sucks having you gone for so long."

"Babe, I know, but what do you expect me to do about it? I'm in trial." He sounded like he was arguing with opposing counsel about jury instructions.

"I don't expect you to do anything. I just need you to know this is tough for me."

"It's tough for me, too. I'm not exactly having fun here."

"I know. And I know I said we don't have to speak on the phone while you are gone, but I was wrong. I need us to speak on the phone every day for just one minute. Just so I can hear the sound of your voice."

"Of course."

A couple of hours later, Laura arrived. By that time, Pippa was asleep in her cradle in the nursery. I had already brushed my teeth and changed into my pajamas. I needed to do only one more thing and then I would be ready for bed.

I put the mirtazapine tablet on my tongue and washed it down with a big sip of water. Maybe it was just having a placebo effect, but that did not matter. What mattered was that I got the sleep I needed to feel like my best self.

When I woke up the next morning, I felt like a new woman.

22

ARE YOU MAD AT ME?

"I'm worried that Nathan doesn't understand the full extent of what the postpartum depression did to me."

The psychologist nodded. "Tell me more about that."

"So much of it happened in my head, and I hid it from him. When I was being admitted to the B Ward, he said, 'The only crazy thing you have ever done is agree to come here.'"

"Would you like to bring Nathan to your session next week? We can talk to him together about what it has been like for you to have postpartum depression."

My shoulders and back muscles tightened reflexively.

"Bring Nathan? Here?"

"Sure, my patients bring spouses and other family members here all the time." The psychologist gestured toward the empty chairs by the window.

———

Two Saturdays later, Nathan was seated in one of the chairs that was usually empty.

"I feel like you are mad at me for having postpartum depression."

"But I'm not," Nathan said. "I'm not mad at all."

"Yeah, I know that's what you say, but it's how I feel."

For the past half hour, the psychologist had been telling Nathan what happens to a woman when she has postpartum depression. Nathan had listened and nodded attentively and said all the right things.

Still, something was nagging at me. I had brought Nathan here so he could understand my experience, but now it felt like we were talking about the wrong things. The conversation we needed to have was about ten miles below the discussion in progress. That's when I blurted the words, "I feel like you are mad at me for having postpartum depression."

The psychologist said, "Courtney, when you are worried that Nathan is mad, what do you do?"

"I ask him if he is mad."

"And then what happens?"

"He says that he is not mad at me."

"And how do you feel after Nathan says that he is not mad at you?"

"I still feel bad. I still think he's mad at me."

"Describe 'bad.'"

"Well . . . it's like . . . it's like guilt."

"For what? You don't have anything to feel guilty about." Nathan looked perplexed.

"I just feel like I have done something wrong. Like I've disappointed you. This should be one of the happiest times of our life. We have a baby and she's beautiful and healthy and so much fun but still I got postpartum depression."

"But that's not your fault."

"It feels that way."

"But that doesn't make any sense." Nathan had not had postpartum depression. He still thought this was something that could be vanquished with reason and logic.

"Yeah, but it's how I feel. Like I did something wrong, and you are mad at me, and I should feel guilty about something."

The psychologist took charge. "It doesn't matter if Courtney's feelings make sense. What's important is they are real, and they are making her uncomfortable. So let's change that."

"How?"

The psychologist smiled. "I want to give both of you homework this week. Courtney, you are not allowed to ask Nathan if he is mad or angry or upset or annoyed with you. And Nathan, if Courtney asks if you are mad or annoyed, you are not allowed to answer her question. You have to ignore her completely. Will you do that for me?"

"Okay," Nathan said, his tone of voice saying, *We are spending how much on this voodoo crap?*

"I know it sounds strange," the psychologist said. "But when Courtney asks if you are angry at her, she is seeking reassurance that you still love her. But when you give her that reassurance, it just reinforces her fear that you might not love her anymore. It's an irrational fear that the postpartum depression caused. We have to squash it completely. So you have to stop answering her questions that seek reassurance of your love. That's the only way to help her get better. If she asks whether you are angry at her, you ignore her. If she tries to get around the homework and seeks reassurance in a different way, like 'Do you still love me?' then you need to ignore her."

"All right," Nathan said. "It sounds silly but I will do it."

NOT LONG AFTER Pippa was born, Nathan and I took her to a small shady park near our house. We sat on a bench and admired

Pippa as she admired the trees, sky, and children running around. It was a lovely Saturday outing.

I was miserable.

If someone had asked me at the time, I would have insisted that I was utterly and completely happy. I was outside enjoying nature with my husband and baby. How could I feel otherwise?

Except I did feel otherwise. I felt like Nathan was angry or at least intensely annoyed with me.

A picnic blanket. That was it. I should have brought a picnic blanket. The bench we were sitting on was not very comfortable. Nathan was mad because I had not thought to bring a blanket.

"Look, baby girl, do you see the Frisbee?" Nathan pointed to some children playing nearby.

Pippa did not see the Frisbee but she did direct an ecstatic coo toward the dirt at our feet.

I started to jiggle my knee up and down while beads of sweat formed on my back. Nathan must be bored. He must hate me for proposing an outing to our neighborhood park. I should have let him stay at home and relax.

"Do you think Pippa needs to eat anytime soon?"

"I fed her right before we left, so she should be good for at least an hour."

"Want to drive over to Langer's to pick up some sandwiches for lunch?"

"Great idea!" I had not had a pastrami sandwich from the legendary Los Angeles deli since before I got pregnant.

I buckled Pippa into her car seat and sat in the back with her. When I sat in the front, I felt as if I were deserting her.

Pippa quickly fell asleep and all was going according to plan until we reached the third freeway. (The twenty-minute drive from our house to the deli involved three freeways—the 210, the 134, and the 2.) Traffic ground to a halt. The freeway was basically a parking lot. A few miles away, smoke billowed.

Nathan turned on the radio. A tanker had overturned near

Dodger Stadium. The fire department had shut down all paths to Langer's.

My stomach was throwing a fit. "I don't think we can make it."

"Hang on!" Nathan somehow made four lane changes in rapid succession and got us off the parking lot. "Yeah, we are so not going to make it. I'll call and cancel."

As Nathan drove home, I silently berated myself. The trip to Langer's had been his idea, but I had endorsed the plan. This was my fault. I should have foreseen there'd be trouble. Now poor Nathan was wasting his precious weekend time on a doomed expedition.

Later, much later, I asked Nathan if he remembered the tanker incident.

"We were going to Langer's, right?"

"Right. I thought you were so mad at me."

"What? You did?"

"Yeah, I thought it was my fault that we got stuck in traffic and you blamed me and we were on the verge of getting a divorce."

"I had no idea."

"Well, of course not, it was all going on in my head."

"Babe, I'm so sorry."

"It's not your fault. You didn't do anything wrong. You were acting like your normal self."

"I was probably exhausted and cranky."

"Yes, *because we had just had a baby*. But I had postpartum depression, and it made me feel guilty and anxious about everything. So I felt responsible for the traffic jam, and that made me feel anxious about our relationship."

<hr />

I PUTTERED AROUND THE KITCHEN, gathering ingredients for dinner. Nathan and Pippa were playing in the next room.

Suddenly, my entire body tensed.

Was Nathan mad at me? Did he hate me?

It would be so easy to say the words—*Are you mad at me?*—and then return to my puttering. It was, however, the day after our joint session with my psychologist, and I had a homework assignment to complete.

My body thrummed with anxiety for several minutes. It was as if some unseen force were pushing against my will, begging me to ask the question—*Are you mad at me? Are you mad at me? ARE YOU MAD AT ME???*

On top of the anxiety, there was guilt. I had not done anything that might warrant guilt—I had not even ordered french toast garnished with cat vomit—but still, the guilt was there.

Guilt is regularly included on official lists of postpartum depression symptoms, and yet, to this day, I still feel a little lame including it on my list of symptoms. To me, it sounds like the mental health equivalent of a runny nose—annoying, but not life-threatening.

Guilt, though, can make you feel physically ill. It can give you stomach cramps or nausea, skin prickles and chills, and the sensation of carrying around extra weight. Guilt can even make you want to die.

Just ask Lady Macbeth.

As I stood in the kitchen, feeling wave after wave of guilt, I knew I had to resist the unseen force. The question—*Are you mad at me?*—felt as imperative as any matter of life or death, but I could not ask it.

For a few minutes, I felt sick. My skin got clammy and I stood by the sink, afraid I was going to puke.

But after those first excruciating minutes, the guilt started to fade until, in less than ten minutes, it had vanished entirely.

A half hour later, I felt another urge to ask Nathan if he was mad. This time, the physical discomfort lasted only five minutes.

By bedtime, the guilt was practically gone—when the question popped into my head, I had to resist for only a few seconds.

———

THE NURSE BENT over Pippa's arm. It was December, and my baby, not quite nine months old, could not stop puking. It was just a stomach bug, but the ER doctor had ordered anti-nausea medications plus an IV to get her hydrated again as quickly as possible. The first nurse had not been able to insert the IV. Neither had the second. Now the third nurse, summoned from the pediatric unit, was preparing to work her magic.

Nathan stood by the door while I held Pippa in my lap. Earlier that morning, as he was getting dressed for work, I warned him that he might need to meet me at the hospital if the puking did not stop. Sure enough, I had to call and have him meet me at the ER less than an hour after he got to the office.

Not so long ago, asking Nathan to meet me at the hospital would have sent me into a tailspin. I would have felt personally responsible for the fact that Pippa had not wet her diaper in over fourteen hours and guilty that Nathan had slogged through his morning commute only to turn around and meet me at the ER.

But on the day Pippa needed an IV, I did not feel a single shudder of guilt. Six weeks had passed since the psychologist told me to stop asking Nathan if he was mad at me. Breaking that habit had been transformational. I no longer felt skittish or insecure around Nathan. I knew he loved me, and when he said something nice, I did not start overanalyzing his facial expressions and inventing phantom problems.

The pediatric nurse was waving a needle around in the air, complaining about how the ER nurses kept paging her during her lunch break. She had still not inserted the IV into puking Pippa's arm.

"I'm trying to enjoy my lunch and my pager is blowing up about some kid in the ER who needs an IV."

That kid in the ER happened to be my baby girl, but I nodded sympathetically. Seeing as the nurse was about to insert an IV into Pippa's arm, I did not want to rile her up anymore. Nathan, on the other hand, looked like he was having a little less success in the anger management department. He was standing by the door, behind the pediatric nurse, and if he had been a cartoon character, there would have been little flames in his eyes and smoke steaming out of his ears.

The nurse finally stopped whining about the ER nurses and actually started to insert the needle into Pippa's vein. I shot Nathan a stern look that told him to calm down.

At long last, the IV was inserted. The pediatric nurse left, and Pippa started getting the fluids she needed.

"I was going to kill her," Nathan said. He looked like he was at the beginning of a rant, but I cut him short.

"This is the Buddha zone. We are calm in this room. Pippa can sense if we are upset, and that makes her upset, so we have to stay Zen."

Nathan huffed.

I did not relent. "Your rage is completely justified. We just can't have it in here. Go outside. Call the grandparents and give them an update. Then get us some snacks. But wait, first help me lie down without getting the IV all tangled."

I curled up on the hospital bed with Pippa, and Nathan arranged the pillows under our heads. The pink was already returning to her cheeks. She fell asleep in my arms, and I quietly watched the rise and fall of her chest.

Nathan returned with candy and chips a half hour later. He was still cranky, but it did not occur to me once to ask if he was mad at me.

23

HOW CBT HELPED ME ANNIHILATE ANXIETY

"I think I'm back to my old myself."

"I agree."

"But I'm still anxious."

The psychologist nodded.

"I think I was an anxious person even before I got pregnant."

"Say more about that."

I took a long moment to think.

"I went to law school and did not feel anxious so long as I was studying. But I remember this time during the first semester when I got a flat tire. I was planning to go home and study some more and when I realized the tire was flat, I started to cry. It was like the whole world was out to get me. Everything was ruined. I was going to fail my exams, never get a good job, and have a miserable life, all because of a flat tire at the beginning of the semester."

"Why do you think you felt that way?"

"I don't know. I lost all sense of perspective. I planned out every moment of my day, and when something out of my control happened, I went straight to thinking it was the end of the world."

"Do you like being in control?"

I had to take another moment to think.

"Yes, I do. I like being in control."

"Was that just during law school?"

"No, I've always liked being in control. At least as an adult."

"Since Kim died?"

My mouth opened.

Ever since those sessions with the therapist in college, I had thought I understood the effect that Kim's death had had on me. She got sick and was hospitalized; the doctors said she would be fine and discharged her; and a few weeks later, she died in her sleep. Her death had been sudden and unexpected. That's why I had become a hypochondriac, overanalyzing every sniffle and headache.

It had never occurred to me that the anxiety went deeper than hypochondria, but as soon as my psychologist mentioned Kim, something clicked and tumbled into place.

I had buried all the negative feelings that tried to surface when Kim died. The very first stab of grief when my parents told me the news was too much. I had never felt so terrible in my life and was not interested in letting the feelings linger. It felt much better to eat ice cream, tell dark jokes, and focus on my studies.

Feelings, though, must be felt. That is their sole purpose. Suppress them, and they do not sigh and flit away. They linger and fester, lurking in the depths of your soul, jamming up your cells, until you let them have their moment.

When I saw the therapist in college, I thought the hypochondria was the sole manifestation of my denied grief. I thought I just needed to tear up in my therapist's office for a few seconds to resolve the old feelings.

Nope.

My grief over Kim's death, buried beneath ice cream and sarcasm, had rotted and morphed into general anxiety, of which the hypochondria was one symptom. The thought of being even a minute late also made me sweat and tremble. The possibility of disappointing someone made me sick to my stomach. That was why I had deliberately sabotaged so many friendships since college. It was easier to have just a few friends than, God forbid, tell someone I could not attend her birthday party. My anxiety even kept me from trying new hobbies that sounded interesting for fear that I would not be any good. Easier never to try than to try and fail.

"Do you think I can become less anxious?"

"Absolutely."

"How? I don't have any more rituals."

"We need to rewire the way you think. This week, I want you to pay attention to your feelings. When you notice you are getting anxious, you need to stop and think about *why* you are feeling anxious. Then, you need to ask yourself two questions: What is the worst thing that can happen? And what is the probability of it happening?"

This sounded less than promising.

But I was desperate.

For almost my entire adult life, I assumed my anxiety was the only thing keeping me safe in a perilous world. Dismantling my rituals had shown me otherwise, but I also assumed that I could eliminate only the anxiety caused by postpartum depression, that I was stuck with all the preexisting anxiety that was part of my genetic makeup.

Now that I knew my anxiety was tied to Kim's death, I was eager to expunge it from my life.

I DUMPED ground beef and chopped onions into a large pot and turned on a burner. As the beef and onions simmered, I gathered the rest of the ingredients for chili: two cans of kidney beans, a jar of salsa, garlic salt, pepper, the magical packet of chili seasoning, one can of tomato sauce, and I just needed one more can of tomato sauce . . . there had to be one somewhere in the pantry . . . maybe behind the raisins . . . or the mustard . . . why did we have so much mustard? . . . WHAT HAD HAPPENED TO MY STOCKPILE OF TOMATO SAUCE?

We were out of tomato sauce.

Dinner was ruined.

My heart started to pound.

Oh.

I stopped pacing.

I was getting anxious.

I hit my internal pause button and searched through my mind. What had the psychologist said I should do when I felt anxious?

Ah, yes, I remembered: *What is the worst thing that could happen?*

I pondered.

Death? Of course not.

Illness? Not even.

Was dinner possibly ruined? Yes.

And if dinner was ruined, might Nathan hate me forever? Yes.

This was not making me feel better.

My temperature started to rise but then I remembered there was a second step to the analysis: *What is the likelihood of the worst-case scenario actually coming to fruition?*

We were talking about a missing can of tomato sauce—not even a proper can but the adorable half can of tomato sauce, of which I only ever used four or five ounces. So instead of the twenty ounces of tomato sauce that the recipe required, we had fifteen. Would a difference of five ounces of tomato sauce render dinner inedible? And even if it did, would that make Nathan hate me forever?

Though the onions and beef were simmering, I forced myself to slow down for a minute and think through my anxiety.

I thought about how I was a resourceful cook and had, on many prior occasions, cobbled together a tasty dinner even when the pantry failed me. In this case, surely some extra salsa would avert the disaster that was not actually a disaster.

I poured out the excess fat from the browned ground beef and started to stir in the ingredients. My heart had already slowed back down to a normal rhythm, but for the sake of the home-work assignment, I decided to keep thinking.

In the absolute worst-case scenario, Nathan divorced me because the chili was inedible. How likely was that?

Slim to nonexistent.

I had ruined meals before because that is what happens when you like to cook: you eat some, you burn some. On more than one occasion, we had needed to run to McDonald's because we simply could not choke down the food on our plates. Would Nathan really decide to end our relationship because the chili lacked its usual oomph?

The question was too ridiculous to answer.

———

We were nearly home.

And then I saw him.

A man.

Walking on the other side of the otherwise empty street.

I started breathing faster.

In order to get home, I would have to walk past that man. He looked like an upstanding citizen. But what if he wasn't?

What if he got angry that I was walking on the same street as him?

What if he started to yell?

What if he ran across the street and pushed the stroller over and—

I was getting carried away by a case of the what-ifs. It was time to hit my inner pause button, take a few deep breaths, and run the two-step analysis.

Step one: *What was the worst-case scenario?*

Well, worst-case scenario, the man was a lunatic who raped and killed me in broad daylight and ran away with Pippa.

Step two: *And what was the likelihood of that happening?*

Approximately 0.00000000000000001 percent. (And that number probably needed a dozen more zeros.)

Still, there was a risk. Maybe I should take the longer way home. I could use the extra exercise—

No. I was letting my anxiety make excuses to justify unnecessary defensive measures, which would just give my anxiety the validation it craved.

My feet kept walking.

I was getting closer to the man.

My heart pounded against my chest.

Closer.

I should have stayed home.

Even closer.

And then.

The man waved and smiled.

I waved back.

The rituals were gone. I no longer obsessed over germs or potential kidnappers. Even my wrists had stopped hurting. The anxiety was getting frantic and scrambling for ways to keep me in its thrall. Just moments ago, I had been gripped by panic that felt real. Now the idea of a harmless neighbor assaulting me and Pippa in broad daylight made me chuckle.

I had been doing the two-step analysis every day for over a week now and then journaling about my thoughts and feelings. Every day, I was getting stronger, and the anxiety was reaching for more ludicrous scenarios. As the scenarios got more ludicrous, I became more adept at dismantling the anxiety.

I was almost ready to confront my biggest fear.

"I'M FEELING A LOT LESS ANXIOUS," I told the psychologist at our next meeting. "Except."

"Except what?"

I took a deep breath. "The worst-case scenario usually gives me a sense of perspective because I realize the worst thing that could happen is not that bad. But sometimes, the worst-case scenario is death. Then it doesn't matter how low the probability of the worst case actually happening is. It's still death. How can I feel calm when there is even a tiny possibility of death?"

"Would it be so bad if you died?"

I could not speak. It was as if the psychologist's question had flattened my windpipe.

"Would it be so bad if you died?" He was speaking with the same voice, but somehow it seemed louder, sterner, more forbidding.

"Yes."

"Why?"

Was he crazy?

"Because I'd be dead."

"And?"

"And I don't know what happens next. I feel like there must be an afterlife, but I don't know if it's heaven up in the clouds or if I retain my memories of this life. I'm not an atheist. I believe there's some bigger force of love out there. But that doesn't mean my soul survives after this body dies. I might die and then, that's it."

"That's it. Would that be so bad?"

I squirmed in my chair. "Well, yeah."

"Why? Why would it be so bad if you cease to exist when you die?"

"Because . . . because . . . because all of this would be gone."

"So?"

"So?" My head was feeling very full now with the suggestion of a headache.

"If you die, and that's it, and you cease to exist, you'll never know."

I shuddered.

"If you die. And that's it." He was speaking slowly and deliberately. "You will never know."

"I guess."

"If you die. And that's it. You will never know."

Now there was a tingling in my chest, a pleasant lightness, as if an old weight was evaporating.

"If I die, and that's it, I won't be around to know it. But there's nothing I can do about that now, so why worry about it?"

"So why worry about it."

I uncrossed and re-crossed my legs and looked out the window toward the mountains.

"Okay, so maybe it's not so terrible if I die. If I die, and there's an afterlife, great. If not, I won't be around to worry about it. But sometimes, my death is not the worst-case scenario. Sometimes, the worst-case scenario is that Nathan or Pippa might die."

"How would you feel if Nathan died?"

"I can't even think about it. My life would be over."

"Would you kill yourself?"

"No, oh no, I couldn't do that. I couldn't do that to Pippa."

"If Nathan died today, would you want to die?"

I did not answer. My psychologist waited.

"No . . . but I would feel awful. I can't even imagine how awful I would feel."

The psychologist nodded. He had a very effective nod.

"But I guess," I said, thinking out loud, "that eventually I would feel okay. Sometimes."

The psychologist nodded.

"And I would keep living."

"Do you think, that if Nathan died, you might eventually be happy again?"

I hesitated. Yes, I thought to myself, yes, I would. It felt like a betrayal even to think that.

The psychologist said, "Many, many people lose their spouses, and it is awful, and they feel miserable but they do keep living and eventually, they are even happy. Do you think you would eventually be happy again if Nathan died?"

"Yes, I would."

"And what is the probability that Nathan is going to die before his time?"

"Low. It's not likely."

"How would you feel if Pippa died?"

"I can't imagine. It would be the worst thing. Unbearable."

"Would it be the first time that a parent lost a child?"

"No."

"So you agree that there are a lot of parents alive in the world today who have lost their children?"

"Yes."

"And how do you think those parents feel?"

"Awful. But they do keep living."

My psychologist nodded.

"And they eventually feel okay and then they can actually make their peace with their child's death and be happy again," I went on. "I'm sure they feel awful whenever they think about their child, but they do not feel that way all the time. I suppose that's how my aunt and uncle feel."

"The parents of your cousin who died?"

"Yes."

"Tell me more about that. How do you think they feel?"

"It's been a long time since Kim died. *I* still sometimes feel awful about it, but she was their daughter. Their baby. They must still feel awful about it."

The psychologist nodded.

"But . . . but they are happy. They adore their grandchildren. They go on trips to Las Vegas and golf. They still have everyone over for Christmas Eve, every year. They laugh. They miss Kim but they have kept living and enjoying their lives. I'm sure that's what Kim would have wanted. She would not have wanted her parents or sisters or son or anyone to freeze up and stop living."

"If Pippa died, do you think you could be like your aunt and uncle and all those other parents who have lost their children?"

I could not speak.

"Do you think," the psychologist pressed, "that you would be able to find happiness and meaning in your life if Pippa died?"

Tears filled my eyes. My heart felt as if it were going to crack in two.

"Do you think, if the worst possible thing happened, and Pippa died, that you could keep living and be happy again?"

"Yes," I said, and as I spoke the word, I realized it was true.

24

SUDDENLY MEH

"Talk to me. How are you?" The psychiatrist waited, hands posed above the keyboard hooked to his iPad, ready to take notes if I said anything important. I preferred the way my psychologist took notes—pen and paper, much easier to ignore—but I was not about to lecture my psychiatrist on the proper way to do his job.

It was late November, almost four months since my discharge from the hospital. The battle of the wits that had started in the hospital now happened during my monthly checkup with the psychiatrist, who was not content with merely monitoring my medications. He wanted to push me even further down the path of recovery.

"I'm pretty good," I said, trying to find a comfortable position on the couch. There were too many throw pillows with needle-point designs, but I felt weird putting them on the floor.

"Good? Convince me."

"I've met some moms in my parenting class."

My psychiatrist frowned. "That's a start. Are you having fun in the class?"

"Fun?"

"Yes, fun. What have you been doing to have fun?"

Ever since our first meeting in the ER, the psychiatrist had been hounding me to have fun. I could not understand his obsession.

"We've been going to the mall once or twice a week, and that is a lot of fun for me."

"The mall is fun?"

"I write every day when Pippa is napping."

"That's something."

"I'm busy, I'm a mom. What do you expect me to do?"

"Get a babysitter."

I slouched back on the couch.

"Courtney, look at me. Sertraline alone is not going to keep you healthy. You have to get off your butt, take care of yourself, and have some fun."

The psychiatrist was so unreasonable. Maybe I needed to work with a female who had kids and sympathized with all the demands on my time—demands that left no room for the active pursuit of fun.

"What am I supposed to be doing that is fun?"

"You have to figure that out for yourself."

No matter what the psychiatrist said or thought, he was wrong. The Parent Education class *was* fun.

The following Monday, I waltzed into the classroom with Pippa on one hip and my diaper bag against the other, scanned the room, and spotted my new friends, sitting in their usual spot on the far side of the room, backs against the toy kitchen set, surrounded by other moms, with no space for me and my cargo.

Well. This was unfortunate.

No matter, I wanted to get to know all the moms. I set up camp in a new spot and laid Pippa on her stomach for tummy time. She promptly rolled onto her back and squawked until I put her in a seated position with an array of toys just within reach.

"Clarissa hates tummy time, too," said the mom to my left.

"I will not miss tummy time," I said.

A few other moms arrived, and soon we were talking about remedies for nasal congestion. I waited for that euphoric feeling that usually came when I was chatting with the moms.

It did not come.

An hour ago, trying to trick Pippa into eating oatmeal, I had felt ready to dance around the world. Now I was being sucked into the core of the earth. The muscles were melting off my bones, and my stomach was turning to dust.

What was wrong with me? It was Monday, my favorite day of the week, but I felt like a zombie staggering around a post-apocalyptic landscape, with somber lighting and leafless trees.

Soon it was time to sing. Singing *always* made me smile, but now, as I moved my fingers like a spider, all I felt was a heaviness pressing against my shoulders.

Was I having a relapse?

This feeling of muscle-melting fatigue was not new. I had first noticed it in the A Ward on the day I got my energy back. I woke up with the urge to sing and dance but after seeing my psychiatrist in the afternoon, I felt so tired that I had to go to my room and lie down in bed. I closed my eyes and could not sleep even though the longer I lay in bed, the more tired I felt. After an hour of resting, I felt as if I had been awake all night. My energy did not return until I went to the common room and colored a picture of a butterfly. That day in the A Ward, I decided the fatigue was just my body's way of adjusting to my new medications.

It never occurred to me that the journey from depressed to exuberantly alive might take longer than seventy-two hours in a hospital.

That Monday morning, four months into my recovery, sitting

among a circle of moms and babies, I truly did not understand what was happening to me. I thought I had done everything necessary to beat depression and was as un-depressed as any person could be. I could not see the link between the fatigue in my body and the postpartum depression diagnosis. I was still having trouble getting my mind around the "depression" part of postpartum depression.

My psychiatrist had told me on numerous occasions that I was in denial of the fact that I was depressed, but as a person who has been depressed, I don't think "denial" is the right word. It's easier to see depression in someone else than it is to see it in yourself. "Denial" connotes consciousness on the part of the doer, like when Peter denied knowing Jesus. With depression, it's more accurate to say that depression has rewired a person's brain so deeply, she cannot see the changes to her normal self.

I needed distance—and healing—from the experience of depression before I could see what it was. The understanding I have now was gained only through time, reflection, and mulling over the many drafts of this memoir. I am describing the journey to my full recovery from depression, but at the time, I did not realize that was what was happening.

After my experience at Parent Education class, I assumed I just needed a trip to the mall to lift my spirits.

———

I WAS RIGHT: I did need a trip to the mall. But it was for different reasons than I anticipated.

At a restaurant that always made me happy, I mashed up bits of avocado for Pippa, then guzzled soda and nibbled a salad with garbanzo beans and salami. It was one of my favorite meals, but I could not shake a feeling of blah. No matter. The carousel, a double-decker with horses and exotic animals, would brighten my mood. I placed Pippa on top of the hippo and gave her lots of kisses, but what had previously felt like a magical bonding moment with my daughter failed to boost my spirits into the celestial sphere. Refusing to accept defeat, I pushed the stroller toward the indoor playground, a walled-off area filled with rubbery structures that looked like animals. While Pippa stood up on her own, balanced carefully with her hands at her side, and crawled through a tunnel, I yawned and felt as if some essential life force were draining out of my body.

I had never been so glad to escape a mall.

Now I was at my desk, writing a journal entry. The muscle-melting fatigue was dragging me down, and my spirits were flatlining. I needed to make some sort of change, that much was obvious, but could not understand what. Hopefully writing would help me make some sense of my feelings.

Could my body still be adjusting to my medications?

Surely not. It had been three months.

Had the sertraline stopped working?

No, it was definitely helping. Otherwise the insomnia and anxiety would be back.

Was I lonely?

No, that was not it either. I had felt the heaviness and fatigue during Parent Education, when I was surrounded by people who wanted to talk. I liked the moms and looked forward to their company.

Was heaviness even the right word? I was journaling about this feeling as if it were a weight pressing me down against the earth. But as I wrote, other words came to mind: an itch, a longing, a hunger for something more . . .

Oh! Forget about depression. I was bored!

I stood up and started walking around the house. No, I needed more than a stretch of the legs. I needed fresh air and sunshine.

With Pippa napping against my chest in the baby carrier, I strode out the front door and walked down the block on the shady side of the street. As my legs moved, my brain whirled. Did I need to go back to work? I had never been bored when I was a lawyer, but I had been finished with the legal field long before I got pregnant. Besides, I had always known in my gut that I wanted to be a stay-at-home mom. Walking around my neighborhood, with Pippa's head against my beating heart, I knew that was still true. Going back to work was not the answer to my boredom.

I crossed the street to avoid the house with the noisy Golden Retriever. I did not miss being a lawyer, but my brain had enjoyed the mental acrobatics of litigation. As a lawyer, I was always learning new things and practicing different skills. Now that I was a stay-at-home mom, I had to find a way to keep my brain happy.

The Parent Education class had, at first, been an adventure because I was so used to huddling in my house all day, feebly shaking rattles for Pippa. Packing my diaper bag, picking a place to sit, making small talk with the other moms, participating in group discussions, taking notes about Pippa's development on a clipboard—those activities had been stimulating and intimidating.

Now they were routine.

The mall outings had been thrilling, too, but now I was a Certified Mall Outings Expert. I could locate all the changing tables, knew all the best places to amuse a baby, and had eaten with Pippa at the restaurants—alone—too many times to count. Changing Pippa's diaper at Nordstrom had lost that daring glow.

Ever since we first met in the ER, my psychiatrist had been nagging me to have fun. For months, I had insisted that watching television and taking Pippa to the mall was fun enough. It was not. I had always been the sort of person who wanted to throw around a Frisbee, ride the Ferris wheel, and explore new places.

Once again, I had not seen my depression for what it was. All I had seen was that I was bored, but hey, I was making progress.

Four months earlier, I would have blamed these feelings on my medications.

THE MALL TRIP had not given my spirits the boost I craved, but it had done something better: it had acted as the catalyst I needed to take the next steps in my mental health home-improvement projects.

Back at my desk, Pippa still asleep in the carrier, I opened a new document. I had some serious writing to do. Another journal entry was not going to cut it.

I typed, *What makes me bored?* Then I sat back and pondered.

That was the wrong question.

I sat back up and typed, *What makes me feel alive?*

There. *That* was the right question.

I wrote all the words that popped into my head, not worrying about diction or grammar. Run-ons, fragments, gibberish didn't matter—I just needed to chip away at all the noise so I could figure out what I needed to do.

I thought about the moments that had made me feel like my best self over the past two months.

There had been the trip I took with Pippa to the Natural History Museum. Nathan had needed to go to the office on a Saturday, so we roamed the dark corridors, admiring dinosaur bones and the gemstone collection.

Then there was the day we took Pippa to the zoo for the first time. I had not been to the zoo in over a year, and it was amazing to look at it through Pippa's eyes. (She liked the fence outside the zebra enclosure the best.)

And of course, there was our day trip on Thanksgiving to Palm Springs, easily one of the best days of the year. The gathering with the extended Henning family had been great, but even the drive, the act of going someplace new and seeing new roads and different buildings, had made me feel awake and invigorated.

Routines were good. They had helped me start the momentum that the social workers loved to harp about in the hospital. Besides, I could not drag Pippa to Palm Springs every day. But there was a fine line between routine and monotony. The Parent Education class and mall outings had given me as much momentum as they could. Now it was time to introduce something fresh to my life as a stay-at-home mom.

It was time to start a list.

25

MY CONTINUED ADVENTURES WITH MOMENTUM

Less than a month after I was discharged from the hospital, my sister Katherine handed me a paperback with a yellow cover.

"*The How of Happiness*. What is this?"

"The author is a psychologist who studies happiness. In the first part of the book, she explains the science behind happiness. Then there's a multiple-choice test that determines your happiness style."

"My 'happiness style'?"

"There are different things that make people happy, but for each of us, there are certain strategies that maximize our happiness. You can use any of the strategies in the book, but the test helps you figure out the ones that will be the most effective for you."

"I don't have time for this crap."

"It's not crap. I know a lot of people—"

"Is this book about postpartum depression?"

"No, it's—"

"Katherine, I have postpartum depression. Some book with a quiz is not going to make me better. I have to take sertraline. I'm doing cognitive behavioral therapy. I have a serious mental illness. Maybe this book is useful for a person who is healthy, but there's nothing that I can do to change the fact that I have post-partum depression. It's all in my hormones."

"Will you just keep the book in case you decide you want to read it?"

"Fine."

This was not the first time my sister had recommended I read a book. When I was a freshman in college, and Katherine a scrappy third grader with an impressive Beanie Baby collection, she insisted I *had* to read a new book. To humor her, I agreed to try a few chapters. By the next morning, I was a Harry Potter convert. Maybe I should humor her again and read just a few chapters of *The How of Happiness*. If I didn't like it, I could just tell her that I was too busy with Pippa for this sort of self-help book.

Within a few pages, I was forced to admit that my sister was really good at recommending books that I needed at certain junctures in my life. In college, I needed Harry Potter as a break from history classes that focused on war and pestilence. And now, as a new mama, I needed this book to push my mental health to the next level. By the time I reached the test about my happiness style, I was ready with a freshly sharpened pencil and blank notebook.

According to my test results, the three activities that would boost my happiness the most were exercise, learning new things, and projects. These strategies resonated with me. They were the activities that in the past had made me feel like my best self. I dove into the relevant chapters for ideas to implement the strategies.

And then, I did nothing.

Or rather, I continued living the way I had been living: taking my medications, doing my CBT homework, attending the Parent Education class, and going to the mall for a thrill. Instead of being inspired to try new things, I used *The How of Happiness* to validate the way I was already living my life.

Exercise? I took walks every day. That counted.

Learning new things? At Parent Education class, we discussed all sorts of child-rearing matters. That was enough.

And projects? I was knitting a blanket for my new niece. As a stay-at-home mom, that was about all I could handle in the way of projects.

When I first read *The How of Happiness*, I was not ready to make changes. I was like a newborn filly, tripping around on shaky legs. I had to learn how to walk before I could run the Kentucky Derby. But three months had passed since I read *The How of Happiness*. I was ready to pick up the pace. It was time to be proactive in creating some happiness. I needed a bigger project than a baby blanket.

Now I sat at my desk with Pippa napping in the carrier. I opened a new document and typed, in a dramatic font, *The Fifty-Two Museums Project*. Over the next year, I would visit a different museum, botanical garden, or other cultural site every week. Libraries counted. Children's museums did not. The boredom had started because I had gotten into a rut of only leaving the house for Parent Education class and the mall, so it made sense to choose a project that would help me get into the habit of going new places.

I started typing a list of places I could go with Pippa. Art museums, historic homes, gardens . . . As I wrote, my excitement grew.

Pippa sighed and stirred. She would be awake soon.

I kissed the top of her head and whispered, "Baby girl, where should we go first?"

"THAT'S SO COOL," said Fiona, a mom at the Monday Parent

Education class, when I told her about my goal to visit fifty-two places by the end of 2014. "Where have you been?"

"The Huntington, LACMA, Descanso, and the Norton Simon."

"I want to do this, too. We just go to the usual baby classes. I never thought about taking Quinn to an art museum. And what was the other project you mentioned?"

It was early January and the first Parent Education class of 2014. The teacher had asked us to pair up with a mom we did not know very well and share three things about ourselves that the rest of the class probably did not know. Telling Fiona about my projects had felt like a gamble but the gamble had paid off. I had discovered a kindred mom spirit.

"So my other project is the One Hundred Podcasts Project. I started listening to podcasts after Christmas one night when I was bored doing the dishes and wanted some brain candy. I've always thought podcasts were something I'd enjoy but never took the effort to find ones that I liked."

"Which one did you try?"

"NPR's *Pop Culture Happy Hour*. They talked about some new movies and television shows, and it made me feel like a grownup again. I let my brain go stagnant during the first months of motherhood and I'm trying to hit the reboot button, so to speak."

"I should check out some podcasts."

When I first realized I was getting bored, I worried that I would have to quit the Parent Education class to find something new. The Fifty-Two Museums Project, however, had given me a new zest for life. Now that I was visiting new places, I could appreciate the parenting class again. The enthusiasm for one enterprise had spilled over into all areas of my life.

CHURN, churn, back and forth, back and forth. I glanced down at the screen. I had been churning for one minute and eighteen seconds.

I changed the intensity and angle, hoping to make the workout feel a little more exciting. This was important. Ever since she had discovered the art of crawling, Pippa could not be bothered to sit in her stroller while mama took her morning walk. There was too much exploring for her to do. Following a baby around my neighborhood, however, did not exactly count as exercise.

I had joined a new gym and registered Pippa for their little day care center so I could get some cardio on the elliptical machines and stair climbers. That was how I had exercised since college. Today I was on a machine near the gym's exercise studio. Yoga had just ended, and people were filtering into the room for the next class: Zumba.

I had wanted to try Zumba for years and had actually taken a few classes at my old gym right before I got pregnant. I stood in the back of the room so no one would see how ridiculous I looked but then I had trouble seeing what the teacher was doing. No matter. It was still as fun as I had expected.

What I had not expected was how much Zumba would kick my ass. After years of logging miles on the elliptical machine, I assumed I was in good enough shape to dance the grapevine. However, thirty minutes into the hour-long class, I thought my right thigh was going to start convulsing. I needed to leave before I hurt myself.

But what would my classmates think?

I had forced myself to stay until the bitter end, even though my knees started to twitch and my lower back was in agony. There was a woman who looked at least eight months pregnant, effortlessly doing the cha-cha. Surely I could keep my feet shuffling until the end of class.

I went back to Zumba once more before returning to the elliptical machines, where the potential for humiliation was much lower. At the time, I would never have admitted it, but Zumba made me anxious.

A lot had happened since my first attempts at Zumba.

I checked the screen on the elliptical I was currently churning. Less than thirty seconds had elapsed. This was torture. I had to give Zumba a second chance.

I sulked into the half-full studio. The teacher was fiddling with the sound system. As I walked toward the back, I noticed an empty spot in the middle of the room. Before I had time to think, I pivoted and claimed the prime spot. If I was going to try Zumba, I might as well give it my best shot.

"Welcome, everyone." The teacher waited for our attention. "Is this anyone's first Zumba class?"

I self-consciously kept my arms at my side. It had been a couple of years, but still, I was telling the truth.

"We have a new song today. Since we have a couple of minutes before class starts, I thought I'd show you some of the more complicated steps. First, we do a little merengue."

As I shifted my weight from side to side, I forgot where I was or that I was surrounded by strangers. I just lost myself in the movement.

"Then we do a twirl, right to left."

I had forgotten the joy of a simple twirl.

"And then some hip bumps . . ."

I spent a lot of time with Pippa balanced on my hip. It felt so good to move and stretch those muscles in a new way.

The studio was full now.

"All right, let's start with a warm-up. Remember, listen to your body and have fun!"

The dancing started.

To my astonishment, I could actually follow the moves. Dance was something I had wanted to try for most of my adult life, but it had not been my thing when I was a kid. I had preferred soccer cleats and basketball hoops over tutus and jazz hands. I assumed I was too old to start dancing.

Another assumption quickly turned to dust.

I could not execute every move perfectly, but so what? A glowing feeling spread across my chest as my body produced endorphins, glorious, magical endorphins. No wonder *The How of Happiness* had pointed me toward exercise. I just had to find the sort of exercise that made me, literally, want to dance.

As I mastered a new move, I realized I was not just exercising. I was learning. Zumba checked the box for not one but two of my optimal happiness strategies. I had recently signed up for an online Spanish class to incorporate more learning into the stay-at-home mom life, but hey, my brain was not going to object to a little more learning. Especially in a way that was so much fun.

Fun. There was that word again. I had protested when my psychiatrist insisted I bring more fun into my life, convinced it was impossible, but now my body was glowing as if I were racing down a water slide or playing video games with Nathan.

I waved my hands around in the air and cheered with my fellow students at the end of a song. And then, I left.

I had danced for only twenty minutes of an hour-long class, but I could tell my body had reached its limit. If I kept dancing, I would pull a muscle and not be able to come back to this class for who knew how long. That was unacceptable. I needed as much Zumba in my life as possible.

I smiled at the other students as I exited the studio, not caring what they thought about my early departure. All that mattered was that I had been dancing, and that I was going to do it again soon.

I WAS BACK at my desk with Pippa asleep against my chest in the carrier. I had been staring at the same paragraph of my novel for at least five minutes. The story that had been so exciting before I had Pippa now seemed so blah.

I opened a new document and started writing a short story about a woman who had postpartum depression, spent four nights in the hospital, dismantled all her rituals, but definitely was not me because she had red hair and lived in Alaska.

Ugh. I leaned back on the chair and started tapping my foot on the floor. This was not right. I did not want to write a fiction-alized version of my postpartum adventures. I wanted—no, *needed*—to write a memoir.

A memoir? Was I crazy? Only a handful of people knew about my illness. A memoir would completely blow my cover.

That did not matter. I had to do it. The longing to write a memoir about my adventures was in every fiber of every cell of my being. It did not matter that my adventures were still in progress. As I opened yet another document and named it Memoir, something inside of me—my heart, my soul, my purpose—sighed with relief.

I did not know quite where I was going, but I knew the momentum was taking me where I needed to be.

But first, I had to deal with a little something called shame.

26

SHAMEFUL

"Your baby's cheeks are so rosy."

"Yes." I smiled. I knew what was coming next.

"She looks too hot. She must have a fever."

I shrugged. "She just has really pink cheeks. All the time."

The stranger sniffed and looked away.

I kissed the top of Pippa's head and shuffled a few steps closer to the airport security check, suppressing a chuckle. It was early November, just over three months since my discharge, and we were headed to Omaha to introduce Pippa to her Nebraska family.

(Whiplash alert! The last two chapters addressed issues that popped up in December 2013 and early January 2014 during my first year postpartum. This chapter steps back into early November 2013, because I have to set the stage for some big stuff that happened on the recovery front in 2014. Whew, I know, it would be so much easier if my recovery proceeded in a precise, linear fashion. When I was hospitalized, my psychiatrist should have given me some tips on how to heal in accordance with a story-friendly timeline.)

The "concerned" stranger in the airport security line was at least the fifth person who had told me Pippa had a fever in the past two weeks. (To the stranger's credit, Pippa's cheeks were so pink, that one of her many nicknames was "Apple Cheeks.") Practically every time we left the house, someone advised me that Pippa's cheeks were too pink. Usually they had advice: take off her socks; she does not need that blanket; call the doctor.

The first time a stranger admonished me regarding Pippa's pink cheeks, I felt a quick flare of panic. By that time, though, I had internalized the two-step analysis.

Step one: What was the worst thing that could happen? The stranger might think I was an incompetent mother.

Step two: And what was the probability of that? Meh. It did not matter if the stranger thought I was the worst mother in the history of humanity. *I* knew I was a good mother. *I* knew my baby's cheeks were perpetually rosy. *I* knew she was healthy. What a stranger thought was simply irrelevant.

Even the first time a stranger commented on Pippa's complexion, the two-step analysis took all of three seconds to complete. I did not have to hit my internal pause button or force myself to take deep breaths. I did not have to remind myself to think through the questions or struggle to remember what they were. The two-step analysis had become a reflex as automatic as breathing. (It never ceases to amaze me how much I accomplished during the first three months of my recovery.)

Now, as we shuffled toward the security check, the concerned stranger, an older woman with grey hair, made a point of ignoring me, as if she did not want to be associated with my gross and obvious child neglect. Not too long ago, this would have made me feel wretched. Oh no! A stranger thinks I'm a bad mom! But the two-step analysis had cured me of that needless worrying. As I slipped off my shoes and put them in a plastic bin, I did not even need to engage in the two-step analysis. I was too confident in my mothering skills to let one stranger unnerve me.

On the other side of the security check, I pulled my shoes back on. "When do we board?"

"Not for an hour."

I followed Nathan through the terminal, weaving through crowds of harried travelers, Pippa snug in the baby carrier.

"Does this spot look good?"

"Fine by me. Pippa looks sleepy so I'm going to walk a bit."

"Have fun, babe."

I walked past restaurants and bookstores, patting Pippa's back gently. After a few minutes, her legs relaxed and she burrowed against my chest. She was asleep.

The popular majority had wanted Pippa to nap in her crib. When I was in the hospital, Laura the doula had taught Pippa to do just that, but only if we followed an elaborate procedure of rocking and swaddling, gently lowering Pippa into the crib, scooping her back up at the slightest sound of fussing, and repeating until Pippa, too exhausted to protest, surrendered to the nap gods and closed her eyes.

Everyone said this was better for me and Pippa, but my intuition was not so sure. If I held her in my arms, Pippa napped for at least an hour, usually more. In the crib, she napped a half hour or less.

After we left my parents' house and returned home to Pasadena, I had tried to follow through on the nap-time regimen, but Pippa sometimes howled so much, she could not sleep. Then she was exhausted and cranky and had even more trouble falling asleep for her next nap.

A month after my discharge, I decided to listen to my intuition and give up on crib naps. Some of the moms in our weekly class let their babies nap in baby carriers. Pippa had refused to nap in the One True Sling when she was three months old, but she was constantly changing. I pulled the most promising carrier out of a drawer and lo, Pippa loved it. If I nestled her inside and took a walk around the neighborhood, she fell asleep and napped against my chest for two hours.

I looped back through the terminal and stopped to browse magazines. The popular majority might cluck their disapproval, but I knew better. The baby carrier gave us so much freedom. Baby carrier naps made adventures like this trip to Nebraska much more civilized.

Walking back to Nathan, I felt a flutter of apprehension in my stomach. We were supposed to have made this trip several months ago when Nathan's youngest cousin got married. The wedding, though, coincided with my admission into the psych ward.

Nathan told the family he was too slammed at work to come. I did not want them to know the truth. Postpartum depression seemed like the sort of thing that should be kept secret.

Now I could not stop myself from wondering. Did his family suspect the real reason we had missed the wedding? Did they hate me?

These were not rational concerns. Since my first trip to Nebraska, during a gloomy Fourth of July weekend when Nathan and I were still dating, his family had been nothing but warm and accepting. I had never felt like I had to prove my worth. I had never felt like an in-law. Postpartum depression, however, was making me question their love and support just as it had made me think Nathan was mad at me.

I pushed my irrational concerns away. No one would ever know. They would learn the truth only if I told them, and that was certainly not going to happen.

Except that did not feel quite right either.

SOMETHING REEKED. I looked at Nathan. He smelled it too.

Poop.

"Do you think . . ." I glanced at Pippa.

Nathan peeked inside her diaper. "Oh yeah. What do we do?"

"Hand her over." Our plane had just bumped through a patch of turbulence and the seat belt sign was still on, but even if I could get up and roam the cabin, our seats seemed like the best place to change a poopy diaper.

A minute later, Pippa was wearing a clean diaper and Nathan was shaking his head in disbelief. "You made that look easy."

"I'm a bad ass."

Just a few months ago, it had taken me a week to emotionally prepare for an expedition to the Target four minutes from our house. Now I was nonchalantly changing poopy diapers at forty thousand feet.

Yet that pesky feeling of apprehension was in my stomach again.

Nathan took Pippa and popped a bottle into her mouth. I turned and looked out at the clouds. Why was I so nervous? Was I really worried that the Novaks might learn the truth about my postpartum illness? Or was I worried that they would never know?

Huh.

Did I want them to know? That was a weird idea.

Or was it?

Changing a poop diaper at high altitude was a major triumph for any new mother, but for a mom recovering from postpartum depression, it was an extra-stupendous triumph. I did not just want a 100 percent. I deserved some extra credit and a standing ovation.

But did I really need extra credit? Was I a third grader seeking my teacher's approval?

No, of course not. I did not care if strangers thought my baby's cheeks were too flushed, and I did not need someone else's approval of my parenting skills. There are too many different approaches to the business of parenthood. If I tried to get every-one's approval, I would drive myself crazy.

But even if I did not need people's approval, I might still want them to know my story. Wasn't that how meaningful connections happened? A little small talk was necessary, but too much was lonely. Lately, the balance between small talk and honest conver-sation in my life seemed to be out of whack. There was far too much chat about butt creams and bibs and not enough dialogue about the real grit of being human.

I leaned my head against Nathan's shoulder. Pippa was asleep but guzzling her bottle. My stomach twisted again, reminding me that I needed to think some stuff through, and then, as if produced by the acids churning in my stomach, a word floated into my conscious thought.

Shame.

That was the feeling twisting my stomach.

I was ashamed that I had postpartum depression.

I assumed I was supposed to plaster a smile on my face and pretend the past few months had been perfect. But if I did that, I was sticking to small talk and avoiding authentic connections with the people in my life. These past few months—becoming a mother, falling into the darkness of depression, fighting my way back—were the most important months of my life, but I was hiding them from almost everyone I knew.

I shivered and drew my cardigan a little tighter.

I felt like I was supposed to hide my illness, but I also wanted everyone to know. I wanted to climb on top of a mountain and shout, "I have postpartum depression!"

What was right? The thoughts in my head or the impulse in my heart? Share my secret or keep it buried forever?

"OH, CRAP."

"What?"

"We left the formula at the hotel. I only have enough to make this bottle for Pippa." Adrenaline flooded my nervous system, but the two-step analysis quickly washed it away. We were in Nebraska, not Siberia. There were plenty of stores that sold formula.

As Pippa drank, I watched the countryside whizzing by, smiling at the now familiar sight of cornfields and farmhouses surrounded by trees. Nathan had grown up in a town three hours west of Omaha. His dad was a farmer. The drive into rural Nebraska usually felt more restorative than a day at a spa. There was something about the dilapidated red barns that recharged my soul batteries. But today, the butterflies of shame were fluttering around my stomach and ruining the scenery.

This was getting annoying.

Couldn't I just forget the past few months and move on with my life?

We stopped at Walmart for formula and diapers. My stomach kept twisting.

The rental car's tires crunched over dirty snow as we parked outside Nathan's grandparents' house. After shedding our extra layers of coats and snow gear, Pippa cuddled with her great-grandparents. Then aunts, uncles, and cousins started to arrive and Pippa was passed from relative to relative. Nathan's cousin Lindsey came with her husband and baby Bennett, who was just two months younger than Pippa. As soon as she could, Pippa plucked her cousin's pacifier from his mouth, even though she had rejected all pacifiers offered since birth.

The Novaks are a close family, just like the Hennings, with lots of gatherings throughout the year. The house was filled with love and joy, laughter and all the things you expect from a movie montage of a happy family.

Still, my stomach was twisting. The shame would not leave me alone.

"How was the flight with Pippa?" Lindsey and I were swapping war stories in the kitchen.

"Not bad at all. I'm so used to being alone with Pippa that it was nice to have Nathan there the whole time. Even if it was because we were stuck on an airplane."

The first floor of the house had an open plan and was very spacious, but still, everyone seemed to be clustered in the same area. (There must have been chips on the kitchen island.) Though we were all jammed together, elbows jostling, the room did not feel claustrophobic. It was cozy.

"Is she sleeping at night?"

"She was, but now she's up once or twice. I think she's teething."

"Bennett's been teething for months."

A few years earlier, when we were dating, Nathan once told me, "Lindsey is the best person I know."

At first, I was offended. Wasn't *I* the best person Nathan knew? But then I thought about it and decided he was right. Lindsey, who is tall, thin, blonde, and gorgeous, has a quality that most people (including myself) lack, one that makes her even more beautiful on the inside than the outside: she knows how to listen. You never get the feeling that she is bored or trying to think of something clever to say. When you are talking to Lindsey, she is listening with every fiber of her soul.

Talking to Lindsey in the kitchen, surrounded by Novaks, with my stomach in agony, I suddenly knew. This was the right person in the right place at the right time.

I glanced around. Everyone seemed too busy with their own conversations to listen to ours. But even if they were listening, it did not matter.

Leaning closer to Lindsey, I whispered, "I had postpartum depression."

For a nanosecond, I had an intense feeling of vertigo, but then

Lindsey leaned closer and said, "Oh no, that's awful. What was it like?"

"I think the worst part was the insomnia." As I started to describe the highlights of my illness, Lindsey nodded emphatically. I think there were tears in her eyes, but I did not look too closely for fear I'd start crying. I was ready for this conversation, but I was not ready to start sobbing in the kitchen in the middle of a family gathering.

At last, the queasiness left my stomach. This was the conversation I had been aching to have.

Staying in the hospital, taking sertraline, doing cognitive behavioral therapy—all of those things had been instrumental to my recovery. Without them, I would still be lost in the darkness of postpartum depression.

But telling Lindsey? That was something more.

Until I told Lindsey, I thought all the Novaks would hate me if they knew the real reason we had missed the recent wedding. I assumed they would think less of me for having a mental illness. That's not the sort of people they are, but that's what I thought. It was easier for me to assume my in-laws would hate me than to face the truth: I was ashamed of myself for having a mental illness.

So when I told Lindsey that I had postpartum depression, it was not about trusting the Novaks with the truth. If I had been honest with myself, I would have known all along that they would continue to love and accept me no matter how many milligrams of sertraline I needed to sleep at night.

When I told Lindsey that I had postpartum depression, I was finally denying the shame I had been feeling ever since I ran searches about *postpartum insomnia* and ignored the results that mentioned depression.

It was just a baby step. After all, Lindsey was the best listener I knew and she was family. It was not like I had told all the moms at my weekly parenting class.

But it was the baby step my entire body had been urging me to take.

I had left California confident in my skills as a mother. When we returned home, I had a fledging confidence in my value as a human being.

I was starting to let go of the shame.

Could I ever let it go completely?

27

SHAMELESS

As I pulled into the parking lot, I spotted Judy, the teacher of the Parent Education class, getting out of her minivan. If I moved quickly enough, maybe I could talk to her without the other moms seeing. I unceremoniously dumped Pippa into the baby carrier and hustled toward the classroom.

Judy looked up as we approached. "Good morning, my dear. Good morning, Pippa."

"Hi, Judy."

I scanned the parking lot.

A few moms were slowly emerging from their vehicles, but they still needed to unbuckle babies from car seats and gather up diaper bags and purses.

This was my chance.

I took a few steps toward Judy and whispered quickly, "I wanted to let you know that I have postpartum depression."

"Okay." Judy looked me straight in the eyes, and with that one word, she conveyed her support, concern, and love. Although her official job description was "teacher," the word was not strong enough for all the wisdom she imparted. Judy did not advocate for one particular parenting style. Instead, she was the patron saint of acceptance. She knew that all babies marched to their own beat and that there was no single way to be a parent. It was more important to love our children and follow their lead.

I had fretted that Judy would think less of me if she knew the truth about my postpartum depression, but once again, I was projecting my personal insecurities onto someone else.

"I was hoping that you could tell the class that there's a mom who has postpartum depression, and if there's anyone who is struggling herself and would like someone to talk to, you can put us in touch."

"That's very generous of you. I will do that today after snack."

I glanced over my shoulder. My classmates were approaching.

"Thank you." I turned and dashed into the classroom. If I lingered any longer, my anonymity might be compromised.

As I set up camp on the floor—diaper bag, iced coffee, Pippa's favorite teether—my body tingled. Soon, the other moms would know: one of us had postpartum depression.

I chatted with some moms about babyproofing. Maybe soon, when they knew, we could have more important conversations.

We sang "Row, Row, Row Your Boat" and "Matilda the Gorilla." What would the other moms think? What would they say? Would they know it was me?

We gathered around toddler-sized tables and ate crackers and grapes while sneaking spoonfuls of mashed bananas into our babies' mouths. Someone was telling the class about an incident concerning a blowout diaper. Everyone seemed horrified.

They did not know the true meaning of horror.

At last, after the longest two hours of my life, it was time. Judy waited until the room was quiet. "There is a mom here who wants to share that she has postpartum depression. She has very generously offered to speak to any other moms who might have it as well."

The moms nodded. I tried to keep a neutral expression on my face.

One mom raised her hand. "I belong to a group offered by my church, and the leader has some experience working with moms who have postpartum depression. I could share her information if the mom here would like it."

Silence.

This was not what I wanted. I had been hoping for a chorus of "me toos" and "that sucks." Maybe moms would ask questions and commiserate. We could have a really meaningful conversation about maternal mental health. I didn't need a referral to another therapist.

Judy waited and looked around the room.

Silence.

"All right, today's topic is sleep."

That was it? That was all anyone had to say about someone having postpartum depression? There were over twenty moms here. At least one out of seven moms experiences a maternal mood disorder. Surely someone had something more to say.

My throat went dry.

By having the teacher tell the class anonymously that I had postpartum depression, I had reinforced the belief that I still needed to hide my diagnosis from other moms. Worse, I had sent the message to my fellow moms that postpartum depression was far too shameful to speak about openly. It was the sort of thing that could be addressed only with hushed whispers and a series of secret handshakes.

As the other moms vented about their babies' sleep habits, I withdrew further into myself. I was not here to learn about sleep training. I could learn that from a book or the internet. I was here to build friendships, but no one knew the real Courtney. They just knew a pale, sanitized version of myself—the non-PPD version that was safe for public consumption. Friendships built on that version of myself were shallow and unsatisfying. I wanted friends who knew the real me.

I had revealed my secrets to Lindsey in November and a few more friends in December, but now it was January, six months after I was first diagnosed. Most people in my life still had no idea that I was recovering from a mental illness.

Why was I still clinging to secrecy? Partly I worried what other people would think if they knew I took sertraline every day and had spent four days in the hospital's psychiatric unit. Mostly, though, it was a matter of etiquette. People talked about the weather, traffic, and their jobs. On the spectrum of appropriate conversation topics, mental illness ranked far below vomit and poop.

Yet my secret was an anchor pulling my soul down, down, down. If I kept my experiences to myself, shame would cast a shadow over my soul for the rest of my life.

THE NEXT TIME I met with my psychologist, I told him about a ritual that I had noticed and nipped in the bud. (I got anxious if I did not unload the dishes while Pippa was eating breakfast, so I forced myself to tackle that chore later in the day.) I spent a long time talking about that ritual before realizing I needed to talk about something else.

"I told the teacher at my Monday class that I have postpartum depression. I asked her to tell the class that one of the moms had postpartum depression and that if anyone wanted to talk, she could put us in touch."

The psychologist smiled. "That was a wonderful thing for you to do."

"Yeah, but it didn't feel right."

"Say more."

"I think I need to tell the class my story for myself. Like I need to come out of the closet, sort of."

The psychologist tapped his pen against his clipboard. "I think that would be an excellent step for you to take. But first, you'll want to rehearse what you want to say."

"Can't I just wing it?"

"That could be overwhelming and frustrating, especially if afterwards you realize you left out an important part of your story."

"I didn't think of that."

"Why don't you think about what you want to say this week? Write about it, practice saying it at home. Then, next week, you can do a dress rehearsal for me and we can talk about it."

"I like that. Okay, that's what I'll do."

———

Two weeks later, the mothers were seated in a circle on the floor while babies squabbled over toys. Snacktime was over. Judy got everyone's attention and said, "Ladies, Courtney has very bravely decided to share a story about her postpartum experience."

My heart started to pound.

I took a deep breath, ignored the adrenaline flooding my body, and started talking. "About four months after Pippa was born, I was diagnosed with postpartum depression. It started in the hospital after she was born . . ."

As I told the twelve-minute version of my story—the anxiety, the insomnia, the dark thoughts—I tried to make eye contact with the other moms. Most of them were nodding, clearly listening to my every word. A few were crying. No one was paying attention to the babies.

"I'm doing much better now. I still think of myself as having postpartum depression, but I don't feel anything like I did six months ago. And I wanted to thank all of you for being here week after week. This class has been a huge part of my recovery."

At the end of class, moms swarmed around me. I lost track of the hugs and thank yous.

Veronica, my first proper mom friend, said, "You just described my postpartum experiences exactly. I wasn't diagnosed with postpartum depression, but I must have had it."

Another mom said, "Wow, you made yourself so vulnerable doing that."

Vulnerable?

As I strapped Pippa into her car seat, the word kept flipping over in my head. *Vulnerable . . . vulnerable . . . vulnerable.*

Something about that word did not feel right.

AT OUR NEXT SESSION, the psychologist wanted to hear all about my "big revelation" at Parent Education class

"It went great. Better than I thought possible. The anticipation was the toughest part."

My psychologist nodded.

"At the end of class, one of the moms came up to me and said I had made myself really vulnerable."

"If I remember correctly, we talked about that last week. How you thought you were making yourself vulnerable by sharing this part of yourself with the other moms."

"That's right. Before I talked to the class, I thought I was making myself vulnerable."

"And now?"

"The word 'vulnerable' feels weird."

"How so?"

"Well . . ." I pondered my coffee cup. "The word 'vulnerable' suggests that I made myself emotionally naked to everyone and risked getting hurt."

"Yes."

"But . . . well, actually, it was the secrecy that made me vulnerable."

My psychologist nodded, more intensely than usual.

"By telling the class what it was like to have postpartum depression, I realized it did not matter what they thought. It was just important for me to get over the fear of telling them. Sharing my secret did not make me vulnerable . . . it made me *in*vulnerable."

"I have been trying for years to have patients with mental illnesses publicly speak about their experiences. And in over twenty years of practice, not a single patient has wanted to step forward and tell people that they have a mental illness."

"Not one?"

"Not one."

"But why not?"

"The stigma of mental illness is so great, most people think they have to keep their illness a secret forever."

"Huh."

I tapped the side of my coffee cup.

"I want to tell everyone."

THE NEXT WEEK, we had a very different conversation. A conversation I could not have imagined having when I first started cognitive behavioral therapy, but which suddenly felt very, very right.

"I think I'm ready to end therapy."

I braced myself for impact. Was I ready? Truly? What would my psychologist think? Was I sabotaging my recovery? Placing myself in danger?

"That's great!"

"Great?"

"Cognitive behavioral therapy should never last indefinitely. The patient should be helped enough by the therapy to not need it anymore. Or, if the patient is not helped, then the therapist should tell the patient that he thinks it is best that they discontinue the treatment since it is not helping the patient. I am glad you feel ready to end your treatment."

"I do feel ready. I *am* ready."

"Tell me why."

"I'm journaling every day. As issues pop up, I address them. Like that new ritual with the dishwasher. I just stopped the ritual and writing about it helped me come to terms with the anxiety."

"That is critical. All your writing helps rewire your brain."

"It feels that way. The past couple of months, I've been coming here to report my victories and triumphs from the past week, but I don't need you to give me a gold star."

"No, you don't."

"So how do we end therapy? Should this be my last session?"

"It can be, but I think you should spend this coming week journaling about your goals for therapy. What were they? Have we accomplished them? Is there anything else you want to accomplish? Then we can reconvene next week and revisit the possibility of ending weekly therapy. I will always be available if you want to come in for booster sessions."

"I can do that?"

"Of course. I have many patients who come in for booster sessions to deal with an issue that needs some extra help."

The next week, I returned with my latest journal pages.

"I listed all my goals for therapy on the first page."

"*Address feelings about having postpartum depression.* Do you feel like we have done that adequately?"

"Yes. Plus now I am writing the memoir and that is forcing me to really dig into those feelings."

"Very good. *Improve relationship with Nathan.* Do you feel we have done that adequately? I remember you were very nervous that he was angry with you."

"I know. It's weird to think that was just a few months ago. The issues were really all in my head. I don't think there's any more work for me to do on that front."

"From what you tell me, it seems like you have a very healthy, supportive relationship. Okay, very good. *Become the master of my anxiety.* Do you feel like we have done that adequately?"

"More than adequately. I never thought it was possible for me to feel this well. I'm happier now than I have ever been in my life."

"Is that so? Many people will tell you that parenthood actually leads to a decrease in overall happiness."

"I've heard that a lot, but most of my life, I've lived with a constant hum of anxiety. To be free of that . . . it's hard to put into words."

"*Tell people about having postpartum depression.* Do you think that was one of your original goals when you first started therapy?"

"No, definitely not. I wanted to keep all of this a big secret."

"And now?"

"It felt so good telling my class. It was like a weight came off my shoulders."

"By telling your class, you helped vanquish some of the shame you have been feeling."

"I did. I want to keep telling people, and sharing my story, and fighting against the stigma, but I don't need weekly therapy to do that."

"You most certainly do not."

My FINGERS DANCED along the keyboard, words and sentences pouring out of me, until suddenly I felt empty. I saved the document—a much rougher version of the book you are now reading —and reconnected my laptop to the Wi-Fi.

It had been over two months since I told my class that I had postpartum depression and ended weekly therapy with my psychologist. At the one-month mark, I went back for a booster session. It felt like a waste of a perfectly good babysitter. I could not wait to leave so I could go across the street to write at a coffee shop.

I was truly recovered. Thanks to the hours I spent in my psychologist's office, I had conquered my obsessive compulsive rituals, mastered my anxiety, faced the awful feelings from having postpartum depression, and even gathered the courage to tell some people about my illness.

So why did I feel restless? Why did I have this nagging feeling that there was something more that I had to do on the postpartum depression front?

I logged on to Facebook. Maybe I could post something about postpartum depression?

No, that was silly. Facebook was for happy photos, not stories of mental illness.

I started scrolling through my friends' updates and liking photos of babies covered in blueberries and—

This was not why I was here.

I kept coming to Facebook, day after day, usually a half dozen times, to flirt with the temptation that was my status update. I used my account only to post cute photos of Pippa—photos that cropped out the dirty laundry on the floor, the frustration, the aggravation, and, of course, the sertraline in my medicine cabinet. I felt like one of those traveling salesmen with two houses, two wives, and two sets of children.

Lately, the itch to do something more was getting stronger and stronger. There was something else I needed to be doing, but what?

All I knew was that even though my brain was screaming

otherwise, my gut said that Facebook was the first step toward figuring out a way to scratch my itch.

I clicked on the spot to update my status and starting typing:

I FEEL a little weird sharing this on Facebook, but as some of you know, I had postpartum depression. I have been doing awesome for many months and am writing a book about it. Now I want to get involved with increasing awareness and support for moms with PPD, so I thought Facebook was as good as any place to start. Please feel free to share my contact info with anyone you know who might need help! And if you have any ideas for ways I can help, please let me know. Thanks!

I HIT publish and sat back. At last, the fact that I had postpartum depression was a matter of public knowledge.

Now I could stop worrying about what people would think if they found out and get to work.

28

THERE'S ALSO A PODCAST

I picked a shady spot on the grass and spread out my picnic blanket. Pippa tottered toward the swings, and for a few minutes, we had the playground all to ourselves.

Maybe no one was coming.

Then a mom pushing a stroller crossed the street and approached the playground. I wanted to run over and introduce myself, but what if it wasn't her?

"Courtney?"

"Yes!" My stomach flipped, but in a good way. "You must be Maureen."

The first meeting of my postpartum depression support group had begun.

In response to my post about wanting to increase awareness about postpartum depression, my Facebook friends made some supportive comments. I had been secretly hoping someone would reveal that she was a maternal mental health advocate and had a Ten Point Plan to jumpstart my work, but that hadn't happened. Still, posting on Facebook made me think and thinking made me write and writing shed light on what I needed to do.

When I was a patient in the psychiatric ward, I assumed that once I was back in the real world, there would be plenty of ways for me to meet other moms who had postpartum depression. It was, after all, the most common complication of childbirth, and I lived in Pasadena, a large city adjacent to Los Angeles, one of the biggest and most progressive cities in the world. Finding a group would not be a problem.

Except it was.

There was a weekly support group led by a psychologist. It cost money, and between the psychiatrist, psychologist, and medications, surely I was already spending enough on my recovery. But more importantly, I worried that too many cooks would spoil the soup. I did not want advice that might undermine the progress I was making in therapy.

All I wanted was a way to informally meet with other moms who could relate to my illness, but that mommy group did not exist. Not in Pasadena or even Los Angeles.

Since coming out of the mental illness closet, I had been able to talk about postpartum depression with my friends and family. That helped a little, but I wanted more. I could not get the idea out of my head that there should be a local mom group dedicated to the topic of postpartum depression.

So I started one myself. I did not know what I was doing, but I did it anyway. I created an account on Meetup, filled in all the information for a new group, and waited for members to join. Within a week, we had a half dozen members.

Maureen sat down on my picnic blanket while her newborn snoozed in the stroller. "Thank you so much for starting this group."

"I've been thinking about it for a long time."

"Yeah, I could not imagine starting something like this right now." Maureen nodded toward her newborn. "I can't remember exactly what you said in your bio. Do you still have postpartum depression?"

"I still see my psychiatrist once a month and I take sertraline and mirtazapine, but I think of the illness as something in the past tense."

"I was just diagnosed last week but I saw it coming. I've struggled with depression in the past . . ."

Over the next hour, we shared our stories. There were a lot of similarities, but also lots of differences. Yet despite the differences, it seemed like Maureen understood everything I was saying more than anyone else I knew. It turned out she felt the same way.

"This might sound weird," she said, picking at a clump of grass, "but I haven't been able to talk about this with anyone else. We've just met, but it's like you already know me better than most of my friends."

No one else attended that first meeting—or the second, or the third. For the first three meetings, it was just me and Maureen, even though a dozen other moms had joined the group online.

But I was not about to give up. For months, my body had been telling me to do this. Now that I had started, I had too much momentum to stop.

"Well, I guess no one is coming today." I smiled at my baby. "Oh well, let's take a walk."

The group's online membership had been growing, but attendance was still spotty. After those first few meetings with Maureen, twenty other moms had eventually attended a support group meeting. Some moms came once and that was all the validation they needed. Other moms attended every meeting for several months in a row. Sometimes it was just me and one mom; other times, there would be four or five attendees.

Two moms had RSVP'd for today's meeting, but one had cancelled first thing in the morning. She had been up all night with a sick baby. The other mom had not shown up. Her night had presumably been so bad, she could not even deal with email.

I was disappointed. The conversations that happened during postpartum depression support group always left me feeling invigorated and inspired. But I was not bitter. I understood too well how unpredictable life with a baby could be. Naptimes shifted. Teething upset the most carefully laid plans. And don't get me started on blowout diapers.

It is difficult to get out of the house with a baby. Add in a little postpartum depression or anxiety, and leaving the house can feel downright impossible. It was a miracle that moms were ever able to attend our humble little support group.

I crossed the street and wandered across Caltech's campus. I like to walk there at least a few times a year on the off chance that I might absorb some spare brain cells from the next Einstein. Also, the scenery is not too shabby. The campus architecture is a mix of gargoyles and Spanish tiles, with plenty of sculptures and fountains watching over the students.

My thoughts wandered. Maybe I needed to schedule more meetings at different times for the postpartum group. That way, more moms could attend. I could host meetings at night for the working moms and throw in the occasional Saturday gathering. I could even schedule meetings outside of Pasadena to help moms in other parts of Los Angeles. If the group got big enough, we could do something elaborate, like spend an evening at a Dodgers game, or have a carnival for the entire family . . .

I parked the stroller and picked up my baby. "Look, turtles!"

In the middle of the Caltech campus, there are two man-made ponds connected by a tiny trickle of a stream. Dozens of turtles call this spot home. One pond is at a slightly higher elevation than the other. To a human, it is just a minor slope, but for a tiny turtle, it is quite the incline. As I pointed, one turtle, smaller than the rest, was trying to climb up the stream that connected the lower and upper ponds. He had his work cut out for him, going against the current up a hill, like a salmon headed back to ancient breeding grounds.

"Ooh, hang on little guy, you've got it."

The turtle lost his footing and slipped back a few inches.

"Keep going!"

He tried a new route and avoided a treacherous rock.

"Just a few more feet."

We watched, mama and baby, as the turtle reached the top of the hill and slid into the upper pond.

"Hooray for turtle!"

We said good-bye to the turtles and headed toward the coffee shop. My thoughts returned to the support group. My schemes about multiple locations and carnivals were probably more than I could manage. Those sorts of efforts would deplete my energy and take away time from the activities that made me feel like my best self.

Still, my brain kept churning. There was an idea trying to make its way out of my subconscious, a little turtle fighting against the current . . .

What if I started a podcast?

A podcast? Me?

I bumped the stroller down a curb.

With a podcast, I could help moms who were too busy—or too depressed—to make it to support group. Naptime might conflict with our gatherings, but a podcast could be listened to at any time of day.

My body started to tingle with the possibilities.

With a podcast, I could help any mom with an internet connection. There were blogs and online support groups dedicated to improving maternal mental health, and I am a great believer in the written word, but there is something so intimate about hearing the inflection of someone's voice. Words were spoken aloud many millennia before they were ever written. To speak and listen is in our DNA.

Sharing my story with my parenting class had been an essential part of my recovery from postpartum depression. Could I heal even more if I told my story on a podcast?

I bent over and adjusted the blankets in the stroller. This was ludicrous. I was a writer, not a broadcaster. I did not know the first thing about podcasting.

Tightening the straps on the car seat, I shoved the thought of a podcast out of my mind. I was writing this memoir and running a peer support group. I did not have the time to think about another project.

That turtle of an idea, however, had gone to great effort to drag itself out of the lower pond of my subconscious. It was not about to slip away quietly.

I WATCHED as the numbers ticked up—20 percent, 45 percent, 70 percent—until the screen announced "Upload Complete." The audio file of my first podcast episode was ready to go. I just had to hit the publish button.

Should I do it?

It was not perfect. I had stuttered and stumbled, mispronounced all sorts of words, and had zero credentials to justify this indulgence.

So what?

I moved the cursor and clicked on the publish button.

The hourglass icon started to turn, and then a pop-up screen appeared.

Your podcast will be available shortly.

I ran out of the bedroom. Nathan was watching television on the other side of the house.

"I did it! I published my first podcast episode."

"Way to go, babe. How was it?"

"It felt weird. But good."

Good was an understatement. Publishing my first podcast episode felt satisfying, magical and right—very, very right, as if some creative force was using me for a greater good. The most difficult part had actually been deciding the podcast was something I wanted to do. I spent about three months trying to come up with reasons for *not* starting a podcast. My brain offered dozens of reasons to ignore the idea: no one would listen; I did not know how to market the show; I had no experience with podcasting; I did not have time to learn some new craft; I needed to focus on writing my book; I would run out of things to say; people would get sick of my story and want to listen to interviews but I did not know the first thing about conducting an interview; and so on and on and on.

No matter what my head said, my intuition kept screaming at me to start the podcast. It was something I *had* to do.

Once I got started, everything fell into place. Lots of people have written How to Podcast blog posts. After reading a few, I invested in a $50 microphone that looked like the love child of a robot and a snowball and downloaded free recording software.

For the very first episode, I set up a temporary recording studio in our backyard. This means I put my laptop on a dirty patio table, plugged the microphone into my laptop, and hit the record button. Then I launched into the story of my adventures of postpartum depression. I babbled for a few minutes and then stuttered mid-sentence.

Crap. I stopped recording and opened a new file. Take two!

I started again at the beginning. This time, after a few minutes, my mind went blank. After several seconds of silence, I hit the pause button again and opened a new file.

Take three!

Around take five or six, I realized I was going to have to either embrace imperfection or abandon the entire enterprise. I watched a bird hopping alongside our pool. Why did I think I could host a podcast?

Because somewhere out there, there was a mom who needed to hear my story. Statistically, I knew there were thousands and thousands of women suffering with postpartum depression but I was not thinking about the thousands. That was too overwhelming. I was thinking about one. Just one mom. If I could help one mom, then it did not matter how many words I mispronounced or how screechy my voice sounded.

I hit the record button again but this time, I kept talking for forty-three minutes and forty-four seconds.

Although I listened to a lot of podcasts, I did not have a model for my show. The podcasts I loved were about pop culture or the indie author industry. They did not talk about mental illness. The week that I launched my show, Dr. Katayune Kaeni, a psychologist in Claremont (thirty minutes from Pasadena) launched another podcast about maternal mental health. We were the pioneers. I love that we are practically neighbors. It's as if the Universe wanted a podcast about maternal mental health and broadcast that idea to a small area in Southern California. Dr. Kat and I were both listening.

After reporting the news of the successful upload to Nathan, I did a nerdy dance move to burn off some exuberance and ran back to my computer. There was a new pop-up screen. It was official. *Adventures with Postpartum Depression* was no longer just a draft of a book on my computer. It was a podcast that any person could download or stream.

"Ooh, I can see where my listeners live."

"That's not at all creepy."

I glared across the room at Nathan. "I can't see their addresses. Just countries and cities."

According to the stats on my account, I had listeners in Los Angeles, Omaha (presumably a Novak), and Atlanta (my friend

274

Kendall) but also more surprising places like Texas, Oregon, Wisconsin and even Brazil.

"Brazil?" Nathan said.

"Yes, even moms in Brazil get postpartum depression."

Now it was Nathan's turn to glare across the room. "I know that. I'm just impressed. You're a big deal in Brazil."

"Actually, from these statistics, it looks like I have several listeners in Brazil. And a few in Africa."

"*Africa?*"

"Kenya and Somalia. Then Australia, England, Canada, China, Poland . . ."

I don't know how my listeners found me, but they did. Only a few hundred people were listening to my episodes, but *holy crap*, a few hundred people were listening to my episodes!

Postpartum depression was the worst experience of my life. It broke me into a thousand pieces and convinced me that my life was over.

But I put myself back together, stronger and better than ever. I did not just vanquish the postpartum depression symptoms. I annihilated the anxiety that had been terrorizing me for almost my entire adult life.

I did not just recover my old self. I rescued and claimed my authentic self.

The self who loves to lift her daughter in the air to play airplane.

The self who writes, dances, and starts support groups.

The self who feels called to start a podcast about postpartum depression and actually heeds the call.

Postpartum depression nearly ended my life, but I emerged from the illness more alive than ever. I am so glad I had postpartum depression.

EPILOGUE

I was a little misleading in the last chapter. You probably assumed I was showing Pippa the turtles, but Pippa was actually at preschool. My baby in the stroller was Julian.

In February 2015, about six weeks before Pippa's second birthday, Nathan and I decided we were ready to have another baby. It was Valentine's Day. We were having lunch at a lovely Italian bistro while my parents watched Pippa.

Ten days later, I took an early detection pregnancy test. When I saw the plus symbol, I felt a rush of pure, unadulterated joy.

The psychiatrist yanked me off my medications. By that time, I had reduced my mirtazapine dose to 15 milligrams at bedtime, but a few months earlier, after a particularly rocky menstrual cycle, the psychiatrist had bumped my sertraline dose from 100 to 150 milligrams a day. For the rest of the pregnancy, I took a medication called buspirone that he thought would be safer for pregnancy.

The nausea hit around week seven, just as it had with Pippa, except now I had a toddler who did not understand why Mama was spending so much time leaning over the bathroom sink. I had to enroll her in a neighborhood day care two blocks from our house so I could spend my days moaning in bed.

I stopped writing, stopped going to Zumba, and stopped scheduling meetings for the peer support group. The nausea had stolen all my energy. It seemed like a good time to schedule a booster session with my psychologist.

"I'm worried that I'm getting depressed again."

"Tell me more."

"All I do is puke all day. I had to stop working on my memoir. I had started taking guitar lessons"—Nathan had bought me a guitar for Christmas; I'd always wanted to learn—"but I quit because I couldn't practice. I've also been painting a lot but I don't have the energy for that anymore. I'm not doing anything. Oh God, can I have the trash can?"

My psychologist waited patiently as I heaved into the waste bin.

"Would you like a toothbrush?"

"That's okay, I'm used to it."

"Are you sure? I have this travel toothbrush that comes with the toothpaste already on the brush."

I declined, worried the toothpaste might make me puke more, and popped an anti-nausea sucking candy instead.

"So you are worried you might be sinking into a depression because you are nauseous all the time and not able to do anything."

"That's right."

"I don't think you are depressed. I think you are just experiencing what many other women experience during the first trimester. You are just more sensitive to the possibility of feeling depressed because of what happened after your last pregnancy."

"So I'm feeling miserable because I'm pregnant, but I'm not depressed?"

"Correct."

That's what I had thought, but wanting to stay on top of my mental health, I had scheduled the appointment. When the receptionist asked if I wanted to schedule another session, I said the one visit with the psychologist had been enough. As I drove away, I knew in my heart that I had the support team and tools I needed to stay as healthy as possible during this pregnancy.

I WAS WEARING a hospital gown and sitting on the edge of a table as the anesthesiologist tried to insert an epidural. A student nurse ran out of the operating room and fainted in the hallway. This caused a bit of a commotion.

"Is that student nurse coming back for the C-section?" By now, my epidural was in place and I was lying on my back, pleasantly numb and excited to meet my baby boy.

"I don't know," the assistant surgeon said. "But if *you* say you don't want her to return, then she won't be allowed back in the OR."

"Yeah, let's not let her back."

Nathan was allowed into the operating room and sat near my head. "Well I didn't expect that to happen. I was worried you'd think I'd fainted."

"I knew it wasn't you because I heard the door slam. But I was worried you would think something had gone wrong with me. Oh hey, I just noticed. The nausea is gone."

It had only taken nine months, a fainting nurse, and an epidural to end the nausea. I had thought it would wear me down into at least a mild depression, but it had not. Despite spending the majority of the first, second, and third trimesters supine in bed, napping and reading novels, I had built up enough momentum to stay in relatively good spirits through the pregnancy. I was too sick to keep the peer support group going, or to keep working on this book, or to keep going to Zumba, but I did what I could: I read, I journaled every day, I listened to podcasts, I gave Pippa all the snuggles her heart desired, and I knit Julian a blanket and cardigan. That was enough.

"All right, Courtney, you are going to feel pressure as I make the first incision." My obstetrician was as excited for the end of this pregnancy as I was. She knew I was at risk for another round of postpartum depression and that the nausea was not doing anything for my mental health.

But I was ready to do everything I could to squelch any signs of postpartum depression. We had hired a night nurse for the first month postpartum. I had decided to skip breastfeeding entirely, so I would be able to sleep all night. Nathan was taking a full month of paternity leave. I would have lots of support so I could rest and recover from the C-section.

I had a new psychiatrist (I'd never clicked with the first), and we had decided I would get back on sertraline within a few days of delivery. I already had an appointment scheduled so I could see her in a couple of weeks. I was not taking any chances with my mental health.

At home, hanging in a prominent place, I had a checklist of all the things I needed to do every day to feel like my best self: write, sing, go outside, open the windows, shower, listen to music, drink tons of water, stretch, get silly with Pippa, and doodle, draw, knit, or craft. Even with the night nurse's help, I would still be exhausted. I knew it would be easy to forget the little things that made a huge difference. Also, the list was there for Nathan's reference. I warned him, many times, that if I stopped doing the things on the list, he needed to call for reinforcements.

"Okay, Courtney, you are doing great. He's almost here. You are going to feel a tugging."

I did not know what to expect, but then I felt something that can really only be described as a tugging at my internal organs. It was weird.

Someone placed my baby on my chest, his head close to my neck. Julian James Novak. He was big—almost ten pounds—and his cheeks were deliciously fat. Nathan and I would later overhear the maternity nurses gushing about the "huge baby."

This delivery was nothing like the first. I never felt a contraction, and I did not have to push anything out my vagina. Still, I was exhausted and felt empty. As I kissed Julian's head and counted his digits, I noticed that once again, I was not experiencing the legendary "fireworks."

I smiled and told Julian how much I loved him. I did not need fireworks to feel connected to my baby. After all, we had shared every breath for the past nine months.

IN LATE JANUARY, when I was not quite three months postpartum, I had trouble sleeping one night. Until that night, I had been doing great: I was walking every day, getting outside and going places with Julian, taking Pippa to preschool and meeting the other parents, writing again, seeing friends and family, and taking plenty of time for self-care. I kept close tabs on my mental health but detected nary a flicker of depression or anxiety—until that night in January.

I tossed and turned and slept only a few hours but decided it must have been a fluke. Maybe I was experiencing a year's worth of PMS all at once.

The next night, it happened again, and then a third night.

This was nothing, I thought. Just some PMS. No need to overreact. Besides, I was seeing my psychiatrist in a few weeks. No need to call her about a little PMS. I just needed to keep doing the things on my self-care list.

I checked the list and remembered I had not yet journaled

that day. I wrote about the way I felt and started to think about my body. There was nothing bothering me emotionally or mentally but I could feel a physical sensation of anxiety: accelerated heartbeat, constricted lungs, that creepy-crawly feeling on my skin.

I stopped writing.

I had watched this horror movie before. I knew how it ended.

One minute later, I was leaving a voicemail for my psychiatrist.

We decided to bump my sertraline dose from 100 to 150 milligrams. I had continued taking the buspirone after delivery but agreed I should switch back immediately to mirtazapine. That night, I took the mirtazapine, slept beautifully, and woke up feeling like myself.

I never again felt a flicker of a maternal mood disorder.

WHEN JULIAN WAS six months old, I woke up one day and decided it was time to restart my mom-to-mom support group. I was not struggling with depression, anxiety, or any of the symptoms I had after Pippa was born. I just knew in my gut that it was time to reboot the group.

Restarting the group gave me the idea for the podcast. The podcast made me feel more serious about the group. Instead of erratic meetings at local parks, it needed a regular time and permanent home. I contacted Karen Stoteraux, the owner of The Family Room in San Marino, California, a local business that has birthing and baby classes, and she was thrilled to let me use the space. On Thursday afternoons, you can find me there, facilitating the group. I imagine I will keep leading the group for many years to come, until another mom is eager to take over.

Then I'll start a peer support group for menopause.

I HAVE A LOT OF HOUSEPLANTS—AT least twenty—and my collection keeps growing. Mostly I choose easy plants that are tough to kill, but sometimes, even the most mellow tangle of ivy can get a little fussy. As the weather changes, and the thermostat fluctuates, they need different amounts of water. Sometimes they demand repotting so they can spread their roots. My favorite divas like to be rotated to different shelves and ledges to get a change in sunlight intensity. I have to pay attention to my houseplants and make tiny adjustments so they can flourish.

My mental health is a lot like my houseplants.

I know the basic things that my soul needs, but just as I sometimes have to try a different shelf for a plant, or even give it some time on the front porch, I need to tweak and occasionally overhaul the things I do to feel like my best self. You can't water a plant once and assume that is all it needs. You can't nourish your soul once and then leave it alone. The soul requires even more careful tending than the most elaborate collection of houseplants.

Like my houseplants, which require water, light, and soil, my soul has some absolute needs: writing, meaningful relationships, time for fun, lots of physical movement, learning, and projects. The ways that I satisfy these absolutes, though, shift.

These days, I'm doing a lot of Zumba. I would not be surprised if I'm dancing for the rest of my life. Then again, I also would not be surprised if I become a water aerobics fanatic or a regular at the roller skating rink. I just need to keep moving in ways that feel exhilarating and fun.

I also do a lot of "making." Writing is my biggest creative pursuit, but there's also cooking, baking, painting, knitting, crocheting, embroidery, sewing, gardening, drawing, and on and on. Every night, after the kids are in bed, I take a moment to consider whether my hunger to make is satiated. If it isn't, I bust out a craft project or grab my pens and doodle while watching reality television with Nathan.

I still have a self-care checklist hanging in a prominent spot in the little nook that functions as my home office. I check it regularly to make sure I am staying on top of my well-being. When I was single and childless, I did not have to be deliberate about my mental health. Even with a busy job, I had enough free time to fit in the activities—hiking, road trips, spa dates—that recharged my batteries for another day in the lawyer salt mines.

I don't have that luxury anymore. Motherhood is time-consuming. I don't just feed myself. I have to convince my kids that breakfast is actually in their best interest. I don't just sleep at night. I have to make sure my kids are well rested. And do not get me started on the matter of skin. Some days, it feels like all I do is manage sunblock distribution.

Postpartum depression helped me become a better version of myself, but I am not done evolving. Motherhood tests my limits constantly, nudging me toward an even stronger version of myself.

Recently, I found it was getting more and more difficult to control my kids. I often lost my temper and screamed. That made me feel terrible. I started reading books, hoping to find a way to trick Pippa and Julian into being little obedient androids, but they refused to mold their personalities to my vision. After a lot of soul searching, I realized that my expectations were unreasonable. I had to let go, become more patient, and learn to live in the moment with my babies. Within weeks of accepting the fact that my kids are far wiser than me, I stopped screaming, relaxed, and started to really enjoy motherhood.

But that's another adventure.

RESOURCES

If you need immediate help, please call 1-800-273-TALK (1-800-273-8255) to reach a twenty-four-hour crisis center in your area.

<u>Online Resources:</u>

Postpartum Support International (PSI) is an organization dedicated to increasing awareness, prevention, and treatment of maternal mood disorders throughout the world. The PSI warmline is a toll-free telephone number that anyone can call to get basic information, support, and resources. Their number is 1-800-944-4PPD (1-800-944-4773). The PSI website, http://www.postpartum.net, has a lot more information.

Postpartum Progress was a nonprofit that started as a blog. Sadly, they ceased operating in early 2017, but the posts on their website are very informative. Everything is still available at http://www.postpartumprogress.com. I especially recommend "The Symptoms of Postpartum Depression & Anxiety (in Plain Mama English)" available at http://www.postpartumprogress.com/the-symptoms-of-postpartum-depression-anxiety-in-plain-mama-english.

The Postpartum Mama is my favorite place to learn about self-care. After a dangerous and traumatizing birth, Graeme Seabrook had postpartum depression and anxiety. Since her recovery, she has become passionate about helping women become pros at taking care of themselves. Start with her website, http://www.postpartummama.org/. On Facebook, she runs the Self Care Squad: https://www.facebook.com/groups/selfcaresquad/. Graeme is also a life coach and recently opened the virtual doors to The Mom Center, a community where mothers feel like people. Learn more at https://themomcenter.mn.co/.

Olivia Scobie has a ton of resources available on her website, http://oliviascobie.com/, including her free *DIY Postpartum Mood Support Planning E-book*. She also offers a free online therapy course as part of a nonprofit that she runs in Toronto. Although the work of that group is specifically for Toronto residents, anyone can use the online courses. Learn more at https://www.postpartumsupporttoronto.com/copy-of-register-for-groups-events.

The Perinatal Mental Health Alliance for Women of Color is a division of PSI dedicated to providing a safe space for clients, families, and professionals of color around perinatal mental health. They are in the process of building a resource list of professionals of color who provide perinatal mental health services. Learn more at https://www.pmhawoc.org.

Tessera Collective is a community for girls and women of color. They have an online support group and a therapist directory. Visit their website at http://www.tesseracollective.org/.

Podcasts

Adventures with Postpartum Depression by Courtney Henning Novak: http://PPDadventures.com. This is my show, so I'm a bit biased, but I think podcasts are a great way to listen to stories and feel less alone. I share interviews with moms who currently have or have conquered a maternal mood disorder. I also share updates on my personal adventures with motherhood and mental health. Warning: I swear. A LOT.

Mom & Mind by Dr. Katayune Kaeni: http://www.momandmind.com/. Dr. Kat is a psychologist who experienced postpartum depression after the birth of her first child. This podcast discusses the things we wish we had been told before we tried to get pregnant and make the transition to motherhood. It includes personal stories as well as interviews with advocates working to change the landscape of maternal mental health.

The Natural Postpartum Support Podcast by Katie Flores: https://katiefloreshealth.podbean.com/. Katie is a certified holistic health coach and postpartum depression survivor. Her monthly podcast addresses natural approaches to treating maternal mood disorders.

Useful Books

Postpartum Depression for Dummies by Shoshana S. Bennett, PhD. This book was my bible during my recovery. I always have several copies on hand to give to moms (or dads!) in need. If I could give one book to every mom in the world, this would be it.

Pregnant on Prozac: The Essential Guide to Making the Best Decision for You and Your Baby by Shoshana S. Bennett, PhD. This book debunks a lot of the myths surrounding pregnancy and medications.

The Postpartum Husband: Practical Solutions for Living with Postpartum Depression by Karen Kleiman, MSW. I did not come across this book until long after my recovery, but I think it would have been very helpful for Nathan. Honestly, it's also helpful for the mama. It's a very quick, easy read.

Bottled Up: How the Way We Feed Babies Has Come to Define Motherhood, and Why It Shouldn't by Suzanne Barston. I did not discover this book until after I had fully recovered from postpartum depression. When I learned about it, I still had some lingering feelings about the way breastfeeding ended for me and Pippa. Barton researched, examined, and probed the politics and science of breastfeeding. Her book put all my crappy guilty feelings to rest and then helped me feel good about my decision to skip breastfeeding entirely with Julian.

The Happiest Mom: Ten Secrets to Enjoying Motherhood by Meagan Francis. Francis applied happiness research to the art of motherhood and showed how a mom in the trenches can still enjoy her life. This is the book that inspired me to read more about postpartum depression.

The How of Happiness: A New Approach to Getting the Life You Want by Sonja Lyubomirsky. This book helped me identify the strategies to maximize my happiness. I still refer to it. It jumpstarted my own self-care practice with lots of practical tips. One of my favorites: make a "Don't Do Now" list.

Memoirs
Down Came the Rain: My Journey through Postpartum Depression by Brooke Shields. This is the memoir that helped me acknowledge and process my feelings about having postpartum depression. Shields writes about her struggles with infertility, her

descent into the darkness, and her recovery, including the issues she had with being medicated.

Dancing on the Edge of Sanity by Ana Clare Rouds. I highly recommend this memoir for health professionals as well as any person who wants to learn more about postpartum depression, anxiety, and maternal mental illnesses. This is an important story about what can go wrong when health professionals do not understand postpartum depression. While I think my time in the hospital was the best thing possible for my health, Rouds' doctors were a bit too eager to have her committed. If you are presently in the throes of a maternal mental illness yourself, I think you should probably wait until you are a bit steadier on your legs before reading this one.

The Warrior within Me: My Postpartum Story by Tabitha Grassmid. A short read packed with a ton of honesty and inspiration. Grassmid describes her journey from having postpartum depression to becoming a maternal mental health advocate.

From Shattered Dreams: My Journey through Postpartum Psychosis by Dorothy R. Ruhwald. A very candid story about Ruhwald's descent into postpartum psychosis and depression. This memoir includes biblical quotes and explores the ways that Ruhwald's faith helped her recovery. Postpartum psychosis is greatly misunderstood and this book helped me understand better what actually happens to a mom with this illness.

Making Mom Friends

If you live in the Pasadena area, I highly recommend the parent education classes offered by Pasadena City College. These are free, non-credit courses open to all caretakers. These classes expose caretakers to different philosophies and strategies for parenting. I made several amazing friends through these classes.

Learn more at https://pasadena.edu/academics/divisions/noncredit/our-programs/parent-education.php. Check your local community college to see if they offer a similar program.

I also made several friends through my local chapter of the MOMS Club. Visit http://www.momsclub.org/ to find your local chapter.

MOPS is another great way to meet moms. MOPS stands for Mothers of Preschoolers, but it's also for moms with newborns and babies. MOPS International helps moms to realize their potential as mothers, women, and leaders. The groups are operated by local Christian churches and yes, Jesus gets mentioned a lot. Even though I am not religious, I belonged to my local MOPS group for two years and really enjoyed the experience. Check out http://www.mops.org/ to learn more.

Meetup is another great way to connect with parents. I use Meetup to run my weekly mom-to-mom support group. Find ways to connect with local parents at https://www.meetup.com/.

If you are ever in the Pasadena area, please join us at the free postpartum mom-to-mom support group at The Family Room in San Marino. We currently meet Thursdays from 1-2:30 p.m. but please visit http://www.familyroomcenter.com/ for the most current information.

Events

The Climb Out of the Darkness is an international event that raises awareness of maternal mood disorders. It is held as close as possible to the longest day of the year to help shine the most light on perinatal mood and anxiety disorders. Participants climb mountains and hike trails (or sometimes just walk through an air conditioned mall) to symbolize the rise out of the darkness of a mental health crisis. I did a solo climb in June 2014 and it was a wonderful opportunity to reflect on my journey. In 2015, I had too much morning sickness to climb, but I joined Team Los Angeles in 2016 and got to meet a lot of wonderful moms. To learn more, visit http://www.postpartum.net/.

QUESTIONS FOR THE TRADITIONAL
BOOK CLUB

By "traditional" book club, I mean the type of book club I belonged to before I had Pippa. It involved a lot of quiches and baked goods. Also, wine. A couple of members were moms, but most of us were not.

1. What motivated the author to write this book? Would you recommend this book to a friend? To a woman expecting her first child?
2. What do you think caused the author's postpartum depression? Was there one main trigger for her depression, or was it more of a perfect storm?
3. Did this memoir give you a better understanding of maternal mental illnesses? Of anxiety? Depression? Obsessive compulsive disorder?
4. Did this book change any of your opinions about motherhood? About breastfeeding? Mental health?
5. Were any parts of the author's journey difficult for you to read?
6. Why did the author decide to call this book *Adventures with Postpartum Depression*? Do you like the title?

7. Ultimately, the author is glad she had postpartum depression. Does this make sense to you? Can you relate? Or do you think she's totally nuts?

QUESTIONS FOR MOM GROUPS

You belong to a moms' group that actually has time to talk about books? That's awesome! Can I join? These questions are a little more specific for the mom crowd, in case you want to dig deeper with your discussion.

1. Before reading this book, what experience, if any, did you have with maternal mood disorders? Had you read any other books on the subject? Talked to friends who suffered from a mood disorder? Suffered from one yourself?

2. When you were pregnant, did your doctor give you any information about maternal mood disorders? What about the pregnancy books you read or any classes you attended?

3. Did the author's description of labor and delivery dredge up any memories or feelings for you? Do you think your experience giving birth affected your transition into motherhood?

4. Hormones. We all have them. We all respond differently to hormonal fluctuations. How did your

hormones treat you during pregnancy? The first postpartum months? Has your body completely bounced back from pregnancy? Or have things seemed to change permanently, e.g., did the pregnancy hormones change your menstrual cycle? (It's okay to rant.)

5. Why do you think the author tried to hide the way she was struggling during those first postpartum months? Could you relate?

6. The author experienced dark, disturbing thoughts about hurting her baby and herself. How did reading about these thoughts make you feel?

7. How do you think you would have felt if your doctor asked you to admit yourself for psychiatric care when your baby was four months old?

8. After the author was discharged from the hospital, her baby did not want to breastfeed. If you had been in the same position, what would you have done? Did you feel any societal pressure to breastfeed? Would you have been devastated if you could not breastfeed?

9. As part of her cognitive behavioral therapy, the author had to stop checking her baby during the night. Do you check your children after they go to bed? Do you think checking a child would increase or decrease your anxiety?

10. The author found herself getting bored when her baby was about eight months old. Have you ever battled boredom as a mother? If so, how do you cope?

11. To overcome postpartum depression, the author focused on improving her self-care. As a mother, do you take care of yourself? How? Or if you are not taking care of yourself, what would you like to do if you had all the time and money in the world?

12. Despite her experiences with postpartum depression,

the author decided to have another baby. Was she being reckless? Brave? Or had she gained enough self-knowledge to know what she was doing?

13. This book is called *Adventures with Postpartum Depression*. What about motherhood? Would you call it an adventure? Or something else?

ACKNOWLEDGMENTS

Thank you, Mom and Dad, for everything from birth to the present day. I would not have been able to recover without your love and support. I could write pages more of gratitude for all you have done and continue to do, but I'm told the Acknowledgments page should be shorter than the book. I love you!

Thank you, Katherine/Pom Pom/Spucky, for listening, talking, laughing, and being ridiculously awesome.

Thank you, Matt and Sara, for all the delicious foods you brought when I was in postpartum hell. Your visits and love kept me going.

Teddy Manolova! I'm so excited I wrote a book because I get to thank you publicly for being my matchmaker. Thank you for nagging and hounding me until I finally relented and agreed to meet Nathan. You were right. Game, set, match. You did find my husband.

Kendall Lioon, my guardian angel, I'm actually crying as I write this because you saved my life. I refused to call my doctor until I read your email. You are the sort of person who can drink a martini in a burning building, so when you told me to get help,

I knew it was time to hit the panic button. Thank you for being you.

To Kelly Finck, I know you did your best to keep me afloat during the postpartum months. Silly me for ignoring my best friend's emails! I know however far apart we live, and however busy we get with our kids, you will always be my dude.

And my other Dartmouth girlfriends—Shialing Kwa, Amy Salomon, and Rebecca Cook-Dubin—thank you for all your love and support during my ordeal.

Lindsey Novak-Kaiser, thank you for being such a compassionate listener. Talking to you was one of the most vital steps in my adventure.

Emily Paz and Julie Silva, how "awesome" was it when I emailed you from the ER and said I was about to be admitted for psychiatric care? I bet you never thought that would happen when we were playing orphans lost in the woods. Thanks for being the sort of cousins that I could lean on for emotional support.

My second therapist, Sheila Honig, thank you so much for getting me to a place where I was emotionally ready to meet my soulmate and have a baby. If not for you, I'd still be a lawyer, denying my authentic self.

Dr. Roberto Zarate, my cognitive behavioral psychologist, thank you for helping me turn my rituals to dust. I'm sorry I didn't mention the hand washing (except not really, because ew gross, you would have made me stay dirty for weeks). Thank you for giving me the time I needed to process my experiences. Thank you for encouraging me to push my recovery farther than necessary so I could become the person I'm meant to be.

My fourth therapist, Victoria Gutierrez-Kovner, you did not make the timeline for this book but you have been an amazing teacher/mentor/cheerleader. You were with me as I revised this book and adjusted to life as a mom of two, and you did so much to empower me. Thank you!

I would like to give a standing ovation to Judy McCord, the teacher at my Parent Education Class. This book barely skims the surface of all the things you have taught me. When are you writing a parenting book??

Lillie, thank you for all our conversations during my recovery. Your words and encouragement did so much to help me heal.

To my second psychiatrist, Dr. Mariel Tourani, thank you for giving me the support and confidence I needed during my second pregnancy and postpartum year. Instead of feeling like an invalid, you made me feel like a collaborator and partner in my mental health plan.

Karen Stoteraux, thank you for opening up The Family Room for my postpartum support group. I love having you in my life!

Sarah King and Ali Hanff, thank you for talking to me about postpartum depression and maternal mental health. You probably thought we were just talking during playdates but no, you were helping me write this book. My therapist Sheila used to promise that I'd make amazing friends once I had children. She was right.

To my babysitter Nelly, thank you for loving my children and making me feel comfortable enough to go away for hours and write this book.

To the occupational therapist! I don't know your name but I hope we meet again someday so I can hug you and thank you for being such a huge part of my recovery.

Dr. Shoshana Bennett and Jane Honikman, thank you for the wonderful weekend that I got to spend with you at the Postpartum Action Institute. I was struggling with my voice and role as a mental health advocate and you helped me reach the next stage in my advocacy. (To any maternal mental health advocates reading, I highly recommend the Postpartum Action Institute. Learn more at http://www.postpartumaction.org/).

A thousand thanks to all the survivors of maternal mood disorders who have encouraged and inspired me. If I tried to name all of you, I'd forget someone important, so I'm not even going to try.

Except I do need to give a special thank you to one PPD survivor: Graeme Seabrook. You, lady, are a rock star. You helped me take self-care to the next level.

And I need to thank every mom who has ever attended my postpartum peer support group. You inspire me to keep doing this work. I always leave our group feeling uplifted.

To everyone who has been a guest on my podcast, thank you thank you thank you! I have had so much fun talking to each and every one one of you.

I cannot thank my lovely editor Anne Horowitz enough. You took a big heaping mess and gave me a crash course in writing a memoir. You helped me keep my sense of humor while pushing me deeper into the raw emotional sewage.

A thousand thanks to Rachel Ake, who designed the cover for this book. I love it! So much!

My babies, Pippa and Julian, thank you for loving me through all our adventures and helping me become a better person every single day. I am so incredibly lucky and blessed to be your mama bear.

Nathan, you are the love of my life. Thank you for bending over backwards (again and again and again) to make sure I got the things I needed to recover. Thank you for never questioning my decision to write a memoir about such a personal experience. Thank you for encouraging me to take the time to write and take care of myself. Thank you for the crayons, foot rubs, popcorn, random detours to hunt for peacocks, trips to Santa Barbara, for trying a bite of that tomato dish, for sometimes letting me beat you at Mario Kart, for reminding me about the brigands, a zillion other things, and of course, the pumpkin.

ABOUT THE AUTHOR

Courtney Henning Novak lives in Pasadena, California, with her husband Nathan, daughter Pippa, son Julian, and an overwhelming menagerie of stuffed animals and plastic dinosaurs. After recovering from postpartum depression, she thought she was supposed to put the experience behind her and move on with her life, but that just did not feel right. She is now a passionate advocate for maternal mental health. She is the host of the podcast *Adventures with Postpartum Depression*, facilitates a weekly postpartum support group, and loves talking about postpartum depression with random strangers. Visit her at http://www.PPDadventures.com for all things postpartum. To hear about her non-postpartum adventures, visit http://www.CourtneyHenningNovak.com.

facebook.com/ppdadventures

instagram.com/courtney.novak

Made in United States
Orlando, FL
15 July 2022

19845601R00189